Capital Cuisine

Cooking
with the Pioneers

Telephone
Pioneers
of America

ANSWERING THE CALL OF THOSE IN NEED

ALEXANDER GRAHAM BELL NO. 15

The Telephone Pioneers of
America would like to
express their appreciation to
Kathleen Wilderson, Graphics,
for her dedication and
assistance in designing the
artwork for this project.

This cookbook is a collection of our favorite recipes
which are not necessarily original recipes.

Published by: Favorite Recipes® Press
P.O. Box 305142
Nashville, Tennessee 37230

Manufactured in the United States of America
First Printing: 1991, 15,000 copies

Library of Congress Catalog Number: 91-3226
ISBN: 0-87197-298-0

CONTENTS

WHAT IS PIONEERING?

The Telephone Pioneer Story

The Telephone Pioneers of America is the largest volunteer association in the United States and in Canada. The Pioneers have over 870,000 members. It was established in 1911 by men and women who were dedicated pioneers of the telephone industry.

The Pioneer triangle was adopted in 1911; its three sides are intended to symbolize the three principal objectives of the Telephone Pioneers: *Fellowship*, *Loyalty* and *Service*.

- *Fellowship*—comes first and is the foundation upon which Loyalty and Service rest.

- *Loyalty*—represented by the left side of the triangle marks the relationship of our members to each other.

- *Service*—signified by the right side of the emblem, is an outgrowth of both fellowship and loyalty and has become an integral part of the Pioneer program.

The Alexander Graham Bell Chapter #15 is made up of four Councils and four Life Member Clubs: Washington D.C., Prince George's County, Montgomery County and Northern Virginia. We are over 10,000 members strong. People caring about people.

Our active members, future pioneers, pioneer partners and Life Members come together as a team to *Answer the Call of Those in Need* and to "Improve the Quality of life in our communities."

Education is high on the list of priorities:

- Pioneers sponsor unique and stimulating educational programs like the Challenger Center Teleconferences through satellite communications.

- Pioneers support the Smithsonian Institute Information Age Exhibit with our volunteers acting as docents and we provide volunteers to assist *7 on Your Side*, Channel 7 News Consumer Program.

- Pioneers have joined the battle against illiteracy by raising money and collecting books for P.L.A.N. (Push Literacy Action Now), a Washington D.C.-based organization that teaches reading to both children and adults.

- Pioneers have combined both a bit of modern technology and lots of old-fashioned caring to bring joy to the visually impaired who play Pioneer Beep Ball. A sound in the ball lets the player know where to swing and a sound from the base lets the player know where to run.

- Pioneers sponsor disabled children each year to enable them to participate in the Pioneer Sports Jamboree in Cairo, West Virginia and Indiantown Gap, Pennsylvania. Special children compete for all they're worth.

- Pioneers sponsor an Easter Egg Hunt for the visually impaired with a sound device inserted in a plastic egg. When the children find the egg, they turn it in for money.

- Pioneers reach out to the elderly, offering comfort and friendship which touches and enriches our own lives as we give to others. We enjoy our visits to many different nursing homes.

- Pioneers give Christmas parties at nursing homes, halfway houses, special care homes and for disabled children. Pioneers give and share with people who might otherwise be forgotten.

- Pioneers make those loveable stuffed Hug-a-Bears for comforting young traumatized accident victims, abused children, and patients in nursing homes and hospitals.

- Pioneers are hope for the sick, fun for the disabled, happiness for the bedridden and food for the homeless. Children look up to us and our senior citizens can't wait to see us.

- Pioneers are *Leaders*, *Thinkers* and *Doers*—Pioneers care.

- Pioneers are very proud of their organization and we thank you for this opportunity to share our story with you.

EXPRESSION OF APPRECIATION

The Alexander Graham Bell Chapter #15, Telephone Pioneers of America, dedicates this Cookbook to all those who have so graciously shared their favorite family recipes.

May all of those who find enjoyment in this Cookbook in the years to come, always remember the *Friendship*, *Loyalty* and *Service* of the Telephone Pioneers of America.

Congratulations to the following people for submitting the winning names of our Cookbook:

Capital Cuisine	Norma Adams, Pioneer
Cooking with the Pioneers	Justine Smith, Future Pioneer

A special thanks to the committee for their help and encouragement in making this Cookbook a success.

COOKBOOK COMMITTEE

Norma Adams	Joyce Michaels
Helen Canter	Mary Pearson
Joanne Colt	Marie Williams
Shirley Jackson	Michael Wilson
Patti Maxwell	Charlotte Wood

On behalf of the Cookbook Committee, I would like to thank our Pioneer Administrator, Janet Sullivan, for her support and guidance on this project.

Sincerely Yours,

Nancy L. Rebar

Nancy L. Rebar
Project Chairperson

A Volunteer's Prayer

I thank Thee, Lord, as a volunteer
    For the chance to serve again this year;
To give of myself in some small way
    To those not blessed as I each day.

My thanks for health of mind and soul
    To aid me ever toward my goal;
For ever to see the good in all,
    A hand to extend before a fall.

For legs to go where the need is great
    Learning to love ... forgetting to hate.
For ears to hear and heart to care
    When someone's cross is hard to bear.

A smile to show my affection true,
    With energy plenty the task I do;
And all I ask, dear Lord, if I may
    Is to serve YOU better, day by day.

Telephone Pioneers of America
Alexander Graham Bell
Chapter #15

District of Columbia Council
Prince George's County Council
Northern Virginia Council
Montgomery County Council
District of Columbia Life Member Club
Prince George's County Life Member Club
Northern Virginia Life Member Club
Montgomery County Life Member Club

LIST OF CONTRIBUTORS

Donna Adams
Norma Adams
Rita Adams
Rita E. Alexander
Bevan Allen
Reba G. Anderson
Georgianne Atzrodt
Patricia Austin
Billie S. Barnes
Virginia (Ginny)
   Barnes
Marlene Bartus
Doris A. Baylor
Deborah L. Bean
Helen Bell
Adelaide Bersbach
Jan Blackford
Bobby Dean Blue
June Bodmer
Shelly Bokman
Eunice Booker
Pat Boyce
Charlene "Joy" Boyd
Georgia Bracy
Dale N. Bradley
Fran Brosius
Linda Bryant
Sadie V. Buck
Kay Burgee
Bill Caldwell
Colleen Campbell
Robert W. Campbell
Sandra Campbell
Helen A. Canter
Jan Carothers
Suzie Carothers
C. Lucinda Carr
Oliver T. Carter
Karen V. Cave
Kathryn B. Cave
Bernie Cavanaugh

Nancy Cavanaugh
Joanne B. Colt
Lou Coale
Mary Cornell
Diane Cotter
Mary L. Cowden
Irene Craig
Brenda N. Crist
Sal D'Adamo
Carolyn Dade
Peggy Dalby
Ruth D. Darby
Cara Davis
Dorothy G. Davis
Mary Ann Davis
Juanda H. Day
Gina Denell
Alice DeStacy
Pamela Dixon
Michael Dutch
Orvylle Mae Dye
Jean Emer
Karen Engle
Brenda Eskildsen
Elise P. Evans
Judy Evans
Heschel Falek
Patricia J. Fingerhut
Dee Fitzpatrick
Marge Fritz
Dawn C. Frizzell
Tonya Gibbs
Patricia S. Giles
Rose M. Gill
Linda Giuliani
Betty Goldbach
Millicent Gooden
Velma L. Graham
Gale Graney
Laura Gray
E. I. Green

Mrs. Melvin J.
   Griggs, Jr.
Dennis A. Grim
Helen C. Guilfoyle
Betty Hainke
Wanda Hall
Audrey Hamm
Alice R. Haywood
Pat Henning
Annie M. Hiatt
Chester Hicks
Tammy Hill
Kimberly P. Hines
Mary M. Hines
Horace G. Holliday
Ann Holman
Martha M. Hottle
Margot Howard
Wade Howard
Shirley Jackson
June Jenkins
Mary Johnson
Patricia Julien
Beverly Kaub
Joyce Kay
Ashby A. Kelley
Grace Kessler
Bonnie Klepp-Egge
Lin Kogle
Kathleen Kondus
Deborah Kulinski
Barbara Kuzniewski
Jewel C. Lacek
Gwynne Lazure
Linda A. Leavitt
Sheila Levine
Matt Lewis
V. Emily Lewis
Judith M. Lindsay
Lisa A. Mack
Lou Ann Maclay

LIST OF CONTRIBUTORS

Carole Marcum
Dorothy Mason
Kathy Matlock
Patti Maxwell
Robert Mayer
Margaret L. McCain
Virginia McCoy
Alice McDonald
Anna K. McNeil
Linda McPherson
Joyce M. Michaels
Ida M. Minifee
Jeannette Mobley
Robert Montgomery
Sharon Ann Moore
Florine W. Mooring
Esther S. Moreland
Deborah J. Morton
Elizabeth Vargo Niles
Kathleen L. Nygard
Catherine O'Malley
Brenda Osborne
Yvonne Outland
Sharon Paceley
Dennis E. Pauley Jr.
Patty Peacock
Mary J. Pearson
Florence P. Perry
Ethel M. Phillips
Deborah Poncheri
Betty R. Powell
Brenda Prestidge
Elizabeth Price
Ruth C. Pyles
Patti Rabuck
Regina Ann Ratliff
Allen M. Rebar

Nancy L. Rebar
Ben Reca
Audrey E. Reid
Sallie Reese
Ginny Ricciuti
M. Irene Richmond
Maggie Riley
Ellen W. Robinett
Gladys Rockenbaugh
Sharon L. Rohrback
Audrey C. Rothman
Donna Sakai
Ginger Sauls
Lori Scarpulla
Jan K. Schmalz
Allen P. Shallcross
Daisy L. Shallcross
Mildred Sheldon
Leona C. Shobe
Pauline F. Simmons
Justine A. Smith
Susan C. Smith
Jean Sorrell
Bea Souder
Hannah L. Spalding
Karen Springfield
Saundra Stalter
Shannon Stilley
Jane Stipe
Frank Stottlemyer
Robert L. Stricker
Mrs. David A. Sturgill
Janet L. Sullivan
Pearl M. Sykes
Helen Taylor
Allan Thomas
Mary Alice Thomas

Anita Thompson
Jean Kiger-Thompson
Reneé Thompson
Frank A. Tinnirella
Sharon Tolley
Betty L. Trapani
Jeanne N. Trapani
Moe Tremblay
David L. Trubey
Lucille H. Turner
Nancy S. Vance
Marie A. Velez
Terri Vieyra
James A. Wallis
Jean S. Ward
Marcia Dark-Ward
Judith E. Ware
Lisa R. Washington
Adelia C. Watson
June Weakley
Martha E. Weeks
Barbara Wheeler
Margaret E. Wiggins
Brenda Williams
June C. Williams
Margaret Williams
Sharon M.
    Willingham
Clarise B. Witcher
Christina J. Wolfe
Charlotte Wood
Tossie Wright
Jack Yaskulski
Cheryl Yoder
Eddie T. Yo
Denise Zeidler
Marie L. Zurick

Nutritional Analysis Guidelines

The editors have attempted to present these family recipes in a form that allows approximate nutritional values to be computed. Persons with dietary or health problems or whose diets require close monitoring should not rely solely on the nutritional information provided. They should consult their physicians or a registered dietitian for specific information.

Abbreviations for Nutritional Analysis

Cal — Calories
Prot — Protein
Carbo — Carbohydrates

Dietary Fiber — Fiber
T Fat — Total Fat
Chol — Cholesterol

Sod — Sodium
gr — gram
mg — milligrams

Nutritional information for these recipes is computed from information derived from many sources, including materials supplied by the United States Department of Agriculture, computer databanks and journals in which the information is assumed to be in the public domain. However, many specialty items, new products and processed foods may not be available from these sources or may vary from the average values used in these analyses. More information on new and/or specific products may be obtained by reading the nutrient labels. Unless otherwise specified, the nutritional analysis of these recipes is based on all measurements being level.

- **Artificial sweeteners** vary in use and strength so should be used "to taste," using the recipe ingredients as a guideline.
- **Artificial sweeteners** using aspertame (NutraSweet and Equal) should not be used as a sweetener in recipes involving prolonged heating which reduces the sweet taste. For further information on the use of these sweeteners, refer to package information.
- **Alcoholic ingredients** have been analyzed for the basic ingredients, although cooking causes the evaporation of alcohol thus decreasing caloric content.
- **Buttermilk**, **sour cream** and **yogurt** are the types available commercially.
- **Cake mixes** which are prepared using package directions include 3 eggs and 1/2 cup oil.
- **Chicken**, cooked for boning and chopping, has been roasted; this method yields the lowest caloric values.
- **Cottage cheese** is cream-style with 4.2% creaming mixture. Dry-curd cottage cheese has no creaming mixture.
- **Eggs** are all large.
- **Flour** is unsifted all-purpose flour.
- **Garnishes**, serving suggestions and other optional additions and variations are not included in the analysis.
- **Margarine** and **butter** are regular, not whipped or presoftened.
- **Milk** is whole milk, 3.5% butterfat. Lowfat milk is 1% butterfat. Evaporated milk is whole milk with 60% of the water removed.
- **Oil** is any type of vegetable cooking oil. Shortening is hydrogenated vegetable shortening.
- **Salt** and other ingredients to taste as noted in the ingredients have not been included in the nutritional analysis.
- If a choice of ingredients has been given, the analysis reflects the first option.

10

Appetizers
and Beverages

Hot Artichoke Seafood Dip

Yield:
132 tablespoons

Approx Per
Tablespoon:
Cal 36
Prot 1 g
Carbo 1 g
Fiber <1 g
T Fat 3 g
Chol 5 mg
Sod 54 mg

2 14-ounce cans artichoke hearts, chopped
2 cups Parmesan cheese
2 cups mayonnaise
12 ounces crab meat
1/2 cup seasoned bread crumbs

Combine artichoke hearts, Parmesan cheese, mayonnaise and crab meat in casserole; mix well. Top with bread crumbs. Bake at 325 degrees for 15 to 20 minutes or until brown.

Marge Fritz

Chili con Queso

Yield:
92 tablespoons

Approx Per
Tablespoon:
Cal 19
Prot 1 g
Carbo <1 g
Fiber <1 g
T Fat 2 g
Chol 5 mg
Sod 108 mg

16 ounces Velveeta cheese, cubed
1 7 1/2-ounce can jalapeño pepper relish
1/2 15-ounce can tomatoes and green chilies, chopped

Combine cheese cubes, jalapeño pepper relish and tomatoes in microwave-safe bowl. Microwave on Medium-High for 3 to 5 minutes, stirring once each minute until cheese is melted. May substitute salsa for tomatoes. May be reheated several times. Add a small amount of milk before reheating if necessary to make of desired consistency. Serve with corn chips, vegetables, pretzels or even sandwiches.

Kathleen T. Matlock

HOT CHILI CHEESE DIP

Yield:
104 tablespoons

Approx Per Tablespoon:
Cal 29
Prot 1 g
Carbo 1 g
Fiber <1 g
T Fat 3 g
Chol 4 mg
Sod 39 mg

1 cup mayonnaise
8 ounces Monterey Jack cheese, shredded
4 3-ounce cans chopped green chilies
1/2 cup Parmesan cheese
1 12-ounce can Mexicorn with green and red peppers

Combine mayonnaise, Monterey Jack cheese, green chilies, Parmesan cheese and Mexicorn in 2-quart microwave-safe casserole. Microwave on High for 8 minutes, stirring several times. May make ahead, store in refrigerator and microwave on High for 10 minutes. May bake at 350 degrees until casserole is heated through.

Adelia C. Watson

CRAB DIP

Yield:
37 tablespoons

Approx Per Tablespoon:
Cal 29
Prot 1 g
Carbo <1 g
Fiber <1 g
T Fat 2 g
Chol 13 mg
Sod 33 mg

8 ounces cream cheese, softened
2 tablespoons chopped onion
1 tablespoon prepared horseradish
2 tablespoons cream
Salt and pepper to taste
Old Bay seasoning to taste
8 ounces lump crab meat

Combine cream cheese, onion, horseradish, cream, salt, pepper and Old Bay seasoning in 1-quart casserole; mix well. Stir in crab meat. Bake at 375 degrees for 15 minutes. Serve with Rye crackers.

Karen Engle

Elegant Crab Dip

Yield:
100 tablespoons

Approx Per Tablespoon:
Cal 37
Prot 1 g
Carbo <1 g
Fiber <1 g
T Fat 3 g
Chol 12 mg
Sod 41 mg

24 ounces cream cheese, softened
16 ounces crab meat
1/2 cup mayonnaise
2 tablespoons prepared mustard
1/2 cup white wine
1 tablespoon confectioners' sugar
1 tablespoon onion juice
1 tablespoon lemon juice

Melt cream cheese in top of double boiler over hot water. Stir in crab meat, mayonnaise, mustard, white wine, confectioners' sugar, onion juice and lemon juice. Heat to serving temperature, stirring occasionally. Keep hot in chafing dish. Serve with assorted vegetables or crackers for dipping.

Betty Goldbach

Hot Crab Dip

Yield:
30 tablespoons

Approx Per Tablespoon:
Cal 43
Prot 1 g
Carbo <1 g
Fiber <1 g
T Fat 4 g
Chol 11 mg
Sod 46 mg

3 ounces cream cheese, softened
1/2 cup mayonnaise
1   6-ounce can crab meat, drained
1/4 cup minced onion
1 tablespoon lemon juice
1/8 teaspoon hot pepper sauce

Beat cream cheese in mixer bowl until smooth. Stir in mayonnaise, crab meat, onion, lemon juice and hot pepper sauce. Spoon into 1-quart casserole. Bake at 350 degrees for 30 minutes or until hot and bubbly.

Wanda Hall

Fruit Dip

Yield:
32 tablespoons

Approx Per Tablespoon:
Cal 46
Prot <1 g
Carbo 4 g
Fiber <1 g
T Fat 3 g
Chol 3 mg
Sod 15 mg

3 ounces cream cheese, softened
2 tablespoons mayonnaise
2 tablespoons maraschino cherry juice
1 tablespoon milk
8 ounces whipped topping
1 to 2 tablespoons finely chopped maraschino cherries
1/4 cup cherry preserves

Combine cream cheese, mayonnaise, cherry juice, milk and whipped topping in bowl. Fold in chopped cherries and cherry preserves. Chill until serving time. Beat lightly. Spoon into serving bowl. Serve with fresh fruit.

Deborah Morton

Piña Colada Fruit Dip

Yield:
40 tablespoons

Approx Per Tablespoon:
Cal 21
Prot <1 g
Carbo 3 g
Fiber <1 g
T Fat 1 g
Chol 2 mg
Sod 18 mg

1 3-ounce package coconut cream instant pudding mix
3/4 cup milk
1/2 cup sour cream
1 8-ounce can crushed pineapple

Combine pudding mix, milk, sour cream and crushed pineapple in blender container. Process until well blended and thickened. Pour into serving bowl. Chill for 10 minutes or longer. Serve with apple, pear and strawberry slices.

Susan C. Smith

Rye Round Bread Dip

Yield:
45 tablespoons

Approx Per Tablespoon:
Cal 62
Prot <1 g
Carbo 1 g
Fiber <1 g
T Fat 7 g
Chol 7 mg
Sod 41 mg

1¹/₃ cups sour cream
1¹/₃ cups mayonnaise
1 teaspoon Beau Monde seasoning
1 teaspoon dillweed
1 tablespoon onion flakes
1 tablespoon parsley flakes

Combine sour cream, mayonnaise, Beau Monde seasoning, dillweed, onion flakes and parsley flakes in bowl; mix well. Chill. Serve in bread bowl. Make bowl by cutting top from rounded rye or Hawaiian loaf. Scoop out center, leaving shell; cut top and center into cubes for dipping. May serve with fresh vegetable dippers.

Nutritional information does not include bread bowl.

Adelia C. Watson

Seven-Layer Dip

Yield:
80 tablespoons

Approx Per Tablespoon:
Cal 22
Prot 1 g
Carbo 1 g
Fiber <1 g
T Fat 2 g
Chol 3 mg
Sod 53 mg

1 4-ounce can bean dip
1 3-ounce can frozen avocado dip, thawed
3 tablespoons mayonnaise
3 tablespoons sour cream
¹/₂ package taco seasoning mix
1 cup shredded Cheddar cheese
1 cup shredded Monterey Jack cheese
1 2-ounce can chopped black olives
1 cup chopped tomato
1 cup chopped green onions

Layer bean dip and avocado dip in 8x10-inch serving dish. Mix mayonnaise, sour cream and taco seasoning mix in small bowl. Spread over avocado layer. Sprinkle with Cheddar cheese, Monterey Jack cheese, black olives, tomato and green onions. May serve immediately or chill until serving time. Serve with corn chips.

Lori Scarpulla

Shrimp Dip

Yield:
96 tablespoons

Approx Per Tablespoon:
Cal 24
Prot 2 g
Carbo 1 g
Fiber <1 g
T Fat 1 g
Chol 10 mg
Sod 111 mg

1 10-ounce can tomato soup
8 ounces cream cheese, softened
1½ envelopes unflavored gelatin
½ cup cold water
½ cup chopped celery
½ cup chopped onion
½ cup mayonnaise-type salad dressing
1 tablespoon salt
2 8-ounce packages frozen shrimp, chopped

Bring tomato soup to a boil in saucepan. Add cream cheese, stirring until melted. Soften gelatin in cold water in small saucepan. Heat until dissolved, stirring constantly. Add to soup; mix well. Remove from heat. Combine celery, onion, salad dressing and salt in bowl; mix well. Stir in shrimp and soup. Pour into mold. Chill for 45 to 60 minutes or until firm. Unmold onto serving plate.

Jan Carothers

Beer Cheese

Yield:
90 servings

Approx Per Serving:
Cal 25
Prot 1 g
Carbo <1 g
Fiber <1 g
T Fat 2 g
Chol 6 mg
Sod 44 mg

16 ounces Cheddar cheese, shredded
2½ ounces bleu cheese, softened
1 tablespoon butter
½ teaspoon dry mustard
¼ teaspoon Tabasco sauce
1 teaspoon Worcestershire sauce
1½ teaspoons grated onion
1 cup (or more) beer

Combine Cheddar cheese, bleu cheese, butter, dry mustard, Tabasco sauce, Worcestershire sauce and onion in blender container. Process at low speed until blended, adding enough beer gradually to make of spreading consistency. Serve in bread bowl prepared by freezing round rye bread loaf, removing top and scooping out center, leaving ½-inch shell. Serve with rye bread cubes, breadsticks or pretzel logs.

Marge Fritz

CHEDDAR CHEESE PINEAPPLE

Yield:
180 servings

Approx Per Serving:
Cal 31
Prot 2 g
Carbo <1 g
Fiber <1 g
T Fat 3 g
Chol 8 mg
Sod 56 mg

8 ounces cream cheese, softened
1/3 cup dark brown mustard
2 1/2 pounds sharp Cheddar cheese, shredded
1 2-ounce jar small green olives, drained

Beat cream cheese and mustard in mixer bowl at medium speed until smooth and creamy. Add Cheddar cheese; beat at low speed until well mixed. Knead on smooth surface until pliable. Mold to resemble pineapple; place on serving platter. Slice green olives crosswise into 1/4-inch slices. Arrange on cheese in straight diagonal rows. Score diagonal line with sharp knife between rows of olive slices. Chill, covered with plastic wrap, until serving time. Garnish with fresh pineapple top. Serve surrounded with assorted crackers and party breads.

Lisa R. Washington

ZESTY CHEESE BALL

Yield:
26 servings

Approx Per Serving:
Cal 47
Prot 1 g
Carbo 1 g
Fiber <1 g
T Fat 5 g
Chol 10 mg
Sod 35 mg

8 ounces cream cheese, softened
4 1/2 teaspoons A-1 sauce
Tabasco sauce to taste
1 clove of garlic, minced
1/2 cup chopped pecans

Combine cream cheese, A-1 sauce, Tabasco sauce and garlic in bowl; mix well. Shape into ball. Roll in chopped pecans. Chill for 2 to 3 hours. Make 1 day before serving for enhanced flavor.

Maggie Riley

FESTIVE CHEESE BALL

Yield:
70 servings

Approx Per Serving:
Cal 39
Prot 1 g
Carbo 1 g
Fiber <1 g
T Fat 4 g
Chol 7 mg
Sod 36 mg

2 cups shredded sharp Cheddar cheese
8 ounces cream cheese, softened
1 2-ounce can chopped black olives
1/3 cup Sherry
1 medium onion, finely chopped
2 cloves of garlic, minced
3 or 4 drops of Tabasco sauce
1 cup chopped pecans

Combine Cheddar cheese, cream cheese, olives, Sherry, onion, garlic and Tabasco sauce in bowl; mix with fork until well mixed. Shape into ball; roll in chopped pecans. Chill, tightly wrapped, for 1 to 2 days for enhanced flavor. May be frozen.

Marge Fritz

HAM AND CHEESE BALL

Yield:
50 tablespoons

Approx Per Tablespoon:
Cal 52
Prot 1 g
Carbo 1 g
Fiber <1 g
T Fat 5 g
Chol 12 mg
Sod 77 mg

16 ounces cream cheese, softened
1 6-ounce can ham
1 small onion, minced
1/4 cup mayonnaise
1 tablespoon garlic powder
1/2 cup finely chopped walnuts

Combine cream cheese, ham and onion in bowl; mix well. Add mayonnaise and garlic powder; mix well. Shape into ball; roll in walnuts. Garnish with cherry on top. Chill, tightly wrapped, overnight for enhanced flavor. May omit walnuts and roll in parsley flakes.

Kay Burgee

HOLIDAY CHEESE BALL

Yield:
90 tablespoons

Approx Per Tablespoon:
Cal 33
Prot 1 g
Carbo 1 g
Fiber <1 g
T Fat 3 g
Chol 6 mg
Sod 152 mg

16 ounces cream cheese, softened
1 small green or red bell pepper, chopped
1 8-ounce can crushed pineapple, drained
1/4 cup chopped green onions
2 tablespoons Season-All seasoning
1 1/2 cups chopped pecans

Combine cream cheese, bell pepper, pineapple, green onions, seasoning and 1/2 cup pecans in bowl; mix well. Chill for 30 minutes. Shape into ball. Roll in remaining pecans. Chill, tightly wrapped, for 24 hours to 2 days.

Helen Taylor

JOAN'S CHEESE SPREAD

Yield:
70 tablespoons

Approx Per Tablespoon:
Cal 85
Prot 4 g
Carbo 1 g
Fiber <1 g
T Fat 7 g
Chol 19 mg
Sod 289 mg

3 pounds Velveeta cheese
1/2 cup mayonnaise
1/4 cup white wine
1 5-ounce jar prepared horseradish

Cut cheese into pieces. Melt in saucepan over low heat, stirring constantly. Combine melted cheese, mayonnaise, wine and horseradish in bowl; mix well. Store in refrigerator. May spoon into small crocks or custard dishes for gifts.

Kay Burgee

PESTO SPREAD

Yield:
50 tablespoons

Approx Per Tablespoon:
Cal 42
Prot 1 g
Carbo 2 g
Fiber 1 g
T Fat 4 g
Chol 3 mg
Sod 70 mg

2 cups sweet basil leaves
2 tablespoons pine nuts
1 teaspoon salt
2 to 6 cloves of garlic
½ cup olive oil
½ cup Parmesan cheese
2 tablespoons Romano cheese
¼ cup melted butter

Purée basil leaves in food processor. Add pine nuts, salt, garlic, olive oil, Parmesan cheese, Romano cheese and butter. Process to consistency of smooth paste. Store in small containers in refrigerator for several weeks or may be frozen. Bring to room temperature; do not heat. Spread over cream cheese on serving plate. Serve with crackers. May toss with hot or cold pasta. My Italian father used to make this sauce using a mortar and pestle.

Linda Giuliani

CRAB SPREAD

Yield:
36 tablespoons

Approx Per Tablespoon:
Cal 29
Prot 2 g
Carbo <1 g
Fiber <1 g
T Fat 2 g
Chol 13 mg
Sod 36 mg

4 to 8 ounces cream cheese, softened
8 ounces crab meat
2 tablespoons minced green onions
1 tablespoon lemon juice
Salt and pepper to taste
1 tablespoon Chesapeake Bay seasoning
Paprika to taste

Combine cream cheese, crab meat, green onions, lemon juice, salt, pepper and Chesapeake Bay seasoning in bowl; mix well. Spoon into buttered 1-quart casserole. Sprinkle with paprika. Bake, covered, at 350 degrees for 20 to 30 minutes or until hot and bubbly. Serve with crackers.

Margaret L. McCain

Seafood Mousse

Yield:
100 tablespoons

Approx Per
Tablespoon:
Cal 33
Prot 1 g
Carbo 1 g
Fiber <1 g
T Fat 3 g
Chol 9 mg
Sod 61 mg

2 teaspoons
  unflavored gelatin
1/3 cup catsup
2 tablespoons
  unflavored gelatin
3/4 cup cold water
1 10-ounce can cream
  of mushroom soup
9 ounces cream cheese,
  softened
1 cup chopped celery
1 cup mayonnaise
7 ounces crab meat
1 6-ounce package
  frozen small
  shrimp, thawed
Pepper to taste

Soften 2 teaspoons gelatin in catsup in saucepan. Heat until dissolved, stirring constantly. Spray 2 lobster molds with nonstick cooking spray. Pour catsup mixture into molds. Chill until firm. Soften 2 tablespoons gelatin in cold water. Heat soup and cream cheese in saucepan until cream cheese is melted, stirring frequently. Add gelatin, stirring until dissolved; remove from heat. Add celery, mayonnaise, crab meat, shrimp and pepper; mix well. Pour into molds. Chill until firm. Loosen edges with knife. Invert onto serving plates. Serve with crackers.

Betty Trapani

Double Shrimp Mold

Yield:
140 tablespoons

Approx Per
Tablespoon:
Cal 33
Prot 2 g
Carbo <1 g
Fiber <1 g
T Fat 3 g
Chol 17 mg
Sod 50 mg

1 envelope unflavored
  gelatin
1/2 cup cold water
1 10-ounce can cream
  of shrimp soup
16 ounces cream
  cheese, softened
1 to 2 pounds shrimp,
  cooked, peeled
1 cup mayonnaise
1/2 cup chopped green
  onions
1 cup chopped celery

Soften gelatin in cold water. Heat soup in saucepan. Add gelatin, stirring until dissolved. Add cream cheese; heat until melted, stirring constantly. Cool mixture slightly. Cut shrimp into halves or thirds. Add mayonnaise, green onions, celery and shrimp to soup mixture; mix well. Spoon into mold. Chill until set. Unmold onto serving plate. Serve with assorted crackers.

Billie S. Barnes

TUNA RING

Yield:
80 tablespoons

Approx Per Tablespoon:
Cal 29
Prot 2 g
Carbo 1 g
Fiber <1 g
T Fat 2 g
Chol 6 mg
Sod 56 mg

2 envelopes unflavored gelatin
1/2 cup cold water
1 10-ounce can tomato soup
8 ounces cream cheese, softened
1/2 cup mayonnaise
2 6-ounce cans water-pack tuna
1 small onion, finely chopped
1 small green bell pepper, finely chopped
Celery salt to taste
Pepper to taste
Hot pepper sauce to taste

Soften gelatin in cold water. Heat soup and cream cheese in saucepan until cream cheese is melted, stirring constantly. Add gelatin, stirring until dissolved. Stir in mayonnaise. Chill for 20 minutes. Combine tuna, onion, green pepper, celery salt, pepper and hot pepper sauce in bowl; mix well. Add to soup mixture; mix well. Spoon into ring mold. Chill until set. Unmold onto serving plate. May substitute crab meat or shrimp for tuna.

Margaret E. Wiggins

ORIENTAL CHICKEN WINGS

Yield:
30 appetizers

Approx Per Appetizer:
Cal 44
Prot 4 g
Carbo 3 g
Fiber <1 g
T Fat 2 g
Chol 11 mg
Sod 305 mg

2 1/2 pounds chicken wings
1/2 cup soy sauce
1/4 cup honey
2 tablespoons oil
2 tablespoons chili sauce
1/4 teaspoon garlic powder

Separate chicken wings at joint. Remove and discard wing tips. Rinse chicken. Place in shallow container. Combine soy sauce, honey, oil, chili sauce and garlic powder in bowl. Pour marinade over chicken. Marinate, covered, in refrigerator for 2 to 4 hours. Drain; reserving marinade. Place chicken in baking dish. Bake at 375 degrees for 30 minutes, basting occasionally with marinade. Turn chicken. Bake for 30 minutes longer, basting occasionally. Serve hot or cold.

Jan Carothers

CHICKEN ROLL-UPS

Yield:
36 appetizers

Approx Per
Appetizer:
Cal 40
Prot 2 g
Carbo 2 g
Fiber <1 g
T Fat 3 g
Chol 11 mg
Sod 42 mg

8 ounces cream cheese, softened
1 6-ounce can chicken
⅛ teaspoon pepper
⅛ teaspoon garlic salt
6 6-inch flour tortillas

Combine cream cheese, chicken, pepper and garlic salt in bowl; mix well. Spread over tortillas. Roll as for jelly roll; cut into 1-inch slices. Serve with picante sauce or salsa. May substitute onion salt for garlic salt.

Sallie Reese

DATE CRACKERS

Yield:
50 servings

Approx Per
Serving:
Cal 91
Prot 1 g
Carbo 14 g
Fiber 1 g
T Fat 4 g
Chol 3 mg
Sod 101 mg

1 14-ounce can sweetened condensed milk
1 8-ounce package chopped dates
½ cup chopped pecans
1 16-ounce package butter-flavored crackers

Heat condensed milk and dates in saucepan until well mixed, stirring constantly; remove from heat. Stir in pecans. Spread on crackers; place on baking sheet. Bake at 350 degrees for 6 to 8 minutes or until heated through.

Tammy Hill

Party Snack Crackers

Yield:
30 servings

Approx Per Serving:
Cal 106
Prot 1 g
Carbo 10 g
Fiber <1 g
T Fat 7 g
Chol 0 mg
Sod 231 mg

³/₄ cup oil
1 envelope ranch salad dressing mix
¹/₂ teaspoon dillweed
¹/₄ teaspoon lemon pepper
¹/₄ teaspoon garlic powder
1 12 to 16-ounce package oyster crackers

Combine oil, salad dressing mix, dillweed, lemon pepper and garlic powder in large bowl; mix well. Add oyster crackers; toss to coat. Spread on baking sheet. Bake at 275 degrees for 15 to 20 minutes or until light brown and crisp.

Terri Vieyra

Mom's Fruit Cocktail

Yield:
6 appetizers

Approx Per Appetizer:
Cal 64
Prot <1 g
Carbo 17 g
Fiber 1 g
T Fat <1 g
Chol 0 mg
Sod 9 mg

1 16-ounce can fruit cocktail
1¹/₂ cups ginger ale

Drain fruit cocktail. Pour ginger ale into metal freezer tray without dividers. Freeze until half frozen. Chop into small pieces. Fill small dessert dishes ¹/₂ full. Spoon fruit cocktail over ginger ale ice. Garnish with parsley sprigs.

Dawn C. Frizzell

Hot Ham and Cheese Rolls

Yield:
36 servings

Approx Per Serving:
Cal 137
Prot 6 g
Carbo 15 g
Fiber 1 g
T Fat 6 g
Chol 22 mg
Sod 367 mg

8 ounces cooked ham, cut into ½-inch cubes
8 ounces Cheddar cheese, cut into ½-inch cubes
4 scallions, thinly sliced
2 hard-boiled eggs, coarsely chopped
½ cup sliced pimento stuffed olives
½ cup tomato paste
2 tablespoons mayonnaise
2 18-count packages small dinner rolls, split

Combine ham, cheese, scallions, eggs, olives, tomato paste and mayonnaise in bowl; mix well. Spread on rolls; place on baking sheet. Bake, covered with foil, at 300 degrees for 15 minutes.

Rose M. Gill

Drunken Dogs

Yield:
20 servings

Approx Per Serving:
Cal 126
Prot 3 g
Carbo 10 g
Fiber <1 g
T Fat 7 g
Chol 12 mg
Sod 351 mg

1 16-ounce package hot dogs
⅔ cup catsup
⅔ cup packed brown sugar
⅔ cup Bourbon

Cut hot dogs into bite-sized pieces. Mix catsup, brown sugar and Bourbon in small saucepan. Bring to a boil. Add hot dogs. Simmer for 3 hours, stirring occasionally.

Linda McPherson

 Make miniature pizzas on party breads, English muffins, split pita rounds or bagels.

Bevan Allen's Pickled Knackwurst

Yield:
50 servings

Approx Per Serving:
Cal 47
Prot 2 g
Carbo 2 g
Fiber <1 g
T Fat 4 g
Chol 9 mg
Sod 211 mg

1½ pounds fully-cooked knackwurst
1 medium onion, thinly sliced
2½ cups water
1¾ cups vinegar
2 tablespoons sugar
1½ teaspoons salt
1 tablespoon pickling spices
1 teaspoon crushed dried red pepper
1 teaspoon whole allspice
¾ teaspoon peppercorns

Cut knackwurst diagonally into ½-inch slices. Separate onion slices into rings. Alternate layers of knackwurst and onions in 2-quart crock or jar. Heat water, vinegar, sugar, salt, pickling spices, red pepper, allspice and peppercorns in saucepan to the boiling point. Pour over knackwurst. Chill, covered, for 3 days. Thread onto wooden picks adding pickled cauliflower and red pepper garnish.

Patti Maxwell

Dyno Meatballs

Yield:
45 appetizers

Approx Per Appetizer:
Cal 88
Prot 5 g
Carbo 11 g
Fiber <1 g
T Fat 3 g
Chol 19 mg
Sod 291 mg

35 butter-flavored crackers, crushed
1 cup milk
1 pound ground beef
8 ounces ground veal
8 ounces ground pork
1 small onion, finely chopped
1 egg
1 teaspoon salt
1 teaspoon pepper
2 12-ounce bottles of chili sauce
1 12-ounce bottle of beer
1 cup packed brown sugar

Combine crushed crackers and milk in bowl. Let stand for several minutes. Add ground beef, veal, pork, onion and egg; mix well. Add salt and pepper; mix well. Shape into small balls. Brown lightly in skillet; drain. Place in baking dish. Combine chili sauce, beer and brown sugar in saucepan; mix well. Simmer for 1 hour. Pour over meatballs. Bake at 350 degrees for 1 hour. May keep warm in Crock•Pot while serving.

Sharon Paceley

STUFFED MUSHROOMS

Yield:
10 appetizers

Approx Per Appetizer:
Cal 84
Prot 4 g
Carbo 4 g
Fiber 1 g
T Fat 6 g
Chol 10 mg
Sod 201 mg

10 large fresh mushrooms
4 ounces bacon
1 small onion, finely chopped
Salt and pepper to taste
Oregano and garlic powder to taste
1/4 bunch fresh parsley, finely chopped
1/4 cup Italian-seasoned bread crumbs

Clean mushrooms. Remove stems; chop finely. Cook bacon in skillet until crisp; remove bacon, reserving pan drippings. Sauté chopped mushroom stems and onion in bacon drippings until onion is clear. May add a small amount of butter if necessary. Add salt, pepper, oregano, garlic powder and parsley; mix well. Add bread crumbs; mix well. Spoon into mushroom caps, mounding stuffing. Place on baking sheet. Bake at 350 degrees for 15 minutes. Place under hot broiler for 3 to 5 minutes or until brown and crisp. Serve as appetizer or side dish.

Frank A. Tinnirella

OYSTERS IN CHAMPAGNE SAUCE

Yield:
4 servings

Approx Per Serving:
Cal 336
Prot 12 g
Carbo 13 g
Fiber 4 g
T Fat 23 g
Chol 126 mg
Sod 303 mg

2 cloves of garlic, thinly sliced
2 tablespoons butter
1 pound small oysters
1 cup dry Champagne
1/2 cup whipping cream
1 pound fresh spinach, rinsed
1 tablespoon butter
1 tablespoon flour
Salt to taste

Sauté garlic in 2 tablespoons butter in skillet for several minutes. Add oyster liquid, Champagne and whipping cream. Simmer until reduced by about 1/3. Add oysters. Place spinach on top. Cook, covered, for several minutes; do not overcook oysters. Cook remaining 1 tablespoon butter and flour in small skillet for several minutes to make a roux, stirring constantly. Remove spinach to serving plate; keep warm. Place oysters on spinach. Add roux to pan juices. Cook until thickened, stirring constantly. Pour sauce over oysters. May serve as main dish with green salad with pesto vinaigrette, risotto with mushrooms, French rolls and Chablis or Chardonnay.

Shirley Jackson

Glazed Pecans

¹/₂ cup sour cream
1¹/₂ teaspoons vanilla
    extract

1¹/₂ cups sugar
4 cups pecan halves

Combine sour cream, vanilla and sugar in saucepan. Cook to 234 to 240 degrees on candy thermometer, soft-ball stage. Add pecan halves; stir until coated. Spread on tray. Let stand until cool and dry. Store in airtight container.

Tammy Hill

Sausage and Cheese Appetizer Balls

2 pounds mild or hot
    sausage
16 ounces sharp
    Cheddar cheese,
    shredded

1 recipe 2-crust pie
    pastry

Combine sausage and cheese in large bowl; mix well. Shape into 1-inch balls; place on large baking sheet. Bake at 400 degrees for 30 minutes or until light brown. Cut pie pastry into strips. Wrap pastry around sausage and cheese balls. Place on baking sheet. Bake for 15 minutes or until brown.

Alice R. Haywood

 *Make **Olive Balls** by mixing ¹/₂ cup softened margarine, 1 cup flour, 3 cups shredded Cheddar cheese and cayenne pepper to taste; shape dough around olives and bake at 400 degrees for 10 minutes.*

Party Shrimp Canapés

Yield:
20 appetizers

Approx Per Appetizer:
Cal 90
Prot 3 g
Carbo 7 g
Fiber <1 g
T Fat 5 g
Chol 19 mg
Sod 149 mg

10 slices white bread
2 tablespoons butter
1/2 teaspoon thyme
2 ounces Swiss cheese, shredded
4 ounces peeled cooked shrimp, finely chopped
1/3 cup mayonnaise
1/4 teaspoon salt

Trim crusts from bread slices; reserve crusts. Cut 2-inch circles, 1 1/2-inch triangles and 1x2-inch rectangles from bread; reserve trimmings. Melt butter with thyme in small skillet. Brush bread shapes with butter; place on baking sheet. Broil just until golden brown. Process reserved crusts and trimmings in blender to make 1/2 cup bread crumbs. Combine bread crumbs, cheese, shrimp, mayonnaise and salt in bowl; mix well. Spread on bread shapes; place on baking sheet. Broil until hot and bubbly. Garnish with dill, radish slices, parsley or capers.

Betty R. Powell

Stuffed Cherry Tomatoes

Yield:
24 appetizers

Approx Per Appetizer:
Cal 40
Prot 1 g
Carbo 1 g
Fiber <1 g
T Fat 4 g
Chol 10 mg
Sod 89 mg

24 cherry tomatoes
8 ounces cream cheese, softened
1 2-ounce jar stuffed green olives, drained, chopped
1 teaspoon Worcestershire sauce
1/4 teaspoon white pepper
1/4 cup finely chopped parsley

Slice tops from tomatoes. Remove pulp with small melon baller; invert on paper towels. Combine cream cheese, olives, Worcestershire sauce and pepper in bowl. Fill tomatoes with cream cheese mixture; roll tops in chopped parsley to coat. Place on serving dish. Chill, tightly covered with plastic wrap, until serving time. May store, tightly wrapped in plastic wrap, for 2 days.

Tossie Wright

EGGNOG

Yield:
30 servings

Approx Per
Serving:
Cal 252
Prot 4 g
Carbo 11 g
Fiber 0 g
T Fat 19 g
Chol 106 mg
Sod 68 mg

6 eggs
1 cup sugar
6 cups half and half

2 quarts eggnog ice
  cream, softened
2 cups whipping cream

Combine eggs and sugar in mixer bowl; beat well. Beat in half and half. Add ice cream; beat well. Beat in whipping cream. Pour into glass container. Chill until serving time. Serve cold.

Brenda Prestidge

BOURBON EGGNOG

Yield:
48 servings

Approx Per
Serving:
Cal 365
Prot 9 g
Carbo 21 g
Fiber 0 g
T Fat 18 g
Chol 257 mg
Sod 122 mg

1 gallon French
  vanilla ice cream,
  softened
8 cups half and half
8 cups Bourbon

1 cup confectioners'
  sugar
1 cup strained honey
4 dozen eggs,
  separated

Combine ice cream, half and half and Bourbon in mixer bowl; beat well. Add sugar and honey gradually, mixing well after each addition. Beat egg yolks in bowl until thick and lemon-colored. Beat egg whites in bowl until frothy. Fold egg yolks and egg whites into ice cream mixture. Garnish with nutmeg.

Mildred Sheldon

MINT JULEP

Yield:
1 serving

Approx Per Serving:
Cal 196
Prot 0 g
Carbo 26 g
Fiber 0 g
T Fat 0 g
Chol 0 mg
Sod 6 mg

Crushed ice
1 jigger whiskey

2 tablespoons mint syrup

Fill glass with crushed ice. Pour in whiskey and mint syrup. Garnish with cherry, orange slice, lemon slice and sprig of fresh mint.

Tossie Wright

GOLDEN PUNCH

Yield:
20 servings

Approx Per Serving:
Cal 303
Prot 2 g
Carbo 72 g
Fiber <1 g
T Fat 2 g
Chol 6 mg
Sod 68 mg

2 3-ounce packages lemon, orange or pineapple gelatin
1½ cups sugar
2 cups boiling water
2 cups cold water
2 6-ounce cans frozen orange juice concentrate

1 6-ounce can frozen lemonade concentrate
1 64-ounce can pineapple juice
½ gallon pineapple sherbet
1 liter ginger ale

Dissolve gelatin and sugar in boiling water in large container. Add 2 cups cold water. Prepare orange juice and lemonade using package directions. Add to gelatin. Stir in pineapple juice. Store in refrigerator. Place sherbet in punch bowl. Add ginger ale to punch; pour over sherbet. May freeze a portion of punch mixture as ice molds to float on punch or freeze entire amount, thaw until slushy and add to punch bowl.

Adelia C. Watson

Dawn's Party Punch

Yield:
30 servings

Approx Per
Serving:
Cal 154
Prot 1 g
Carbo 37 g
Fiber <1 g
T Fat 1 g
Chol 4 mg
Sod 62 mg

4 46-ounce cans Hawaiian punch, chilled

½ gallon orange sherbet
½ lemon, sliced
½ lime, sliced

Pour cold Hawaiian punch into punch bowl. Add sherbet by scoopfuls; mix lightly. Float lemon and lime slices on top. May substitute 1 quart raspberry sherbet for 1 quart orange sherbet.

Dawn C. Frizzell

Versatile Party Punch

Yield:
30 servings

Approx Per
Serving:
Cal 145
Prot <1 g
Carbo 37 g
Fiber <1 g
T Fat <1 g
Chol 0 mg
Sod 11 mg

3 packages any flavor unsweetened drink mix
1 46-ounce can orange juice

3 cups sugar
3 quarts water
4 to 8 liters ginger ale, chilled

Combine drink mix, juice, sugar and water in large container; mix well. Pour into containers; freeze. Unmold; place in punch bowl. Pour ginger ale over top just before serving. May freeze a portion of the punch in decorative ice rings, adding cherries and orange, lemon and lime slices.

Terri Vieyra

ED AND JONI'S WEDDING WINE PUNCH

Yield:
20 servings

Approx Per Serving:
Cal 177
Prot <1 g
Carbo 29 g
Fiber 0 g
T Fat <1 g
Chol 0 mg
Sod 13 mg

1 quart frozen punch mix
1 quart wine
1 quart sparkling Champagne
1 quart ginger ale

Place punch mix in punch bowl 1 hour before serving time. Add wine, Champagne and ginger ale, stirring to mix. Use red wine with pink punch mix and white wine with green punch mix.

Justine Smith

CONNIE'S SLUSH

Yield:
15 servings

Approx Per Serving:
Cal 201
Prot <1 g
Carbo 35 g
Fiber 1 g
T Fat <1 g
Chol 0 mg
Sod 9 mg

1 6-ounce can frozen orange juice concentrate, thawed
1 12-ounce can frozen lemonade concentrate, thawed
1 8-ounce jar maraschino cherries
6 ounces vodka
6 ounces apricot or peach Brandy
6 ounces light rum
1 quart Squirt soft drink
1 16-ounce can crushed pineapple

Prepare orange juice using package directions. Combine lemonade concentrate, orange juice, undrained maraschino cherries, vodka, Brandy, rum, Squirt and undrained pineapple in large freezer container; mix well. Freeze for 24 hours. Place in punch bowl. Garnish with peach slices, mandarin oranges or strawberries.

Adelia C. Watson

Soups
and Stews

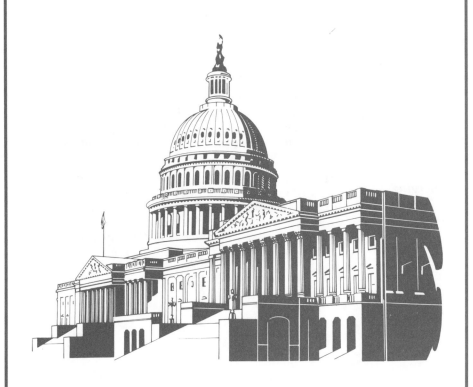

CREAM OF BROCCOLI AND CHEESE SOUP

2 cups chopped celery
1 cup finely chopped onion
1   10-ounce package frozen chopped broccoli
1 cup cottage cheese
2 cups milk
1   10-ounce can cream of chicken soup
Salt and pepper to taste

Combine celery, onion and broccoli in 2½-quart covered glass dish. Microwave on High for 6 minutes, stirring after 3 minutes; do not drain. Process cottage cheese in blender or food processor until very smooth. Add milk slowly, processing constantly. Add chicken soup; blend well. Add to cooked vegetables in dish. Microwave on High for 3 minutes or until heated through; do not boil. Season with salt and pepper.

Joyce M. Michaels

NAVY BEAN SOUP

1 pound dried navy beans
2 quarts cold water
1 meaty ham bone
1 bay leaf
½ teaspoon salt
6 whole peppercorns
1 medium onion, sliced

Soak beans in water in large stockpot overnight; do not drain. Add ham bone, bay leaf, salt and peppercorns. Simmer for 2 hours. Remove bone from soup; cut ham from bone and return to soup. Add onion. Cook for 1 hour to 1½ hours or until beans and onion are tender. Remove bay leaf and peppercorns.

Lou Ann Maclay

Maryland Crab Soup

Yield:
6 servings

Approx Per Serving:
Cal 419
Prot 24 g
Carbo 20 g
Fiber <1 g
T Fat 27 g
Chol 146 mg
Sod 866 mg

1/2 cup butter
3 beef bouillon cubes, crushed
1/4 cup flour
1/8 teaspoon pepper
2 quarts milk
1 pound crab meat
1 teaspoon (or more) Old Bay seasoning

Melt butter in 4-quart saucepan. Stir in crushed bouillon, flour and pepper. Add milk gradually. Cook over medium heat until mixture thickens, stirring constantly. Add crab meat and seasoning. Cook until heated through; do not boil.

Saundra Stalter

She-Crab Soup

Yield:
6 servings

Approx Per Serving:
Cal 339
Prot 18 g
Carbo 10 g
Fiber <1 g
T Fat 25 g
Chol 133 mg
Sod 711 mg

6 tablespoons butter
1 tablespoon flour
2 cups milk
2 cups half and half
1 pound crab meat and roe
1/2 teaspoon Worcestershire sauce
1/4 teaspoon mace
1 teaspoon grated lemon rind
1 teaspoon salt
1/4 teaspoon white pepper
3 crackers, crumbled
3 tablespoons dry Sherry

Melt butter in double boiler over rapidly boiling water. Blend in flour. Stir in milk and half and half. Add crab meat, Worcestershire sauce, mace and lemon rind; mix well. Cook over low heat for 20 minutes. Season with salt and white pepper. Stir in cracker crumbs; remove from heat. Let stand over hot water for 10 to 15 minutes. Ladle into heated soup bowl. Add 1 1/2 teaspoons wine to each bowl. Garnish with dollop of whipped cream and sprinkle of paprika.

Sadie V. Buck

TIM'S CREAM OF CRAB SOUP

Yield:
6 servings

Approx Per
Serving:
Cal 781
Prot 20 g
Carbo 14 g
Fiber 1 g
T Fat 70 g
Chol 285 mg
Sod 532 mg

3 tablespoons melted
  butter
3 tablespoons flour
1 medium onion,
  finely minced
2 tablespoons butter
1 quart half and half
2 cups whipping cream

1/2 cup finely chopped
  parsley
1/4 teaspoon salt
1/4 teaspoon white
  pepper
1 pound crab meat
6 tablespoons butter
11/2 jiggers Scotch

Blend 3 tablespoons melted butter and flour in small saucepan. Cook until roux is browned as desired. Sauté onion in 2 tablespoons butter in small skillet. Heat half and half and whipping cream just to the simmering point in large saucepan; do not boil. Add onion and roux, stirring constantly. Stir in parsley, salt, white pepper, crab meat and 6 tablespoons butter. Cook until heated through. Stir in Scotch. This recipe has been handed down from my great-grandmother.

Allan Thomas

NORWEGIAN FISH CHOWDER

Yield:
6 servings

Approx Per
Serving:
Cal 462
Prot 25 g
Carbo 38 g
Fiber 3 g
T Fat 26 g
Chol 89 mg
Sod 932 mg

2 leeks, sliced
2 carrots, sliced
2 tablespoons butter
11/2 pounds haddock
  filets
2 cups water
1 teaspoon salt
1 10-ounce can cream
  of celery soup

3 cups thawed frozen
  O'Brien potatoes
1 small cucumber
1 tablespoon butter
3 cups hot milk
1 tablespoon chopped
  fresh dill

Sauté leeks and carrots in 2 tablespoons butter in stockpot for 4 to 5 minutes or until tender but not brown. Cut fish into serving pieces. Add to stockpot with water and salt. Bring to a boil; reduce heat. Simmer, covered, for 15 minutes or until fish flakes easily. Remove fish with slotted spoon. Add celery soup and potatoes to stockpot. Bring to a boil; reduce heat. Simmer for 5 minutes. Peel cucumber and cut into halves lengthwise, discarding seed. Cut into 1/8-inch slices. Sauté in 1 tablespoon butter in skillet. Add to stockpot with milk, dill and fish. Heat just to the boiling point.

Yvonne Outland

Abraham's Gumbo

Yield:
6 servings

Approx Per
Serving:
Cal 975
Prot 124 g
Carbo 40 g
Fiber 5 g
T Fat 32 g
Chol 616 mg
Sod 3544 mg

3 crabs
2½ pounds shrimp,
  peeled
8 ounces cocktail
  shrimp
1 pint oysters
1 chicken, cut into
  small pieces
1½ pounds ham,
  chopped
3 hot sausage links,
  sliced ½ inch thick
8 ounces frankfurters,
  sliced ½ inch thick
2 hot peppers
2 bell peppers
½ stalk celery
2 medium onions
1 bunch green onions
½ clove of garlic
¼ bottle of gumbo filé
2 16-ounce cans
  tomato sauce
2 cups cooked rice
2 teaspoons chili
  powder
2 tablespoons meat
  tenderizer
4 bay leaves
Salt and pepper to taste

Remove legs from crabs. Remove meat from crab shell. Combine crab legs, crab meat and next 7 ingredients in large stockpot. Chop peppers, celery, onions, green onions and garlic. Add to stockpot. Add gumbo filé. Cook for 30 minutes. Add tomato sauce and remaining ingredients; mix well. Simmer until cooked through and of desired consistency, adding water as needed. Remove bay leaves.

Nutritional information does not include gumbo filé.

Laura Gray

Ham Soup

Yield:
8 servings

Approx Per
Serving:
Cal 289
Prot 20 g
Carbo 40 g
Fiber 8 g
T Fat 6 g
Chol 17 mg
Sod 1527 mg

1 medium onion, sliced
3 carrots, sliced
1 tablespoon oil
2 cloves of garlic,
  crushed
8 ounces ham, chopped
8 cups chicken broth
1 29-ounce can
  tomatoes
1 16-ounce can
  kidney beans
8 ounces uncooked
  rotini
Salt and pepper to taste

Sauté onion and carrots in oil in large saucepan for 5 minutes or until tender. Add garlic and ham. Cook for 2 minutes. Add chicken broth, tomatoes and beans. Bring to a boil; reduce heat. Simmer for 20 minutes. Cook pasta using package directions just until tender; drain. Add to soup. Season to taste. This is a good way to use leftover ham.

Karen Springfield

Hot and Sour Soup

Yield:
4 servings

Approx Per
Serving:
Cal 208
Prot 20 g
Carbo 9 g
Fiber 2 g
T Fat 11 g
Chol 70 mg
Sod 1433 mg

4 dried black
mushrooms
4 ounces ham, slivered
1/2 cup slivered
bamboo shoots
1 tablespoon soy sauce
4 cups chicken stock
Salt and freshly ground
pepper to taste
1 cup finely sliced soft
bean curd

3 tablespoons red
wine vinegar
2 tablespoons
cornstarch
3 tablespoons cold
water
1 egg, slightly beaten
1 tablespoon sesame
oil

Soak mushrooms in warm water to cover in bowl until softened; drain. Slice caps, discarding stems. Combine with ham, bamboo shoots, soy sauce and chicken stock in large saucepan. Bring to a boil over high heat; reduce heat. Simmer for 3 minutes. Season to taste. Add bean curd and vinegar. Bring to a boil. Stir in mixture of cornstarch and cold water. Cook until slightly thickened, stirring constantly. Stir in egg very gently; remove from heat. Stir in oil. Ladle into soup bowls. Garnish with finely chopped green onions. May add green onions with bean curd if preferred.

Terri Vieyra

Vegetable Soup

Yield:
12 servings

Approx Per
Serving:
Cal 152
Prot 17 g
Carbo 11 g
Fiber 3 g
T Fat 5 g
Chol 43 mg
Sod 1182 mg

2 pounds beef stew
meat
8 cups water
14 beef bouillon cubes
2 cups sliced carrots
2 cups sliced celery
2 cups chopped onions
2 cups chopped
cabbage

2 cups quartered
yellow squash slices
2 cups quartered
zucchini slices
1   32-ounce can
tomatoes, chopped
2 cloves of garlic,
sliced
Salt and pepper to taste

Brown beef on all sides in skillet sprayed with non-stick cooking spray. Combine with water in large saucepan. Cook for 15 minutes. Add bouillon cubes, vegetables, tomatoes, garlic, salt and pepper; mix well. Cook for 1 hour. May substitute ground beef for stew beef if preferred.

James A. Wallis

CABBAGE AND VEGETABLE SOUP

Yield:
12 servings

Approx Per Serving:
Cal 145
Prot 2 g
Carbo 14 g
Fiber 2 g
T Fat 9 g
Chol 32 mg
Sod 308 mg

1/2 medium cabbage, chopped
4 medium potatoes, peeled, chopped
1 bunch green onions, chopped
2 carrots, sliced
3 stalks celery, chopped
5 1/2 cups water
1 cup whipping cream
2 tablespoons butter
1/2 teaspoon parsley
1/2 teaspoon sweet basil
1 1/2 teaspoons salt
1/2 teaspoon pepper

Combine cabbage, potatoes, green onions, carrots, celery and water in large stockpot. Bring to a boil; reduce heat. Simmer, covered, for 15 to 20 minutes. Stir in whipping cream, butter, parsley, basil, salt and pepper. Cook until butter melts and soup is heated through, stirring constantly. Ladle into soup bowls. Garnish with Parmesan cheese.

Chester Hicks

VEGETABLE BEEF SOUP

Yield:
8 servings

Approx Per Serving:
Cal 383
Prot 29 g
Carbo 49 g
Fiber 5 g
T Fat 9 g
Chol 64 mg
Sod 3676 mg

2 pounds stew beef
3 quarts water
1   16-ounce can tomatoes
2 teaspoons Worcestershire sauce
2 teaspoons parsley
1 tablespoon MSG
2 tablespoons salt
1/4 teaspoon pepper
1 cup sliced carrots
1 cup chopped celery
1 medium onion, chopped
1 cup sliced potatoes
1 cup shredded cabbage
1 turnip, chopped
1   16-ounce can green beans
1   16-ounce can white corn
2 cups uncooked egg noodles

Brown beef slowly on all sides in heavy saucepan sprayed with nonstick cooking spray. Add water, tomatoes, Worcestershire sauce, parsley, MSG, salt and pepper. Simmer for 2 1/2 to 3 hours. Add carrots. Cook for 15 minutes. Add celery, onion, potatoes, cabbage and turnip. Simmer for 45 minutes or until tender. Add green beans and corn. Cook until heated through; remove from heat. Stir in noodles. Let stand until heat cooks noodles. Flavor improves if chilled overnight and reheated.

Wade Howard

ZUCCHINI SOUP

Yield:
6 servings

Approx Per Serving:
Cal 256
Prot 15 g
Carbo 20 g
Fiber 5 g
T Fat 15 g
Chol 41 mg
Sod 1315 mg

1½ pounds sweet
   Italian sausage
2 zucchini, chopped
2 28-ounce cans
   peeled tomatoes
1 small head cabbage,
   chopped
2 cups chopped celery
1 cup chopped onion

1 teaspoon sugar
1 teaspoon oregano
½ teaspoon basil
½ teaspoon garlic
   powder
1 teaspoon salt
1 green bell pepper,
   chopped

Crumble sausage into large saucepan. Cook until brown, stirring constantly; drain. Add zucchini, tomatoes, cabbage, celery, onion, sugar, oregano, basil, garlic powder and salt; mix well. Simmer for 45 to 50 minutes. Add green pepper. Simmer for 20 minutes longer.

Kay Burgee

BEEF STEW

Yield:
6 servings

Approx Per Serving:
Cal 388
Prot 27 g
Carbo 55 g
Fiber 8 g
T Fat 7 g
Chol 64 mg
Sod 335 mg

1½ pounds stew beef
1 cup chopped celery
6 carrots, sliced
1 large onion, sliced
4 medium white
   potatoes, cut into
   quarters

1 32-ounce can
   tomatoes
1 tablespoon sugar
2 tablespoons tapioca
MSG, salt and pepper
   to taste

Combine beef, celery, carrots, onion, potatoes, tomatoes, sugar, tapioca, MSG, salt and pepper in bowl; mix well. Spoon into baking dish. Bake, covered, at 250 degrees for 5 hours; do not remove top during baking time.

Janet Sullivan

 Freeze leftover rice, barley or bulgur in ice cube trays, then store in plastic bags in the freezer. Add a few cubes to thicken and enrich soups.

POP'S STEW SOUPPE

Yield:
12 servings

Approx Per Serving:
Cal 337
Prot 25 g
Carbo 40 g
Fiber 5 g
T Fat 9 g
Chol 61 mg
Sod 398 mg

3 pounds 1-inch beef cubes
1/2 cup flour
Salt and pepper to taste
2 tablespoons oil
2 envelopes onion soup mix
6 cups water
1 pound carrots, chopped
2 pounds potatoes, chopped
1/2 head cabbage, chopped
1 pound yellow onions, chopped
1 16-ounce can tomatoes
1 16-ounce can corn
1/2 teaspoon parsley flakes
1/4 teaspoon onion salt
2 bay leaves
1/4 teaspoon salt
1/2 teaspoon liquid smoke

Coat beef cubes with mixture of flour and salt and pepper to taste. Brown on all sides in oil in large saucepan; drain. Add onion soup mix, water, carrots, potatoes, cabbage and onions. Bring mixture to a boil; reduce heat. Simmer for several minutes. Add tomatoes, corn, parsley flakes, onion salt, bay leaves and 1/4 teaspoon salt. Simmer until beef is tender. Stir in liquid smoke. Remove bay leaves. Use your imagination on this soup. Add leftovers, pasta, smoked sausage, hot dogs, broccoli or other vegetables, for example.

Oliver T. Carter

CHILI

Yield:
4 servings

Approx Per Serving:
Cal 436
Prot 34 g
Carbo 39 g
Fiber 13 g
T Fat 17 g
Chol 74 mg
Sod 1142 mg

1 pound ground beef
1 cup chopped onion
3/4 cup chopped green bell pepper
1 16-ounce can dark red kidney beans, drained
1 16-ounce can stewed tomatoes
1 8-ounce can tomato sauce
1 to 2 teaspoons chili powder or to taste
1 bay leaf
1 teaspoon salt

Brown ground beef with onion and green pepper in heavy skillet, stirring frequently; drain. Stir in beans, tomatoes, tomato sauce, chili powder, bay leaf and salt. Simmer, covered, for 1 hour. Remove bay leaf.

Linda Leavitt

Easy Chili

Yield:
8 servings

Approx Per
Serving:
Cal 302
Prot 29 g
Carbo 31 g
Fiber 10 g
T Fat 7 g
Chol 64 mg
Sod 1656 mg

2 pounds ground chuck
1   15-ounce can whole
    tomatoes, crushed
2   15-ounce cans dark
    red kidney beans
2   15-ounce cans
    tomato sauce
1 envelope chili
    seasoning mix

Brown ground chuck in medium saucepan, stirring until crumbly; drain. Add tomatoes, beans, tomato sauce and chili seasoning; mix well. Bring to a boil; reduce heat. Cook for 1 hour, stirring occasionally.

Jack Yaskulski

Matt Lewis' Famous Chili

Yield:
12 servings

Approx Per
Serving:
Cal 368
Prot 27 g
Carbo 28 g
Fiber 8 g
T Fat 17 g
Chol 74 mg
Sod 1697 mg

2 large onions,
    chopped
2 stalks celery,
    chopped
2 quarts water
2 envelopes chili
    seasoning mix
2 tablespoons sugar
1 tablespoon salt
1 tablespoon black
    pepper
2   16-ounce cans
    stewed tomatoes
2   16-ounce cans
    kidney beans
1   6-ounce can tomato
    paste
3 pounds ground
    round
Chili powder and red
    pepper to taste

Combine onions, celery, water, chili mix, sugar, salt and black pepper in saucepan. Cook, covered, over medium heat for 35 minutes. Mash tomatoes and beans. Add to saucepan with tomato paste. Simmer for 15 minutes, stirring frequently. Brown ground round in large saucepan, stirring until crumbly; drain. Add enough of the tomato sauce mixture to make of desired consistency, reserving any remaining sauce for another use. Add chili powder and red pepper, adjusting other seasonings as needed.

Matt Lewis

TOMATO CHILI WITH BEANS

Yield:
8 servings

Approx Per Serving:
Cal 423
Prot 32 g
Carbo 38 g
Fiber 15 g
T Fat 18 g
Chol 74 mg
Sod 1297 mg

2 pounds ground beef
3 medium onions, chopped
1 medium green bell pepper, finely chopped
2 cloves of garlic, minced
1 28-ounce can tomatoes
1 6-ounce can tomato paste
1 4-ounce can chopped green chilies, drained
3 tablespoons chili powder
2 teaspoons cumin
2 teaspoons salt
2 20-ounce cans red kidney beans, drained

Brown ground beef with onions, green pepper and garlic in 5-quart saucepan, stirring frequently; drain. Stir in tomatoes, tomato paste, green chilies, chili powder, cumin and salt. Bring to a boil; reduce heat. Simmer, covered, for 1½ hours, stirring occasionally. Stir in beans. Simmer for 15 minutes longer. Serve with shredded Cheddar cheese. May add hot peppers or 1 tablespoon sugar if desired.

Maurice Tremblay

EASY CHICKEN STEW

Yield:
10 servings

Approx Per Serving:
Cal 482
Prot 44 g
Carbo 47 g
Fiber 6 g
T Fat 13 g
Chol 122 mg
Sod 451 mg

2 chickens
1 large onion, chopped
2 pounds carrots, chopped
3 pounds potatoes, chopped
1 10-ounce can cream of mushroom soup
1 envelope onion soup mix

Rinse chickens inside and out. Combine with water to cover in 10-quart saucepan. Cook until tender. Remove chicken to cool, reserving broth. Add onion, carrots and potatoes to broth. Cook until tender. Bone and chop chicken; add to saucepan. Stir in mushroom soup and onion soup mix. Cook until heated through. Serve over biscuits.

Pat Boyce

Grandma's Chicken and Dumpling Soup

1 2½-pound chicken, cut up
6 cups cold water
3 chicken bouillon cubes
6 peppercorns
3 whole cloves
1 10-ounce can chicken broth
1 10-ounce can cream of chicken soup
1 10-ounce can cream of mushroom soup
1 cup chopped celery
1½ cups chopped carrots
¼ cup chopped onion
1 cup chopped potato
1 cup fresh or frozen peas
1 small bay leaf
1 teaspoon seasoned salt
2 cups flour
4 teaspoons baking powder
1 teaspoon salt
¼ teaspoon white or black pepper
1 egg, beaten
2 tablespoons melted butter
⅔ cup (about) milk

Rinse chicken well. Combine with water, bouillon cubes, peppercorns and cloves in stockpot. Bring to a boil; reduce heat. Simmer for 1½ hours or until chicken is tender. Remove chicken to cool, reserving broth; cut chicken into bite-sized pieces. Strain and skim broth. Combine chicken, reserved broth, canned broth, canned soups, celery, carrots, onion, potato, peas, bay leaf and seasoned salt in stockpot; mix well. Simmer, covered, for 2½ hours. Sift flour, baking powder, salt and pepper into bowl. Add egg, butter and enough milk to make a stiff but moist batter. Drop by teaspoonfuls into simmering soup. Cook, covered, for 18 to 20 minutes or until dumplings are cooked through; do not remove cover during cooking time. Remove bay leaf.

Joyce M. Michaels

Salads

The Lincoln Memorial

BLUEBERRY SALAD

Yield:
12 servings

Approx Per Serving:
Cal 255
Prot 3 g
Carbo 44 g
Fiber 1 g
T Fat 9 g
Chol 25 mg
Sod 122 mg

2 3-ounce packages grape or blackberry gelatin
2 cups boiling water
1 21-ounce can blueberry pie filling
1 20-ounce can crushed pineapple

1/2 cup sour cream
8 ounces cream cheese, softened
1/2 cup sugar
1 teaspoon vanilla extract

Dissolve gelatin in boiling water in bowl. Stir in pie filling and pineapple. Spoon into dish. Chill until firm. Combine sour cream, cream cheese, sugar and vanilla in bowl; mix until smooth. Spread over congealed layer. Chill for 2 hours. May substitute cherry or strawberry pie filling for blueberry pie filling if preferred.

Virginia McCoy

BLUEBERRY AND CREAM CHEESE MOLD

Yield:
12 servings

Approx Per Serving:
Cal 313
Prot 5 g
Carbo 36 g
Fiber 1 g
T Fat 18 g
Chol 38 mg
Sod 137 mg

1 8-ounce can crushed pineapple
1 1/2 cups water
2 3-ounce packages grape or black cherry gelatin
1 21-ounce can blueberry pie filling

8 ounces cream cheese
2 cups sour cream
1/4 cup sugar
1 teaspoon vanilla extract
1/2 cup chopped pecans

Drain pineapple, reserving juice. Bring reserved juice and water to a boil in saucepan. Stir in gelatin until dissolved. Stir in pie filling and pineapple. Spoon into glass dish. Chill for 2 hours or until congealed. Combine cream cheese, sour cream, sugar, vanilla and pecans in bowl; mix well. Spread over congealed layer. Chill until serving time.

Shannon Stilley

FROZEN CRANBERRY SALAD

Yield:
8 servings

Approx Per Serving:
Cal 331
Prot 4 g
Carbo 36 g
Fiber 2 g
T Fat 20 g
Chol 35 mg
Sod 133 mg

8 ounces cream cheese, softened
2 tablespoons mayonnaise
2 tablespoons sugar
1 16-ounce can whole cranberry sauce
1 8-ounce can crushed pineapple
1/2 cup chopped pecans
1 envelope whipped topping mix

Blend cream cheese, mayonnaise and sugar in mixer bowl until smooth. Add cranberry sauce, pineapple and pecans; mix well. Prepared whipped topping mix using package directions. Add to cranberry mixture; mix well. Spoon into 9x9-inch pan. Freeze until firm. Let stand at room temperature for 30 minutes before serving.

Ellen W. Robinett

CRANBERRY SALAD RING

Yield:
20 servings

Approx Per Serving:
Cal 215
Prot 2 g
Carbo 45 g
Fiber 2 g
T Fat 4 g
Chol 0 mg
Sod 55 mg

4 3-ounce packages black raspberry gelatin
2 cups boiling water
1/2 cup cold water
2 cups sugar
2 cups ground cranberries
2 unpeeled oranges, ground
2 unpeeled apples, ground
1 15-ounce can crushed pineapple
1 cup chopped pecans

Dissolve gelatin in boiling water in bowl. Stir in cold water. Chill until consistency of egg white. Combine sugar, cranberries, oranges, apples, undrained pineapple and pecans in bowl; mix well. Fold into thickened gelatin. Spoon into 10-cup ring mold. Chill until set. Unmold onto lettuce-lined serving plate. Serve with mayonnaise in center and garnish of orange slices.

Patricia J. Fingerhut

Fruit Salad with Orange Dressing

Yield:
2 servings

Approx Per Serving:
Cal 277
Prot 17 g
Carbo 52 g
Fiber 7 g
T Fat 2 g
Chol 5 mg
Sod 467 mg

1/2 cup orange juice
2 teaspoons honey
1 1/2 teaspoons lemon juice
1 teaspoon cornstarch
1/4 teaspoon curry powder
1 cup fresh or canned 3/4-inch pineapple chunks
1/2 cup fresh blueberries

2 medium kiwifruit, cut into 3/4-inch cubes
1 large navel orange, peeled, cut into 1-inch cubes
4 medium strawberries, cut into halves
1 cup dry-curd low-fat cottage cheese

Combine orange juice, honey, lemon juice, cornstarch and curry powder in small heavy saucepan. Cook over medium heat for 3 minutes, stirring constantly. Chill, covered, for 30 minutes or until cool. Combine pineapple, blueberries, kiwifruit and orange in bowl. Chill, covered, until serving time. Add strawberries and dressing to fruit mixture at serving time; toss gently to mix. Spoon onto serving plates. Spoon cottage cheese onto plates.

Helen Canter

Fruit and Pudding Salad

Yield:
8 servings

Approx Per Serving:
Cal 179
Prot 1 g
Carbo 46 g
Fiber 2 g
T Fat <1 g
Chol 0 mg
Sod 147 mg

1   16-ounce can pineapple tidbits
2   8-ounce cans mandarin oranges
1/2 cup orange juice
1   4-ounce package vanilla pudding and pie filling mix

1   4-ounce package vanilla tapioca pudding mix
1 cup green grapes

Drain pineapple and oranges, reserving juice. Combine enough reserved juice with 1/2 cup orange juice to measure 3 cups. Combine with pudding mixes in saucepan; mix well. Cook until thickened, stirring constantly. Fold in pineapple, oranges and grapes. Chill until serving time. Garnish with kiwifruit, strawberries and/or maraschino cherries. May substitute bananas for grapes if preferred.

Hannah L. Spalding

Aunt Elsie's Lime Salad

Yield:
8 servings

Approx Per Serving:
Cal 307
Prot 5 g
Carbo 37 g
Fiber 1 g
T Fat 17 g
Chol 26 mg
Sod 99 mg

2 3-ounce packages
   lime gelatin
1 cup boiling water
1/2 cup chopped pecans

1 20-ounce can
   crushed pineapple
2 cups sour cream

Dissolve gelatin in boiling water in bowl. Add pecans and undrained pineapple. Cool slightly. Stir in sour cream. Spoon into salad mold. Chill for 2 hours or until firm. Unmold onto serving plate.

Catherine O'Malley

Moon Cheese

Yield:
12 servings

Approx Per Serving:
Cal 222
Prot 5 g
Carbo 25 g
Fiber 1 g
T Fat 12 g
Chol 30 mg
Sod 134 mg

1 16-ounce can
   crushed pineapple
1 13-ounce can
   evaporated milk
8 ounces cream cheese,
   chopped, softened

1 6-ounce package
   lime or strawberry
   gelatin
1/2 cup chopped pecans

Combine undrained pineapple, evaporated milk and cream cheese in large saucepan. Heat until cream cheese melts, stirring constantly. Add gelatin, stirring to dissolve completely. Stir in pecans. Spoon into salad mold. Chill until firm. Unmold onto lettuce-lined serving plate. This is a pretty holiday salad.

Maggie Riley

 *For a **Fruit Salad Dressing**, mix 1/2 cup mayonnaise, 1/2 cup whipped cream, 1 tablespoon maraschino cherry juice and 4 chopped cherries.*

Frozen Peach Salad

Yield:
15 servings

Approx Per Serving:
Cal 180
Prot 1 g
Carbo 18 g
Fiber 1 g
T Fat 12 g
Chol 29 mg
Sod 77 mg

2 tablespoons mayonnaise
3 ounces cream cheese, softened
1/4 teaspoon salt
1 cup whipping cream, whipped
1 2/3 cups miniature marshmallows
1 16-ounce can sliced peaches, drained
1 20-ounce can pineapple chunks, drained
1/2 cup sliced maraschino cherries
1/2 cup chopped pecans

Cream mayonnaise and cream cheese in mixer bowl until smooth. Add salt; mix well. Fold in whipped cream and marshmallows. Fold in peaches, pineapple, cherries and pecans. Spoon into rectangular dish. Freeze until firm. Cut into squares.

Marge Fritz

Spiced Peach Mold

Yield:
8 servings

Approx Per Serving:
Cal 103
Prot 2 g
Carbo 26 g
Fiber 1 g
T Fat <1 g
Chol 0 mg
Sod 38 mg

1 16-ounce can sliced peaches
1 1/2 cups (about) orange juice
12 whole cloves
1 cinnamon stick
3 tablespoons cider vinegar
1 3-ounce package lemon gelatin

Drain peaches, reserving juice; pat peaches dry. Add enough orange juice to reserved peach juice to measure 2 cups. Combine with cloves, cinnamon and vinegar in saucepan. Bring to a boil; reduce heat. Simmer for 10 minutes. Strain into gelatin in bowl; stir to dissolve gelatin completely. Chill until thickened to consistency of egg white. Stir in peaches. Spoon into 4-cup mold. Chill, tightly covered, until firm or for up to 2 days. Unmold onto plate at serving time.

Hannah L. Spalding

Pink Panther Salad

Yield:
15 servings

Approx Per
Serving:
Cal 296
Prot 3 g
Carbo 39 g
Fiber 1 g
T Fat 15 g
Chol 9 mg
Sod 54 mg

1   14-ounce can
sweetened
condensed milk
1   16-ounce can
crushed pineapple

16 ounces whipped
topping
1 cup chopped pecans
1   21-ounce can cherry
pie filling

Combine condensed milk, pineapple, whipped topping and pecans in large bowl; mix well. Stir in pie filling. Spoon into 9x13-inch pan or mold. Chill or freeze overnight. Let frozen salad stand at room temperature for 30 minutes before serving. May serve as dessert if preferred.

Pamela Dixon

Sawdust Salad

Yield:
10 servings

Approx Per
Serving:
Cal 419
Prot 7 g
Carbo 56 g
Fiber 2 g
T Fat 21 g
Chol 49 mg
Sod 155 mg

2   3-ounce packages
raspberry or orange
gelatin
2 cups boiling water
1   16-ounce can
crushed pineapple
3 bananas, sliced
1 cup miniature
marshmallows

2 tablespoons flour
1/2 cup sugar
1 egg
2 envelopes whipped
topping mix
8 ounces cream cheese,
softened
1 cup finely chopped
pecans

Dissolve gelatin in boiling water in bowl. Drain pineapple, reserving juice. Stir pineapple, bananas and marshmallows into gelatin. Spoon into 9x13-inch dish. Chill until firm. Combine reserved pineapple juice with flour and sugar in small saucepan. Beat in egg. Cook until thickened, stirring constantly. Spread over congealed layer. Prepare whipped topping mix using package directions. Add cream cheese; mix until smooth. Fold in pecans. Spread over top of salad. Chill until serving time.

Carole Marcum

Dot's Strawberry and Banana Salad

Yield:
15 servings

Approx Per
Serving:
Cal 245
Prot 5 g
Carbo 45 g
Fiber 2 g
T Fat 7 g
Chol 13 mg
Sod 126 mg

3   6-ounce packages
strawberry gelatin
4 cups boiling water
2   10-ounce packages
frozen strawberries

3 bananas, chopped
1   20-ounce can
crushed pineapple,
drained
2 cups sour cream

Dissolve gelatin in boiling water in large bowl. Add strawberries, bananas and pineapple; mix gently. Spoon half the mixture into 9x13-inch dish. Chill until set. Spread with sour cream. Spoon remaining gelatin mixture over sour cream. Chill until set.

Janet L. Sullivan

Strawberry Salad

Yield:
15 servings

Approx Per
Serving:
Cal 283
Prot 9 g
Carbo 38 g
Fiber 3 g
T Fat 12 g
Chol 13 mg
Sod 94 mg

1 envelope unflavored
gelatin
1/2 cup cold water
2   6-ounce packages
strawberry gelatin
1 1/2 cups boiling water
1   20-ounce can
crushed pineapple

1   16-ounce package
frozen strawberries,
partially thawed
3 bananas, sliced
1 cup chopped pecans
2 cups sour cream

Soften unflavored gelatin in 1/2 cup cold water. Dissolve strawberry gelatin in boiling water in bowl. Stir in unflavored gelatin until dissolved. Add pineapple, strawberries, bananas and pecans; mix gently. Spoon half the mixture into 9x13-inch dish. Chill until set. Spread sour cream over congealed layer. Top with remaining gelatin mixture. Chill until set.

Linda Bryant

Taco Salad

1 head lettuce, shredded
3 large tomatoes, chopped
1 cup shredded Cheddar cheese
1 medium onion, chopped
1/2 cup (or more) French salad dressing
1 pound lean ground beef
1 16-ounce can red kidney beans
1 12-ounce jar taco sauce
1 8-ounce package tortilla chips, coarsely crushed

Combine lettuce, tomatoes, cheese, onion and enough salad dressing to moisten as desired in large bowl; toss lightly to mix. Brown ground beef in skillet, stirring until crumbly; drain. Add beans and taco sauce; mix well. Add to lettuce mixture; mix lightly. Serve over tortilla chips.

Mrs. David A. Sturgill

Easy Taco Salad

1 pound ground beef
1 11-ounce package tortilla chips, broken
2 cups shredded Cheddar cheese
1 onion, chopped
2 tomatoes, chopped
1 head lettuce, torn
1 16-ounce bottle of Catalina salad dressing

Brown ground beef in skillet, stirring until crumbly; drain. Combine tortilla chips, cheese, onion, tomatoes, lettuce, ground beef and salad dressing in order listed in large bowl; toss to mix well.

Brenda Osborne

Tuna Gelatin Salad

Yield:
6 servings

Approx Per Serving:
Cal 517
Prot 37 g
Carbo 8 g
Fiber 5 g
T Fat 38 g
Chol 56 mg
Sod 818 mg

2 envelopes unflavored gelatin
1/2 cup cold water
3 ounces cream cheese
1 10-ounce can cream of mushroom soup
1 cup mayonnaise
1 tablespoon Worcestershire sauce
1 small onion, grated
1 cup chopped celery
1 6-ounce can water-pack tuna

Soften gelatin in cold water. Combine cream cheese, soup, mayonnaise and Worcestershire sauce in saucepan. Heat until bubbly. Add gelatin; stir until dissolved. Stir in onion, celery and tuna. Spoon into 8x8-inch dish. Chill until set. Cut into squares.

Ethel M. Phillips

Pasta Tuna Salad

Yield:
12 servings

Approx Per Serving:
Cal 244
Prot 15 g
Carbo 35 g
Fiber 5 g
T Fat 4 g
Chol 19 mg
Sod 349 mg

1 16-ounce package three-color pasta
3 stalks celery, chopped
1 medium onion, chopped
1/2 teaspoon each Old Bay seasoning, salt and pepper
1/4 cup mayonnaise
1 15-ounce can dark red kidney beans, drained
1 12-ounce can water-pack tuna, drained, flaked

Cook pasta using package directions; drain and rinse with cold water. Combine with celery, onion, seasonings and mayonnaise in large bowl; mix well. Add kidney beans and tuna; mix well. Garnish with Parmesan cheese.

Bonnie Klepp-Egge

Serve chicken or seafood salad in avocado halves, tomato cups, melon rings or pineapple boats. This is an easy way to dress up leftovers.

Seafood Salad

Yield:
6 servings

Approx Per
Serving:
Cal 399
Prot 37 g
Carbo 40 g
Fiber 5 g
T Fat 9 g
Chol 171 mg
Sod 518 mg

1   7-ounce can backfin crab meat, rinsed
1   7-ounce can water-pack tuna, drained, flaked
1 pound shrimp, peeled, cooked
1 onion, chopped
1 green bell pepper, chopped
2 stalks celery, chopped
2 tablespoons (or more) sweet pickle relish
8 ounces macaroni or shell pasta, cooked
1/4 cup mayonnaise
Dry mustard, salt and pepper to taste
1   10-ounce package frozen green peas

Combine crab meat, tuna and shrimp in bowl; mix gently. Add onion, green pepper, celery, relish, pasta, mayonnaise, dry mustard, salt and pepper; mix gently with wooden spoon. Rinse peas under cold water until thawed. Add to salad. Serve on lettuce-lined plates. Garnish with sliced hard-boiled eggs, parsley and orange slice twists.

Millicent Gooden

Shrimp and Macaroni Salad

Yield:
8 servings

Approx Per
Serving:
Cal 240
Prot 13 g
Carbo 25 g
Fiber 2 g
T Fat 10 g
Chol 69 mg
Sod 743 mg

1 envelope Italian salad dressing mix
8 ounces uncooked elbow macaroni
2   11-ounce cans chicken broth
1   10-ounce package frozen cooked shrimp
1 green bell pepper, chopped
1 onion, chopped
3 stalks celery, chopped
25 Spanish olives, chopped

Prepare salad dressing mix using package directions. Chill overnight. Cook pasta in chicken broth in 3-quart saucepan until liquid is nearly absorbed. Add shrimp during last few minutes of cooking time; drain. Stir in half the salad dressing. Combine with green pepper, onion, celery and olives in serving bowl; mix well. Chill until serving time. Stir in remaining salad dressing just before serving. This is a good salad for a potluck or picnic because it has no mayonnaise.

Gina Denell

SHRIMP AND TORTELINI SALAD

Yield:
8 servings

Approx Per
Serving:
Cal 660
Prot 26 g
Carbo 39 g
Fiber 4 g
T Fat 46 g
Chol 199 mg
Sod 830 mg

6 cups water
2 tablespoons oil
1 teaspoon salt
12 ounces uncooked
  tortelini
1/4 cup Paul Newman's
  salad dressing
1 red bell pepper,
  chopped
4 stalks celery,
  chopped
3 kosher pickles,
  chopped
1 4-ounce can sliced
  black olives
2 onions, chopped
1 1/2 pounds cooked
  shrimp
1 tablespoon prepared
  horseradish
1 egg
3 tablespoons lemon
  juice
1/2 teaspoon dry
  mustard
2 tablespoons white
  Worcestershire sauce
1 1/4 cups oil
1 teaspoon sugar
1/2 teaspoon salt

Bring water, 2 tablespoons oil and 1 teaspoon salt to a boil in saucepan. Add tortelini. Cook until tender; drain. Toss with salad dressing in salad bowl. Let stand for 1 hour. Add bell pepper, celery, pickles, olives, onions, shrimp and horseradish; mix well. Chill overnight. Combine egg and remaining ingredients in blender container; process until smooth. Add to salad; toss lightly to coat well.

Anita Thompson

PEPPERY PASTA SALAD

Yield:
12 servings

Approx Per
Serving:
Cal 428
Prot 11 g
Carbo 35 g
Fiber 2 g
T Fat 32 g
Chol 18 mg
Sod 467 mg

1 16-ounce package
  rigatoni
1 medium onion,
  chopped
1 red bell pepper,
  chopped
1 green bell pepper,
  chopped
6 ounces Cheddar
  cheese, cubed
4 ounces sliced
  pepperoni
1 16-ounce bottle of
  Italian salad dressing
1 bottle of Salad
  Supreme seasoning

Cook pasta using package directions; drain and rinse with cold water. Combine with onion, bell peppers, cheese, pepperoni, salad dressing and seasoning in large bowl; mix well. Chill until serving time. May add salami, mushrooms and other items of choice.

Nutritional information does not include Salad Supreme seasoning.

Sharon Tolley

Pasta à la DeStacy

Yield:
12 servings

Approx Per Serving:
Cal 315
Prot 9 g
Carbo 31 g
Fiber 2 g
T Fat 18 g
Chol 45 mg
Sod 356 mg

1 16-ounce package three-color pasta
2 large tomatoes, chopped
2 large green bell peppers, chopped
1 16-ounce bottle of Caesar salad dressing
1/2 bottle of Salad Supreme seasoning

Cook pasta using package directions until done to taste; drain and rinse in cool water in colander. Combine with tomatoes, green peppers, salad dressing and seasoning in bowl; toss to mix well. Chill until serving time. May add onions, carrots, mushrooms and nuts as desired.

Nutritional information does not include Salad Supreme seasoning.

Alice DeStacy

Shell Pasta Salad

Yield:
12 servings

Approx Per Serving:
Cal 326
Prot 5 g
Carbo 35 g
Fiber 2 g
T Fat 23 g
Chol 0 mg
Sod 187 mg

1 16-ounce package shell pasta
1 small onion, chopped
1 cucumber, seeded, chopped
1 green bell pepper, chopped
1 small tomato, chopped
1 16-ounce bottle of Italian salad dressing
1/2 bottle of Salad Supreme seasoning
Salt and pepper to taste

Cook pasta using package directions; drain and rinse in cold water. Combine with onion, cucumber, green pepper, tomato, salad dressing and seasonings in large bowl; toss to mix well. Chill in refrigerator overnight.

Nutritional information does not include Salad Supreme seasoning.

Joyce Day

BROCCOLI SALAD

Yield:
12 servings

Approx Per Serving:
Cal 223
Prot 3 g
Carbo 14 g
Fiber 4 g
T Fat 23 g
Chol 0 mg
Sod 214 mg

2½ pounds broccoli
2 8-ounce cans sliced water chestnuts, drained

1 green bell pepper, chopped
2 8-ounce bottles of Italian salad dressing

Cut broccoli into small flowerets; chop stems. Combine with water chestnuts, green pepper and salad dressing in heavy plastic bag or airtight refrigerator container; mix well. Chill for 24 hours, turning frequently. Serve chilled or at room temperature.

Deborah Poncheri

BROCCOLI AND BACON SALAD

Yield:
8 servings

Approx Per Serving:
Cal 238
Prot 4 g
Carbo 14 g
Fiber 2 g
T Fat 20 g
Chol 18 mg
Sod 231 mg

4 cups chopped fresh broccoli
¼ cup raisins
¼ cup chopped onion
¾ cup mayonnaise

1 tablespoon white vinegar
¼ cup sugar
8 slices crisp-fried bacon, crumbled

Combine broccoli, raisins, onion, mayonnaise, vinegar and sugar in bowl; mix well. Fold in bacon. Chill for 3 hours.

Martha M. Hottie

FRUITED BROCCOLI SALAD

Yield:
8 servings

Approx Per Serving:
Cal 436
Prot 8 g
Carbo 37 g
Fiber 4 g
T Fat 31 g
Chol 31 mg
Sod 260 mg

1 bunch broccoli, chopped
1 cup raisins
1 apple, chopped
1/2 cup slivered almonds
1 cup shredded white Cheddar cheese
1 cup mayonnaise
1/2 cup sugar
1 tablespoon white vinegar

Combine broccoli, raisins, apple, almonds and cheese in bowl; mix well. Combine mayonnaise, sugar and vinegar in small bowl; mix well. Add to salad; toss gently until coated. Chill, covered, for several hours to overnight.

Joyce Kay

BROCCOLI AND YOGURT SALAD

Yield:
12 servings

Approx Per Serving:
Cal 140
Prot 4 g
Carbo 9 g
Fiber 2 g
T Fat 11 g
Chol 9 mg
Sod 134 mg

4 cups broccoli flowerets
1 cup seedless grapes
1/2 cup chopped almonds
1/2 cup sliced red onion
10 slices crisp-fried bacon, crumbled
1/2 cup plain low-fat yogurt
1/3 cup cholesterol-free reduced-calorie mayonnaise
2 tablespoons wine vinegar
2 tablespoons sugar
1 teaspoon Old Bay seasoning

Combine broccoli, grapes, almonds, onion and bacon in bowl; mix well. Combine yogurt, mayonnaise, vinegar, sugar and seasoning in small bowl; mix well. Add to salad; mix well. Chill for several hours to overnight.

Lou Coale

CAESAR SALAD

Yield:
2 servings

Approx Per Serving:
Cal 342
Prot 8 g
Carbo 3 g
Fiber 1 g
T Fat 34 g
Chol 117 mg
Sod 256 mg

1 small clove of garlic, crushed
1 teaspoon anchovy paste
1 egg yolk
Juice of 1/2 lemon
1/4 cup olive oil
8 large romaine lettuce leaves
1/3 cup Parmesan cheese

Whisk garlic and anchovy paste in salad bowl until well mixed. Whisk in egg yolk and lemon juice. Whisk in olive oil. Tear lettuce leaves into bowl; toss to coat well. Top with cheese. Garnish with croutons. Serve with wine.

Tossie Wright

CAROLINA COLESLAW

Yield:
12 servings

Approx Per Serving:
Cal 192
Prot 1 g
Carbo 22 g
Fiber 1 g
T Fat 12 g
Chol 0 mg
Sod 189 mg

1 large head cabbage, chopped
1 green bell pepper, chopped
1 medium onion, sliced
3 carrots, shredded
1 cup sugar
1 teaspoon dry mustard
1 teaspoon celery flakes
1 cup cider vinegar
2/3 cup oil
1 teaspoon salt

Combine cabbage, green pepper, onion and carrots in large bowl; mix well. Combine sugar, dry mustard, celery flakes, vinegar, oil and salt in saucepan. Bring to a boil over medium heat, stirring until sugar dissolves. Pour over salad; mix well. Let stand for 1 hour. Chill, covered, for 6 hours to several days.

Karen Springfield

Overnight Salad

Yield:
10 servings

Approx Per
Serving:
Cal 452
Prot 9 g
Carbo 9 g
Fiber 3 g
T Fat 43 g
Chol 41 mg
Sod 583 mg

½ head lettuce, torn
½ bunch broccoli, chopped
½ cauliflower, chopped
1 medium red onion, thinly sliced
1 pound bacon, crisp-fried, crumbled
1 10-ounce package frozen peas, thawed
2 cups mayonnaise
½ cup Parmesan cheese
1 teaspoon sugar
Pepper to taste

Layer lettuce, broccoli, cauliflower, onion, bacon and peas in salad bowl. Combine mayonnaise, cheese, sugar and pepper in small bowl; mix well. Spread over salad, sealing to edge. Chill overnight. Toss at serving time.

Shannon Stilley

Cheesy Green Pea and Carrot Salad

Yield:
4 servings

Approx Per
Serving:
Cal 79
Prot 4 g
Carbo 9 g
Fiber 3 g
T Fat 3 g
Chol 7 mg
Sod 100 mg

1 cup fresh or frozen green peas
1 medium carrot, chopped
½ stalk celery, chopped
¼ cup mozzarella cheese cubes
2 tablespoons plus 1 teaspoon buttermilk
2 green onions, finely chopped
1 tablespoon plain low-fat yogurt
1½ teaspoons mayonnaise
½ teaspoon red wine vinegar
¼ teaspoon sugar
½ teaspoon basil
⅛ teaspoon pepper

Bring 1 inch water to a boil in small heavy saucepan. Add peas and carrots. Cook for 5 minutes; drain and rinse under cold water. Combine with celery and cheese in bowl; toss to mix well. Combine buttermilk, green onions, yogurt, mayonnaise, vinegar, sugar, basil and pepper in small bowl; mix well. Add to salad; toss to mix. Chill, covered, for up to several days. This is a good lunchbox salad because there are no greens to wilt.

Helen Canter

Potato Salad

Yield:
8 servings

Approx Per
Serving:
Cal 376
Prot 7 g
Carbo 31 g
Fiber 3 g
T Fat 26 g
Chol 149 mg
Sod 816 mg

4 cups cooked
chopped russet
potatoes
1 cup coarsely
chopped celery
5 hard-boiled eggs,
coarsely chopped
1/4 cup sweet pickle
relish

1 1/2 teaspoons celery
seed
2 teaspoons salt
Pepper to taste
1 onion
1 teaspoon prepared
mustard
3/4 to 1 cup mayonnaise

Combine potatoes with celery, eggs, relish, celery
seed, salt and pepper in bowl; mix well. Cut onion
into quarters; cut quarters into thin slices. Add to
salad; mix well. Blend mustard and mayonnaise in
small bowl. Add to salad; mix lightly.

Linda Leavitt

Spinach Salad

Yield:
8 servings

Approx Per
Serving:
Cal 379
Prot 4 g
Carbo 29 g
Fiber 3 g
T Fat 29 g
Chol 53 mg
Sod 220 mg

1 pound fresh spinach,
torn
1 cup drained bean
sprouts
1 cup drained sliced
water chestnuts
2 hard-boiled eggs,
sliced

1 cup oil
3/4 cup sugar
1 medium onion,
coarsely chopped
1/4 cup vinegar
2 tablespoons
Worcestershire sauce
1/3 cup catsup

Combine spinach, bean sprouts, water chestnuts
and eggs in bowl; mix lightly. Combine oil, sugar,
onion, vinegar, Worcestershire sauce and catsup in
blender container; process until smooth. Add to
salad. Chill for 45 minutes before serving.

Velma L. Graham

BLEU CHEESE SALAD DRESSING

Yield:
40 tablespoons

Approx Per
Tablespoon:
Cal 67
Prot 1 g
Carbo 1 g
Fiber <1 g
T Fat 7 g
Chol 10 mg
Sod 113 mg

1 cup mayonnaise
1 tablespoon lemon
  juice

1 cup half and half
8 ounces bleu cheese,
  crumbled

Blend mayonnaise, lemon juice and half and half in bowl. Stir in cheese. Store in refrigerator.

Marge Fritz

BOILED SALAD DRESSING

Yield:
24 tablespoons

Approx Per
Tablespoon:
Cal 46
Prot 1 g
Carbo 3 g
Fiber <1 g
T Fat 4 g
Chol 27 mg
Sod 65 mg

1 teaspoon (heaping)
  flour
1 teaspoon (heaping)
  dry mustard
1/2 teaspoon salt

1/4 cup butter
5 tablespoons sugar
2 egg yolks
1 cup half and half
1/2 cup vinegar

Blend flour, dry mustard and salt with enough water to moisten in small bowl. Melt butter in saucepan; remove from heat. Stir in sugar and egg yolks. Stir in flour mixture. Add half and half and vinegar; mix well. Cook until mixture is thickened, stirring constantly. Store in refrigerator. This was my grandmother's recipe.

Mary J. Pearson

German Salad Dressing

Yield:
16 tablespoons

**Approx Per
Tablespoon:**
Cal 31
Prot <1 g
Carbo <1 g
Fiber <1 g
T Fat 3 g
Chol 0 mg
Sod <1 mg

¼ cup chopped green
onions
¼ cup garlic-flavored
red wine vinegar

¼ cup oil
¼ cup water
Salt to taste

Combine green onions, vinegar, oil, water and salt in bowl; mix well. Serve on vegetable salads. May substitute tomatoes or white onions for green onions if preferred.

Patricia Austin

North African Lemon Salad Dressing

Yield:
16 tablespoons

**Approx Per
Tablespoon:**
Cal 82
Prot <1 g
Carbo 1 g
Fiber <1 g
T Fat 9 g
Chol 0 mg
Sod 200 mg

¼ cup lemon juice
Grated rind of 2
lemons
2 cloves of garlic,
minced
⅔ cup olive oil
1 teaspoon sugar
½ teaspoon dry
mustard

½ teaspoon cumin
½ teaspoon paprika
½ teaspoon coriander
⅛ teaspoon red
pepper or Tabasco
sauce
1½ teaspoons salt

Combine lemon juice, lemon rind, garlic, olive oil, sugar, dry mustard, cumin, paprika, coriander, red pepper sauce and salt in jar; cover and shake vigorously. Store in refrigerator. Shake well before using. Serve on fruit and cottage cheese salad or arranged salad of tomatoes, sweet onions, cucumbers and green pepper rings.

Marcia Dark-Ward

Meats

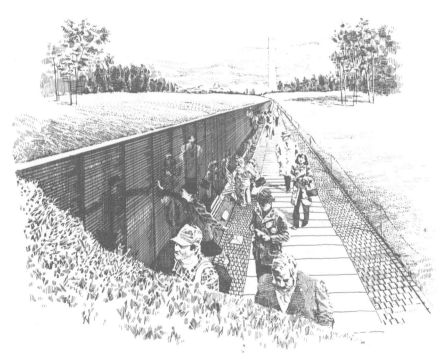

The Viet Nam Wall

BEEF DIABLO

Yield:
10 servings

Approx Per Serving:
Cal 314
Prot 43 g
Carbo 4 g
Fiber <1 g
T Fat 13 g
Chol 128 mg
Sod 127 mg

2 tablespoons flour
1 tablespoon mustard
1 tablespoon chili sauce
1 tablespoon Worcestershire sauce
1 teaspoon vinegar
1 teaspoon sugar
1 5-pound sirloin tip roast
1 large onion, thinly sliced

Combine flour, mustard, chili sauce, Worcestershire sauce, vinegar and sugar in small bowl; mix to form smooth paste. Spread over top of roast. Place roast in slow cooker; spread onions over top. Cook on Low for 12 hours or until tender.

Patti Maxwell

MARINATED BRISKET

Yield:
8 servings

Approx Per Serving:
Cal 337
Prot 43 g
Carbo 9 g
Fiber 1 g
T Fat 13 g
Chol 128 mg
Sod 452 mg

1 4-pound beef brisket
1 cup catsup
1 cup water
1 tablespoon mustard
2 tablespoons vinegar
1 tablespoon prepared horseradish
Salt and pepper to taste

Place brisket on piece of heavy-duty foil. Combine catsup, water, mustard, vinegar, horseradish, salt and pepper in bowl; mix well. Pour over brisket; seal foil. Marinate for several hours to overnight if desired. Place foil packet in roasting pan. Roast at 350 degrees for 2 hours. Slice brisket. Return to roaster. Roast, covered, for 1 hour longer. Serve with parslied potatoes and minted peas and carrots.

Karen V. Cave

 When comparing the cost of different cuts of meat, consider cost per serving rather than cost per pound. A boneless roast may yield more servings than a cheaper cut with bone.

HILTON HEAD POT ROAST

Yield:
8 servings

Approx Per Serving:
Cal 380
Prot 44 g
Carbo 8 g
Fiber 1 g
T Fat 18 g
Chol 128 mg
Sod 590 mg

2 onions, chopped
1 cup water
1/4 cup soy sauce
2 tablespoons molasses
2 tablespoons wine or
  cider vinegar
2 tablespoons sesame
  seed
1 teaspoon garlic
  powder
Pepper to taste
1 4-pound beef roast
2 tablespoons oil
2 tablespoons
  cornstarch
2 tablespoons water

Combine onions, 1 cup water, soy sauce, molasses, vinegar, sesame seed, garlic powder and pepper in bowl; mix well. Add roast, coating well. Marinate in refrigerator for 3 to 4 hours, turning several times. Drain, reserving marinade. Brown roast in oil in heavy saucepan. Add reserved marinade. Simmer, covered, for 3 hours. Remove roast to serving plate. Add enough water to pan juices to measure 2 cups. Stir in mixture of cornstarch and 2 tablespoons water. Cook until thickened, stirring constantly. Serve gravy over roast.

Marge Fritz

SAUERBRATEN

Yield:
8 servings

Approx Per Serving:
Cal 356
Prot 43 g
Carbo 6 g
Fiber <1 g
T Fat 17 g
Chol 129 mg
Sod 880 mg

1/2 cup vinegar
1/2 cup water
1 onion, thinly sliced
1 clove of garlic,
  chopped
1 teaspoon each mixed
  cloves, allspice and
  celery seed
1/2 teaspoon dry mustard
1 tablespoon salt
1 4-pound rump or
  chuck roast
2 tablespoons oil
1 tablespoon sugar
1/4 cup crushed
  gingersnaps

Combine vinegar, water, onion, garlic, spices, dry mustard and salt in dish; mix well. Add roast. Marinate in refrigerator for 2 days, turning roast once. Drain, reserving marinade. Brown roast on all sides in oil in heavy saucepan; drain. Add reserved marinade and sugar. Simmer for 2 to 3 hours or until tender, adding water as needed for desired consistency. Remove roast to serving plate. Strain pan juices. Stir crushed gingersnaps into strained juices in saucepan. Cook until heated through. Serve with new potatoes, rice, dumplings or noodles. May thicken gravy with browned flour if preferred.

Helen A. Canter

Tenderloin Deluxe

Yield:
4 servings

Approx Per Serving:
Cal 460
Prot 43 g
Carbo 2 g
Fiber <1 g
T Fat 25 g
Chol 159 mg
Sod 701 mg

2 tablespoons butter, softened
1 2-pound beef tenderloin
¼ cup chopped green onions
2 tablespoons butter
2 tablespoons soy sauce
1 teaspoon Dijon mustard
¾ cup cooking Sherry
Freshly ground pepper to taste

Spread 2 tablespoons butter on tenderloin. Place on rack in shallow roasting pan. Roast at 400 degrees for 20 minutes. Sauté green onions in 2 tablespoons butter in saucepan. Add soy sauce, mustard, wine and pepper. Bring just to a boil. Pour over tenderloin. Roast for 20 to 25 minutes longer or until done to taste, basting frequently.

Judy Evans

Flank Steak

Yield:
6 servings

Approx Per Serving:
Cal 417
Prot 22 g
Carbo 6 g
Fiber <1 g
T Fat 34 g
Chol 64 mg
Sod 721 mg

¼ cup soy sauce
1 tablespoon honey
2 tablespoons vinegar
¾ cup oil
½ teaspoon ginger
½ teaspoon garlic powder
1 1½-pound flank steak
1 medium onion, sliced

Combine soy sauce, honey, vinegar, oil, ginger and garlic powder in bowl; mix well. Pound steak with meat mallet to tenderize. Add to marinade; top with onion. Marinate in refrigerator overnight, turning once. Place on rack in broiler pan. Broil for 5 minutes on each side or until done to taste.

Nutritional information includes the entire amount of marinade.

E.I. Green

MILDRED'S SWISS STEAK

Yield:
6 servings

Approx Per Serving:
Cal 270
Prot 24 g
Carbo 17 g
Fiber 1 g
T Fat 12 g
Chol 64 mg
Sod 364 mg

1½ pounds sirloin steak
½ cup flour
Salt and pepper to taste
2 tablespoons shortening
1 10-ounce can tomato soup
1 large onion, sliced
1 large green bell pepper, sliced into rounds

Cut steak into serving pieces. Pound flour, salt and pepper into both sides of steak with meat mallet. Brown on both sides in shortening in skillet. Remove to 9x13-inch baking dish. Spread soup over top. Bake, covered, at 250 degrees for 2 hours. Top with onion and green pepper. Bake, covered, for 1 hour longer.

Brenda Eskildsen

AUNT ROSE'S BEEF BARBECUE

Yield:
12 servings

Approx Per Serving:
Cal 249
Prot 30 g
Carbo 12 g
Fiber 2 g
T Fat 9 g
Chol 85 mg
Sod 230 mg

4 pounds lean stew beef or chuck
4 cups tomatoes
3 medium onions, chopped
3 green bell peppers, chopped
1 cup chopped celery
½ cup catsup
½ cup vinegar
¼ cup Worcestershire sauce
4 cups water
2 cloves of garlic, chopped
Tabasco sauce, salt and pepper to taste

Cut beef into 1-inch cubes. Combine with tomatoes, onions, green peppers, celery, catsup, vinegar, Worcestershire sauce, water, garlic, Tabasco sauce, salt and pepper in saucepan; mix well. Cook for 6 hours or until beef is very tender.

Janet L. Sullivan

Beef in Beer

Yield:
6 servings

Approx Per
Serving:
Cal 603
Prot 46 g
Carbo 18 g
Fiber 2 g
T Fat 36 g
Chol 190 mg
Sod 464 mg

3 pounds beef cubes
3/4 cup butter
1/2 cup flour
3 onions, chopped
1 clove of garlic,
  crushed
1 1/2 cups beef broth
1 1/2 cups beer

1 tablespoon brown
  sugar
1 1/2 teaspoons
  chopped parsley
1 1/2 teaspoons thyme
2 bay leaves
Salt and pepper to
  taste

Brown beef on all sides in butter in saucepan. Stir in flour, coating beef well. Add onions, garlic, beef broth, beer, brown sugar, parsley, thyme, bay leaves, salt and pepper; mix well. Spoon into 2-quart baking dish. Bake, uncovered, at 300 degrees for 3 hours. Remove bay leaves. We serve this for Christmas Eve dinner; it was my mother's recipe.

Peggy Dalby

Quick Pepper Steak

Yield:
4 servings

Approx Per
Serving:
Cal 229
Prot 23 g
Carbo 10 g
Fiber 2 g
T Fat 11 g
Chol 64 mg
Sod 857 mg

1 pound cubed steak
1 tablespoon oil
4 green bell peppers,
  cut into strips
1 cup water

1 envelope brown
  gravy mix
2 tablespoons soy
  sauce

Cut steak into 1/2-inch strips. Brown in oil in large skillet. Add green peppers, water, gravy mix and soy sauce; mix well. Bring to a boil, stirring constantly; reduce heat. Simmer for 10 to 15 minutes or until beef is tender.

Mrs. David A. Sturgill

 *Make a delicious and easy **Beef Burgundy** with 3 pounds of stew beef, 3 cans of cream of mushroom soup and 1 envelope dry onion soup mix. Bake, covered, at 325 degrees for 3 hours, add canned mushrooms and serve over rice or noodles.*

STIR-FRY STEAK AND BROCCOLI

Yield:
6 servings

Approx Per Serving:
Cal 425
Prot 34 g
Carbo 46 g
Fiber 3 g
T Fat 11 g
Chol 85 mg
Sod 61 mg

1¹/₂ cups uncooked rice
3 cups water
2 pounds beef steak
1 tablespoon shortening
1 medium green bell pepper, coarsely chopped
1 medium onion, coarsely chopped
1 10-ounce package frozen broccoli
3 tablespoons flour
1 cup water
1 tablespoon Kitchen Bouquet
Salt and pepper to taste

Cook rice in 3 cups water in saucepan for 20 minutes; keep warm. Slice beef into 1-inch strips. Stir-fry in shortening in 9-inch skillet until lightly browned. Add green pepper, onion and broccoli. Stir-fry until vegetables are tender and steak is brown. Stir in mixture of flour and 1 cup water. Cook until thickened, stirring constantly. Stir in Kitchen Bouquet, salt and pepper. Serve over rice with soy sauce.

Nutritional information does not include Kitchen Bouquet.

Reneé Thompson

ANDY'S BEEF STROGANOFF

Yield:
8 servings

Approx Per Serving:
Cal 360
Prot 19 g
Carbo 37 g
Fiber 1 g
T Fat 15 g
Chol 45 mg
Sod 208 mg

1 pound beef cubes
1¹/₂ cups chopped onions
1¹/₄ cups chopped green bell peppers
2 tablespoons oil
1 tablespoon catsup
¹/₈ teaspoon dillweed
3 tablespoons flour
1 10-ounce can beef broth
1 2-ounce can chopped mushrooms
8 ounces sour cream
12 ounces wide egg noodles, cooked

Brown beef cubes with onions and green peppers in oil in large skillet. Remove with slotted spoon. Stir catsup and dillweed into pan juices in skillet. Add flour, 1 tablespoon at a time, alternately with beef broth, mixing well after each addition. Add beef mixture, mushrooms and sour cream; mix well. Simmer, covered, for 5 minutes. Serve over noodles.

Bonnie Klepp-Egge

BAKED BURGERS

<table>
<tr><td>

Yield:
8 servings

</td></tr>
</table>

2 pounds ground beef
1/4 cup water
1 teaspoon salt
4 ounces Roquefort
 cheese

1 envelope Shake 'N
 Bake seasoned
 coating mix for
 hamburgers

<table>
<tr><td>

*Approx Per
Serving:*
Cal 320
Prot 25 g
Carbo 7 g
Fiber 0 g
T Fat 21 g
Chol 87 mg
Sod 808 mg

</td></tr>
</table>

Combine ground beef, water and salt in bowl; mix well. Shape into 16 patties. Crumble cheese onto half the patties. Top with remaining patties; press edges to seal. Shake gently 1 at a time in seasoned coating mix. Place in shallow baking pan. Bake at 450 degrees for 10 minutes.

Deborah J. Morton

BEEF BARBECUE

<table>
<tr><td>

Yield:
12 servings

</td></tr>
</table>

3 pounds ground beef
2 cups chopped celery
1 cup chopped onion
1 cup chopped green
 bell pepper
2 tablespoons vinegar

2 14-ounce bottles of
 catsup
2 tablespoons
 Worcestershire sauce
2 tablespoons
 prepared mustard

<table>
<tr><td>

*Approx Per
Serving:*
Cal 314
Prot 23 g
Carbo 20 g
Fiber 2 g
T Fat 17 g
Chol 74 mg
Sod 830 mg

</td></tr>
</table>

Brown ground beef in saucepan, stirring until crumbly; drain. Add celery, onion, green pepper, vinegar, catsup, Worcestershire sauce and mustard; mix well. Simmer for 1½ to 2 hours. Serve with favorite toppings in hot dog buns. May add sugar to taste if desired.

Deborah J. Morton

When browning ground beef, invert a metal colander over the skillet. This will allow steam to escape but reduces spattering.

MOTHER'S CABBAGE ROLLS

<table>
<tr><td>

Yield:
12 servings

Approx Per Serving:
Cal 398
Prot 26 g
Carbo 20 g
Fiber 3 g
T Fat 24 g
Chol 104 mg
Sod 717 mg

</td></tr>
</table>

1 head cabbage
3 pounds ground beef
1 pound pork sausage
1 large onion, chopped
1 egg
1/2 cup uncooked rice
1 16-ounce package sauerkraut
1/2 cup uncooked barley
1 32-ounce can tomato juice
2 cups water
Salt and pepper to taste

Cook cabbage in water to cover in saucepan, removing leaves as they become tender; drain well. Remove tough veins from leaves. Combine ground beef, sausage, onion, egg and 1/3 cup rice in bowl; mix well. Spoon onto cabbage leaves. Roll to enclose filling, tucking in ends. Spread 1/4 of the sauerkraut in large saucepan. Alternate layers of cabbage rolls, barley, remaining sauerkraut and remaining rice in saucepan until all ingredients are used. Add tomato juice, water, salt and pepper. Cook over medium heat for 2 hours.

Allen Rebar

CREAMY BEEF AND CORN CASSEROLE

<table>
<tr><td>

Yield:
4 servings

Approx Per Serving:
Cal 768
Prot 33 g
Carbo 53 g
Fiber 3 g
T Fat 48 g
Chol 140 mg
Sod 1843 mg

</td></tr>
</table>

1 pound ground beef
1/2 cup chopped onion
8 ounces cream cheese, cubed
1 10-ounce can cream of mushroom soup
1/4 teaspoon salt
1 12-ounce can whole kernel corn, drained
1/4 cup chopped pimento
Pepper to taste
1 8-ounce can buttermilk biscuits

Brown ground beef in saucepan, stirring until crumbly; drain. Add onion. Cook until onion is tender. Add cream cheese and soup; mix well. Stir in salt, corn, pimento and pepper. Spoon into 1 1/2-quart baking dish. Separate biscuits. Cut each biscuit into 2 half-circles. Place cut side down around edge of baking dish. Bake at 375 degrees for 20 minutes or until biscuits are brown.

Linda Bryant

ENCHILADA CASSEROLE

1 pound ground beef
1/4 cup chopped onion
1 clove of garlic,
   minced
1   8-ounce can tomato
   sauce
1/2 cup water

1 1/2 to 2 1/2 teaspoons
   chili powder
1/2 teaspoon salt
1/2 teaspoon pepper
4 corn tortillas
2 cups shredded sharp
   Cheddar cheese

Mix ground beef, onion and garlic in 2-quart glass dish. Microwave on High for 5 to 9 minutes or until beef is no longer pink, stirring once; drain. Add tomato sauce, water, chili powder, salt and pepper; mix well. Microwave on High for 6 to 10 minutes or until of desired consistency, stirring once and rotating dish. Alternate layers of tortillas, meat sauce and cheese in 1 1/2-quart glass dish. Microwave on High for 1 to 3 minutes or until cheese melts. Let stand for 2 to 3 minutes.

Gina Denell

ITALIAN CASSEROLE

1 1/2 pounds ground
   beef
1 large onion, chopped
48 ounces stewed
   tomatoes
2 teaspoons Italian
   seasoning

Salt and pepper to
   taste
3 cups elbow macaroni
12 ounces mozzarella
   cheese, shredded

Brown ground beef in skillet, stirring until crumbly; drain. Add onion. Cook until onion is tender. Stir in tomatoes, Italian seasoning, salt and pepper. Simmer for several minutes. Cook pasta using package directions; drain. Layer meat sauce, pasta and cheese in 9x13-inch baking dish. Bake at 350 degrees for 30 to 40 minutes or until bubbly.

Linda A. Leavitt

CROCK•POT LASAGNA

Yield:
8 servings

Approx Per
Serving:
Cal 748
Prot 39 g
Carbo 64 g
Fiber 4 g
T Fat 37 g
Chol 108 mg
Sod 1240 mg

1   16-ounce package
    regular spaghetti
12 ounces small-curd
    cottage cheese
8 ounces sour cream
1/4 teaspoon each
    garlic powder, salt
    and pepper
1 pound ground beef
1 beef bouillon cube
1   32-ounce jar
    spaghetti sauce
8 ounces Cheddar
    cheese, shredded
8 ounces mozzarella
    cheese, shredded

Cook spaghetti using package directions; drain. Combine spaghetti with cottage cheese, sour cream, garlic powder, salt and pepper in bowl; mix well. Brown ground beef in skillet, stirring until crumbly; drain. Add bouillon. Cook for 10 minutes. Add spaghetti sauce; mix well. Mix Cheddar cheese and mozzarella cheese in bowl. Layer meat sauce, spaghetti mixture and cheeses 1/3 at a time in Crock•Pot. Cook on Low for 3 to 5 hours or until edges are bubbly and center is heated through.

Lin Kogle

ENCHILADA LASAGNA

Yield:
12 servings

Approx Per
Serving:
Cal 619
Prot 38 g
Carbo 35 g
Fiber 6 g
T Fat 37 g
Chol 124 mg
Sod 1198 mg

2 pounds ground beef
1 large onion, chopped
2 envelopes taco
    seasoning mix
2   12-count packages
    corn tortillas
16 ounces Cheddar
    cheese, shredded
16 ounces Monterey
    Jack cheese, shredded
1   10-ounce can mild
    enchilada sauce

Brown ground beef with onion in saucepan, stirring until crumbly; drain. Add taco seasoning mix, using package directions. Cut tortillas into halves. Line large baking dish with 1/3 of the tortillas. Reserve 1/3 of the cheeses. Layer meat sauce, cheeses and remaining tortillas 1/2 at a time in prepared dish. Top with reserved cheeses. Pour enchilada sauce over layers. Bake at 375 degrees until cheese melts and top begins to brown. Let stand for 20 minutes before serving. Serve with sour cream and guacamole. May substitute ground turkey for ground beef.

Dennis A. Grim

LASAGNA

Yield:
8 servings

*Approx Per
Serving:*
Cal 773
Prot 54 g
Carbo 55 g
Fiber 5 g
T Fat 38 g
Chol 142 mg
Sod 1065 mg

1½ pounds ground
  beef
1 16-ounce can
   tomato paste
1 29-ounce can
   tomato purée
½ teaspoon garlic salt
1 teaspoon basil
1 teaspoon oregano
¼ cup sugar

Salt and pepper to taste
2 bay leaves
9 lasagna noodles
16 ounces small-curd
   cottage cheese
1 cup Parmesan cheese
6 cups shredded
   mozzarella cheese
½ cup Parmesan
   cheese

Brown ground beef in skillet over medium heat, stirring until crumbly; drain. Combine with tomato paste, tomato purée, garlic salt, basil, oregano, sugar, salt, pepper and bay leaves in large saucepan. Simmer to desired consistency, adding water if needed. Remove bay leaves. Cook noodles in boiling salted water in large saucepan for 10 minutes, stirring occasionally; drain. Mix cottage cheese and 1 cup Parmesan cheese in bowl. Arrange 3 noodles in 9x13-inch baking dish. Layer ⅓ of the meat sauce, half the cottage cheese mixture and ⅓ of the mozzarella cheese in prepared dish. Repeat layers. Top with remaining noodles, remaining mozzarella cheese and ½ cup Parmesan cheese. Bake at 350 degrees for 1 hour or until top is brown and cheese is melted. Let stand for 10 to 15 minutes before serving. May assemble in advance and refrigerate until baking time.

Martha E. Weeks

OLD-FASHIONED LASAGNA

1 pound ground beef
1 large onion, sliced
2   29-ounce cans
   Italian tomatoes
1   29-ounce can
   tomato purée
1   8-ounce can tomato
   paste
1/2 cup red wine
1 teaspoon oregano
1 clove of garlic,
   crushed
1 teaspoon parsley
1 teaspoon salt
1/2 teaspoon crushed
   peppercorns
1   16-ounce package
   lasagna noodles
1 teaspoon olive oil
16 ounces ricotta
   cheese
1 egg
1/4 cup Parmesan
   cheese
16 ounces mozzarella
   cheese, sliced
1/4 cup Parmesan
   cheese

Brown ground beef in skillet, stirring until crumbly; drain. Add onion. Cook until onion is transparent. Combine with tomatoes, tomato purée, tomato paste, wine, oregano, garlic, parsley, salt and peppercorns in large saucepan. Simmer, covered, for 1 hour, stirring occasionally. Combine noodles with olive oil and water to cover in saucepan. Cook for 10 to 12 minutes or until tender. Drain on paper towel. Mix ricotta cheese, egg and 1/4 cup Parmesan cheese in bowl. Spread layer of meat sauce in baking dish. Arrange 1/3 of the noodles in prepared dish. Layer half the ricotta cheese mixture, half the mozzarella cheese, half the remaining meat sauce and half the remaining noodles in dish. Top with remaining ricotta mixture, mozzarella, noodles and meat sauce. Sprinkle with 1/4 cup Parmesan cheese. Bake at 375 degrees for 1 hour. Let stand for 15 minutes before serving.

Ben Reca

Barbecued Meatballs

Yield:
6 servings

Approx Per Serving:
Cal 340
Prot 20 g
Carbo 22 g
Fiber <1 g
T Fat 20 g
Chol 97 mg
Sod 952 mg

1 10-ounce can onion soup
1 10-ounce can tomato soup
2 tablespoons cornstarch
1/4 cup vinegar
3 tablespoons brown sugar
1 tablespoon Worcestershire sauce
1/8 teaspoon hot sauce
1 pound ground beef
8 ounces sausage
1/2 cup fresh bread crumbs
1 egg, slightly beaten

Combine soups, cornstarch, vinegar, brown sugar, Worcestershire sauce and hot sauce in bowl; mix well to dissolve cornstarch. Combine ground beef, sausage, bread crumbs and egg in bowl; mix well. Shape into 24 meatballs. Brown in skillet; drain. Add sauce. Simmer, covered, for 20 minutes. May bake meatballs if preferred.

Judith E. Ware

Meatball Casserole

Yield:
8 servings

Approx Per Serving:
Cal 258
Prot 16 g
Carbo 21 g
Fiber 1 g
T Fat 13 g
Chol 53 mg
Sod 694 mg

1 1/2 pounds lean ground beef
3/4 cup oats
1 cup evaporated milk
1 tablespoon onion flakes
1 teaspoon salt
Pepper to taste
1 cup catsup
2 tablespoons vinegar
1/2 cup water
2 tablespoons sugar

Combine ground beef, oats, evaporated milk, onion flakes, salt and pepper in bowl; mix well. Shape into 8 large meatballs; place in 2-quart baking dish. Combine catsup, vinegar, water and sugar in bowl; mix well. Pour over meatballs. Bake at 350 degrees for 1 1/4 to 1 1/2 hours or until done to taste. Serve with rice or noodles.

Ruth C. Pyles

SPEED BALLS

Yield:
4 servings

Approx Per Serving:
Cal 360
Prot 24 g
Carbo 13 g
Fiber 1 g
T Fat 24 g
Chol 94 mg
Sod 375 mg

1 pound ground beef
1/2 cup bread crumbs
1/2 cup milk
1/2 cup chopped onion
2 tablespoons butter
1 envelope onion soup mix
1 cup water

Combine ground beef, bread crumbs, milk and chopped onion in bowl; mix well. Shape into 8 large balls. Brown on all sides in butter in skillet; drain. Combine soup mix and water in bowl. Add to skillet. Simmer for 15 minutes. Serve on rice or noodles. May substitute beer or wine for water if preferred.

Irene Craig

SWEDISH MEATBALLS

Yield:
6 servings

Approx Per Serving:
Cal 318
Prot 25 g
Carbo 9 g
Fiber <1 g
T Fat 20 g
Chol 111 mg
Sod 518 mg

2/3 cup fine bread crumbs
1/2 cup milk
1 egg, slightly beaten
2 tablespoons minced onion
1 teaspoon salt
1/2 teaspoon pepper
1/8 teaspoon each allspice, ginger, cloves and nutmeg
1 pound ground beef
8 ounces ground pork
2 tablespoons oil

Combine bread crumbs, milk, egg, onion, salt, pepper, spices, ground beef and ground pork in order listed in bowl, mixing well. Shape into 1-inch balls. Brown on all sides in oil in skillet. May thicken pan drippings for gravy if desired. This recipe is from my Swedish grandmother who came to this country in the 1880s.

Adelaide Bersbach

SWEET AND SOUR MEATBALLS

Yield:
4 servings

Approx Per
Serving:
Cal 502
Prot 26 g
Carbo 60 g
Fiber 2 g
T Fat 19 g
Chol 130 mg
Sod 992 mg

1 pound ground beef
1/2 cup dry bread
  crumbs
1/4 cup milk
2 tablespoons chopped
  onion
1/2 teaspoon
  Worcestershire sauce
1 egg
1 teaspoon salt

1/2 cup packed brown
  sugar
1 tablespoon
  cornstarch
1   13-ounce can
  pineapple chunks
1/3 cup vinegar
1 tablespoon soy sauce
1 green bell pepper,
  coarsely chopped

Combine ground beef, bread crumbs, milk, onion, Worcestershire sauce, egg and salt in bowl; mix well. Shape into twenty 1½-inch balls; place in 9x13-inch baking pan. Bake at 400 degrees for 20 to 25 minutes or until light brown. Mix brown sugar and cornstarch in large saucepan. Stir in undrained pineapple, vinegar and soy sauce. Bring to a boil, stirring constantly; reduce heat. Add meatballs. Simmer, covered, for 10 minutes, stirring occasionally. Stir in green pepper. Simmer, covered, for 5 minutes or until green pepper is tender-crisp. Serve over rice.

Elizabeth Price

EASY MEAT LOAF

Yield:
8 servings

Approx Per
Serving:
Cal 279
Prot 23 g
Carbo 6 g
Fiber <1 g
T Fat 18 g
Chol 127 mg
Sod 307 mg

2 pounds ground beef
1½ cups fresh bread
  crumbs
2 eggs, slightly beaten

1/3 cup catsup
3/4 cup water
1 envelope onion soup
  mix

Combine ground beef, bread crumbs, eggs, catsup, water and soup mix in bowl; mix well. Pack into loaf pan. Bake at 350 degrees for 1 hour.

Ida M. Minifee

MEAT LOAF

Yield:
6 servings

Approx Per Serving:
Cal 309
Prot 24 g
Carbo 15 g
Fiber 2 g
T Fat 18 g
Chol 110 mg
Sod 1132 mg

1½ pounds ground beef
1 egg, beaten
1 cup fresh bread crumbs
1 medium onion, chopped
1 clove of garlic, crushed
1   15-ounce can tomato sauce
Worcestershire sauce to taste
1½ teaspoons salt
¼ teaspoon pepper
2 tablespoons brown sugar
2 tablespoons prepared mustard
2 tablespoons vinegar
1 cup water

Combine ground beef, egg, bread crumbs, onion, garlic, half the tomato sauce, Worcestershire sauce, salt and pepper in bowl; mix well. Shape into loaf; place in 9x13-inch baking dish. Bake at 350 degrees while preparing sauce. Combine remaining tomato sauce, brown sugar, mustard, vinegar and water in bowl; mix well. Pour over meat loaf. Bake for 1½ hours, basting occasionally.

Annie M. Hiatt

ITALIAN MEAT LOAF

Yield:
6 servings

Approx Per Serving:
Cal 415
Prot 32 g
Carbo 14 g
Fiber 1 g
T Fat 25 g
Chol 139 mg
Sod 910 mg

1½ pounds extra-lean ground beef
1 egg, slightly beaten
¾ cup dry bread crumbs
½ cup chopped onion
⅓ cup tomato sauce
½ teaspoon oregano
1 teaspoon salt
¼ teaspoon pepper
2 cups shredded mozzarella cheese
⅔ cup tomato sauce

Combine ground beef, egg, bread crumbs, onion, ½ cup tomato sauce, oregano, salt and pepper in bowl; mix well. Shape into 10x12-inch rectangle on waxed paper. Sprinkle with cheese. Roll to enclose cheese; press edges to seal. Place in shallow baking dish. Bake at 350 degrees for 1 hour. Pour ¾ cup tomato sauce over top. Bake for 15 minutes longer.

Mrs. David A. Sturgill

MEXICAN MEAT LOAVES

Yield:
4 servings

Approx Per Serving:
Cal 379
Prot 29 g
Carbo 15 g
Fiber 3 g
T Fat 23 g
Chol 142 mg
Sod 788 mg

1 pound ground beef
1/2 cup oats
1 egg
1 8-ounce can tomato sauce
1 4-ounce can chopped green chilies
1 tablespoon onion flakes
1 teaspoon chili powder
1/2 teaspoon salt
1 teaspoon onion flakes
1/4 teaspoon garlic powder
2 ounces Cheddar cheese, shredded

Combine ground beef, oats, egg, 1/4 cup tomato sauce, 2 tablespoons green chilies, 1 tablespoon onion flakes, chili powder and salt in bowl; mix well. Shape into four 2x4-inch loaves; place in 9x9-inch baking dish. Bake at 375 degrees for 20 to 25 minutes. Combine remaining tomato sauce, remaining green chilies, 1 teaspoon onion flakes and garlic powder in saucepan. Heat to serving temperature. Place meat loaves on serving plates; spoon sauce over tops. Sprinkle with cheese.

Margot Howard

SHALLCROSS RIGATONI

Yield:
8 servings

Approx Per Serving:
Cal 683
Prot 41 g
Carbo 61 g
Fiber 3 g
T Fat 32 g
Chol 96 mg
Sod 1223 mg

1 16-ounce package extra-wide noodles
11/2 pounds ground round
3 stalks celery, chopped
1 large onion, chopped
1 small green bell pepper, chopped
1 teaspoon oregano
1 14-ounce can tomato sauce
1 16-ounce jar spaghetti sauce
1 14-ounce can stewed tomatoes
2 teaspoons garlic powder
16 ounces provolone cheese, sliced

Cook pasta using package directions; drain. Brown ground round with celery, onion and green pepper in saucepan; drain. Add oregano, tomato sauce, spaghetti sauce, tomatoes and garlic powder; mix well. Simmer for 15 minutes. Layer pasta, meat sauce and cheese 1/2 at a time in 9x13-inch baking dish. Bake at 350 degrees for 40 minutes.

Allen P. Shallcross

STUFFED MANICOTTI

Yield:
6 servings

Approx Per Serving:
Cal 688
Prot 22 g
Carbo 53 g
Fiber 4 g
T Fat 43 g
Chol 180 mg
Sod 2384 mg

8 ounces ground beef
8 ounces sausage
1 cup minced celery
1/2 cup minced onion
1/2 cup minced canned
   mushrooms, drained
1 teaspoon salt
1/2 teaspoon seasoned
   pepper
1/2 cup butter
1/2 cup seasoned bread
   crumbs
2 egg yolks
1 tablespoon tomato
   paste

1/4 cup white wine
3 tablespoons butter
3 tablespoons flour
2 1/4 cups milk
1/4 teaspoon nutmeg
1/2 teaspoon salt
1/8 teaspoon pepper
3 tablespoons
   Parmesan cheese
12 uncooked manicotti
1 tablespoon salt
6 quarts water
1   10-ounce can
   spaghetti sauce

Sauté ground beef and sausage with celery, onion, mushrooms, 1 teaspoon salt and 1/2 teaspoon pepper in 1/2 cup butter in large skillet for 20 minutes, stirring until meats are crumbly; drain. Stir in bread crumbs, egg yolks, tomato paste and wine. Melt 3 tablespoons butter in double boiler or heavy saucepan. Stir in flour, milk, nutmeg, 1/2 teaspoon salt and 1/8 teaspoon pepper. Cook until thickened, stirring constantly. Stir in Parmesan cheese; set Béchamel sauce aside. Cook 4 manicotti at a time with 1 tablespoon salt in boiling water in saucepan for 8 minutes; remove to greased bowl. Stuff manicotti with meat mixture. Layer half the Béchamel sauce and half the spaghetti sauce in 9x13-inch baking dish. Arrange manicotti in prepared dish; cover with foil. Chill manicotti and remaining sauces until baking time. Layer remaining Béchamel sauce and spaghetti sauce over manicotti. Bake, covered, at 400 degrees for 30 minutes. Garnish with additional Parmesan cheese.

Carole Marcum

 Bake meat loaf in greased muffin cups for a speedy supper.

German Spaghetti

Yield:
6 servings

Approx Per
Serving:
Cal 656
Prot 32 g
Carbo 60 g
Fiber 7 g
T Fat 35 g
Chol 95 mg
Sod 1260 mg

1 pound lean ground beef
2 green bell peppers, chopped
2 medium onions, chopped
1 clove of garlic, chopped
1 tablespoon butter
8 ounces uncooked thin spaghetti
Salt to taste

1 10-ounce can tomato soup
1 20-ounce can cream-style corn
1 4-ounce can mushrooms
1 8-ounce can pitted black olives, drained
8 ounces extra-sharp Cheddar cheese, shredded

Brown ground beef with green peppers, onions and garlic in butter in saucepan, stirring until ground beef is crumbly; drain. Cook spaghetti using package directions; drain. Add to beef mixture. Add salt, soup, corn, mushrooms and olives; mix well. Layer meat sauce and cheese 1/2 at a time in baking dish. Bake at 350 degrees for 30 minutes.

Helen A. Canter

Skillet Spaghetti

Yield:
6 servings

Approx Per
Serving:
Cal 427
Prot 26 g
Carbo 42 g
Fiber 5 g
T Fat 18 g
Chol 69 mg
Sod 779 mg

8 ounces uncooked spaghetti
1 pound ground beef
1 cup chopped onion
1 clove of garlic, minced
1 16-ounce can tomatoes, crushed
1 6-ounce can tomato paste

1 6-ounce can mushrooms, drained
1 tablespoon Italian seasoning
1 teaspoon sugar
1 teaspoon salt
1 cup shredded Cheddar or Colby cheese

Cook spaghetti using package directions; drain. Brown ground beef with onion and garlic in large skillet, stirring until ground beef is crumbly; drain. Add tomatoes, tomato paste, mushrooms, Italian seasoning, sugar and salt; mix well. Simmer for 15 minutes. Stir in spaghetti and cheese. Simmer, covered, for 5 minutes.

Jan Carothers

Spaghetti Pie

Yield:
8 servings

Approx Per
Serving:
Cal 424
Prot 26 g
Carbo 27 g
Fiber 2 g
T Fat 23 g
Chol 126 mg
Sod 613 mg

6 ounces uncooked
  spaghetti
2 tablespoons butter
1/3 cup Parmesan
  cheese
2 eggs, beaten
1 cup cottage cheese

1 pound ground beef
1 small onion, chopped
1   15-ounce jar
  spaghetti sauce
8 ounces mozzarella
  cheese, shredded

Cook spaghetti using package directions; drain. Stir in butter and Parmesan cheese. Place in 10-inch pie plate, shaping to form crust. Combine eggs and cottage cheese in bowl; mix well. Spread over crust. Brown ground beef with onion in skillet, stirring until ground beef is crumbly; drain. Stir in spaghetti sauce. Spoon into prepared pie plate. Bake at 350 degrees for 20 minutes. Sprinkle with mozzarella cheese. Bake for 5 minutes longer.

Norma Adams

Chili Relleno Pie

Yield:
4 servings

Approx Per
Serving:
Cal 885
Prot 59 g
Carbo 17 g
Fiber 3 g
T Fat 65 g
Chol 421 mg
Sod 1165 mg

1 pound ground beef
1 green bell pepper,
  chopped
1 medium onion,
  chopped
1 clove of garlic,
  chopped
1/4 teaspoon oregano
Salt and pepper to
  taste
1   7-ounce can green
  chili peppers

8 ounces Monterey
  Jack cheese,
  shredded
8 ounces sharp
  Cheddar cheese,
  shredded
4 eggs, slightly beaten
1 cup half and half
1 tablespoon flour
1   8-ounce can tomato
  sauce

Brown ground beef with green pepper, onion, garlic, oregano, salt and pepper in skillet, stirring until ground beef is crumbly; drain. Cut chili peppers into sections. Layer chili peppers, ground beef mixture and cheeses in baking dish. Combine eggs, half and half and flour in bowl; mix well. Pour over layers. Bake at 375 degrees for 45 minutes. Spread tomato sauce over top. Bake for 10 minutes longer. May omit ground beef for a meatless main dish.

Dorothy Mason

GROUND BEEF AND POTATO PIE

Yield:
8 servings

Approx Per
Serving:
Cal 410
Prot 17 g
Carbo 40 g
Fiber 2 g
T Fat 20 g
Chol 44 mg
Sod 800 mg

1 small onion, chopped
1 clove of garlic,
   chopped
2 tablespoons oil
2 medium potatoes,
   chopped
1 pound ground beef
1/2 cup milk

1   4-ounce can sliced
   mushrooms
1   10-ounce can cream
   of mushroom soup
Salt and pepper to
   taste
2 cups baking mix
1 cup milk

Sauté onion and garlic in oil in skillet. Add potatoes and ground beef. Cook until ground beef is brown and crumbly, stirring frequently; drain. Add 1/2 cup milk, mushrooms, soup, salt and pepper. Cook for 5 minutes. Spoon into 2-quart baking dish. Blend baking mix and 1 cup milk in bowl. Spoon over ground beef mixture. Bake at 350 degrees for 40 minutes or until golden brown.

Sharon Ann Moore

STIR-FRIED GROUND BEEF AND VEGETABLES

Yield:
6 servings

Approx Per
Serving:
Cal 345
Prot 30 g
Carbo 8 g
Fiber 2 g
T Fat 22 g
Chol 99 mg
Sod 275 mg

2 pounds ground beef
1 medium onion,
   chopped
1   10-ounce package
   frozen mixed
   vegetables

1 tablespoon soy sauce
Garlic powder and
   MSG to taste
Pepper to taste

Brown ground beef in hot skillet for 3 minutes, stirring until crumbly. Add onion and mixed vegetables. Stir-fry over low heat for 5 minutes. Add soy sauce, garlic powder, MSG and pepper. Cook for 2 minutes. Serve with rice, noodles or mashed potatoes.

Patricia Julien

Vietta's Surprise Indiana Casserole

Yield:
6 servings

Approx Per Serving:
Cal 425
Prot 26 g
Carbo 34 g
Fiber 4 g
T Fat 21 g
Chol 69 mg
Sod 760 mg

1 pound ground beef
1 tablespoon oil
1/2 cup chopped onion
1   16-ounce can tomatoes
1   8-ounce can tomato sauce
1   8-ounce can sliced mushrooms
Celery salt, salt and pepper to taste
1 1/4 cups uncooked fine noodles
1   8-ounce can small green peas
4 ounces Cheddar cheese, shredded

Brown ground beef in oil in saucepan, stirring until crumbly. Add onion. Cook until onion is light brown; drain. Add tomatoes, tomato sauce, un-drained mushrooms, celery salt, salt and pepper. Bring to a boil. Stir in noodles. Simmer over low heat for 30 minutes or until noodles are tender. Stir in peas. Spoon into medium baking dish. Top with cheese. Bake at 350 degrees for 15 minutes.

Michael Dutch

Ham Loaf

Yield:
8 servings

Approx Per Serving:
Cal 389
Prot 38 g
Carbo 15 g
Fiber 1 g
T Fat 19 g
Chol 109 mg
Sod 1050 mg

2 pounds lean pork shoulder, ground
1 pound uncooked ham, ground
1 cup bread crumbs
1 cup milk
Salt and pepper to taste
1 cup tomato soup

Combine ground pork, ground ham, bread crumbs, milk, salt, pepper and half the soup in bowl; mix well. Shape into loaf; place in loaf pan. Make indentation in top of loaf. Spoon remaining tomato soup into indentation. Bake at 350 degrees for 1 1/2 hours. Serve with hot mustard sauce. May substitute ground veal for ground ham or cracker crumbs for bread crumbs if desired.

Jan K. Schmalz

Ham Loaves with Tippy Sauce

Yield:
12 servings

Approx Per Serving:
Cal 482
Prot 38 g
Carbo 30 g
Fiber <1 g
T Fat 23 g
Chol 177 mg
Sod 1506 mg

2 pounds lean smoked ham, ground
2 pounds lean fresh pork, ground
1½ cups cracker crumbs
⅓ cup chopped onion
4 eggs, beaten
2 cups milk
1¼ teaspoons salt
1 cup (heaping) packed brown sugar
½ cup vinegar
1½ tablespoons dry mustard
½ cup mayonnaise
½ cup sour cream
2 tablespoons prepared horseradish

Combine ham, pork, cracker crumbs, onion, eggs, milk and salt in bowl; mix well. Shape into 2 loaves; place in 5x9-inch loaf pans. Combine brown sugar, vinegar and dry mustard in bowl. Bake ham loaves at 350 degrees for 30 minutes. Baste with brown sugar sauce. Bake for 30 minutes longer, basting as desired. Mix mayonnaise, sour cream and horseradish in small bowl. Serve with ham loaves.

Marge Fritz

Ham and Potato Bake

Yield:
6 servings

Approx Per Serving:
Cal 268
Prot 11 g
Carbo 40 g
Fiber 4 g
T Fat 8 g
Chol 21 mg
Sod 728 mg

4 cups sliced potatoes
1 cup chopped cooked ham
1 small onion, chopped
1 tablespoon butter
1 10-ounce can cream of mushroom soup
½ cup milk
Paprika and pepper to taste

Alternate layers of potatoes, ham and onion in buttered 2-quart baking dish, ending with potatoes. Dot with butter. Combine soup, milk, paprika and pepper in bowl; mix well. Spread over layers. Bake, covered, at 375 degrees for 1 hour. Bake, uncovered, for 15 minutes longer. May heat soup mixture to reduce baking time if desired. May substitute cream of celery or chicken soup for mushroom if preferred.

Sharon L. Rohrback

 Chop leftover ham and add to macaroni and cheese, scrambled eggs, quiche or dried beans or lentils.

JOYCE'S HAM ROLLS

Yield:
4 servings

Approx Per Serving:
Cal 473
Prot 26 g
Carbo 26 g
Fiber 1 g
T Fat 30 g
Chol 142 mg
Sod 1254 mg

1/4 cup minced onion
3 tablespoons butter
1 cup bread crumbs
1/2 cup Parmesan cheese
2 tablespoons minced parsley
1 egg, beaten
8 ham slices
1 cup sour cream
2 tablespoons prepared horseradish
2 tablespoons flour

Sauté onion in butter in skillet until golden brown. Add bread crumbs, cheese and parsley; mix well. Heat until bubbly. Stir in egg. Cook for several minutes, stirring connstantly. Spoon onto ham slices; roll to enclose filling. Arrange in lightly buttered rectangular baking dish. Combine sour cream, horseradish and flour in bowl; mix well. Spoon over ham rolls. Bake at 350 degrees for 20 minutes.

Dawn C. Frizzell

HOT DOGGIE CASSEROLE

Yield:
8 servings

Approx Per Serving:
Cal 538
Prot 19 g
Carbo 35 g
Fiber 4 g
T Fat 36 g
Chol 65 mg
Sod 968 mg

4 medium potatoes
Salt to taste
1/2 cup chopped onion
6 tablespoons margarine
1/4 cup flour
1 1/2 cups milk
1 1/2 cups shredded Cheddar cheese
1   10-ounce package frozen chopped spinach
1   16-ounce package hot dogs
1/2 cup shredded Cheddar cheese

Cook potatoes in salted water to cover in saucepan for 30 minutes or until tender. Drain and cool slightly. Peel potatoes and slice 1/4 inch thick. Sauté onion in margarine in heavy saucepan over low heat. Stir in flour. Cook for 1 minute, stirring constantly. Add milk gradually. Cook over medium heat until thickened, stirring constantly; remove from heat. Stir in 1 1/2 cups cheese. Cook spinach using package directions; drain well. Stir into cheese sauce. Reserve 4 hot dogs. Cut remaining hot dogs into 1/2-inch pieces. Layer half the potatoes in greased 8x12-inch baking dish. Layer hot dogs pieces and half the spinach mixture over potatoes. Top with remaining potatoes and spinach mixture. Slice reserved hot dogs lengthwise into 4 slices, leaving 1 end intact. Arrange on casserole, fanning out slices. Bake, covered, for 40 minutes. Sprinkle with 1/2 cup cheese. Bake for 5 minutes longer.

Shelly Bokman

MOM'S PORK AND BEAN BAKE

Yield:
4 servings

Approx Per Serving:
Cal 695
Prot 21 g
Carbo 78 g
Fiber 12 g
T Fat 35 g
Chol 75 mg
Sod 1772 mg

1 28-ounce can pork and beans
1 16-ounce can pineapple chunks, drained
2 tablespoons molasses
2 teaspoons prepared mustard
¼ cup packed brown sugar
⅛ teaspoon cinnamon
Cloves to taste
8 hot dogs
2 tablespoons melted butter

Combine beans, pineapple, molasses, mustard, brown sugar, cinnamon and cloves in bowl; mix well. Spoon into 2-quart baking dish. Score hot dogs lengthwise. Arrange over casserole; brush with butter. Bake at 350 degrees for 30 minutes.

Dawn C. Frizzell

APPLE-GLAZED PORK CUTLETS

Yield:
2 servings

Approx Per Serving:
Cal 860
Prot 49 g
Carbo 23 g
Fiber 1 g
T Fat 61 g
Chol 263 mg
Sod 2295 mg

1½ tablespoons finely chopped yellow onion
1½ tablespoons finely chopped green onions
⅛ teaspoon finely chopped garlic
1 teaspoon basil
2 tablespoons butter
Dry mustard to taste
1 pound pork tenderloin
3 tablespoons flour
1½ teaspoons salt
1½ teaspoons pepper
6 tablespoons butter
¼ cup white wine
½ cup chicken stock
1½ tablespoons spiced apple jelly

Sauté onion, green onions, garlic and basil in 2 tablespoons butter in small saucepan for 2 minutes. Stir in dry mustard. Cut pork into 2-inch slices. Pound to ¾-inch thickness with meat mallet. Coat with mixture of flour, salt and pepper. Brown lightly on both sides in 6 tablespoons butter in skillet. Remove to warm plate; drain skillet. Add wine, stirring to deglaze. Cook until nearly reduced. Add chicken stock and sautéed vegetables. Stir in jelly. Cook over medium heat until reduced to thin glaze. Add pork, turning to coat well. Place pork on serving plate; pour sauce over top.

Robert L. Stricker

BARBECUED SPARERIBS

Yield:
6 servings

Approx Per Serving:
Cal 671
Prot 45 g
Carbo 17 g
Fiber 1 g
T Fat 46 g
Chol 183 mg
Sod 1101 mg

3 pounds spareribs
1 lemon, sliced
1 medium onion, sliced
1/3 cup Worcestershire sauce
1 cup catsup
2 cups water
2 dashes of Tabasco sauce
1 teaspoon chili powder
1 teaspoon salt

Cut spareribs into serving pieces. Arrange in 10x12-inch baking pan. Top with lemon and onion. Combine Worcestershire sauce, catsup, water, Tabasco sauce, chili powder and salt in saucepan. Bring to a boil. Pour over spareribs. Bake at 450 degrees for 30 minutes; reduce oven temperature to 350 degrees. Bake for 1 hour longer, basting every 15 minutes.

Grace Kessler

SAUSAGE AND BROCCOLI PASTA BAKE

Yield:
8 servings

Approx Per Serving:
Cal 242
Prot 9 g
Carbo 23 g
Fiber 1 g
T Fat 13 g
Chol 22 mg
Sod 664 mg

1 7-ounce package macaroni and cheese dinner
1 10-ounce package frozen broccoli spears, thawed, drained
1 pound smoked sausage
1 10-ounce can cream of celery soup
1/4 cup sliced green onions

Prepare macaroni and cheese dinner using package directions. Cut broccoli into 1-inch pieces; cut sausage into 1/2-inch pieces. Combine dinner with broccoli, sausage, soup and green onions in bowl; mix well. Chill, covered, until serving time. Spoon into 2-quart baking dish. Bake, covered, at 350 degrees for 50 minutes. May microwave on High for 8 minutes or until heated through, turning dish after 4 minutes. Flavor improves with reheating.

Shelly Bokman

 Rib, blade, arm and loin end pork chops are just as delicious and nutritious as center-cut and cost less.

SAUSAGE AND EGG CASSEROLE

Yield:
6 servings

Approx Per Serving:
Cal 581
Prot 29 g
Carbo 19 g
Fiber 1 g
T Fat 43 g
Chol 308 mg
Sod 836 mg

6 slices bread, crusts trimmed
2 cups milk
1 pound sausage
6 eggs, beaten

12 ounces sharp Cheddar cheese, shredded
1/2 teaspoon dry mustard
Salt to taste

Soak bread in milk in bowl. Brown sausage in skillet, stirring until crumbly; drain. Add to bread mixture. Add eggs, cheese, dry mustard and salt; mix well. Spoon into baking dish. Bake at 350 degrees for 40 minutes. May prepare in advance and refrigerate overnight. We serve this dish at breakfast on Christmas morning.

Anna K. McNeil

SAUSAGE AND EGG STRATA

Yield:
8 servings

Approx Per Serving:
Cal 321
Prot 15 g
Carbo 14 g
Fiber <1 g
T Fat 23 g
Chol 201 mg
Sod 717 mg

1 pound sausage
6 slices bread
6 eggs
2 cups milk

1 teaspoon dry mustard
1 teaspoon salt
1 cup shredded Cheddar cheese

Brown sausage in skillet, stirring until crumbly; drain. Layer bread and sausage in 9x13-inch baking dish. Beat eggs in bowl. Add milk, dry mustard and salt; mix well. Pour over layers. Sprinkle with cheese. Chill overnight. Bake, covered with foil, at 350 degrees for 20 minutes. Bake, uncovered, for 20 to 25 minutes or until set. We serve this on Christmas morning.

Linda A. Leavitt

Tortelini and Kielbasa

Yield:
12 servings

Approx Per
Serving:
Cal 399
Prot 16 g
Carbo 34 g
Fiber 3 g
T Fat 21 g
Chol 50 mg
Sod 797 mg

1 onion, chopped
1 green bell pepper,
  chopped
1 red bell pepper,
  chopped
2 stalks celery, sliced 1
  inch thick
2 cloves of garlic,
  minced
1 tablespoon pepper
2 tablespoons oil

3 pounds kielbasa,
  sliced 1/2 inch thick
16 ounces tortelini,
  cooked
1 8-ounce can stewed
  tomatoes
8 slices mozzarella
  cheese
1 8-ounce can tomato
  sauce

Sauté onion, bell peppers, celery and garlic with pepper in oil in skillet until tender. Remove to dish. Add kielbasa to skillet. Cook until heated through. Alternate layers of vegetable mixture, kielbasa, pasta, tomatoes and cheese in 3-quart baking dish until all ingredients are used. Top with tomato sauce. Place dish on baking sheet. Bake at 350 degrees for 1 hour.

Alice McDonald

Sloppy Giuseppe

Yield:
6 servings

Approx Per
Serving:
Cal 437
Prot 15 g
Carbo 55 g
Fiber 4 g
T Fat 18 g
Chol 28 mg
Sod 1458 mg

1 pound Italian link
  sausage, sliced
1 large onion, coarsely
  chopped
2 large green bell
  peppers, coarsely
  chopped

1 32-ounce jar
  meatless spaghetti
  sauce
6 English muffins,
  split, toasted

Brown sausage in saucepan; drain. Add onion, green peppers and spaghetti sauce; mix well. Simmer for 30 minutes. Serve over English muffins.

Justine A. Smith

VEAL DELIGHT

Yield:
6 servings

Approx Per Serving:
Cal 417
Prot 40 g
Carbo 18 g
Fiber 2 g
T Fat 20 g
Chol 214 mg
Sod 1018 mg

1/2 cup cornflake crumbs
1/2 cup cracker meal
1/4 teaspoon each paprika, salt and pepper
1 medium onion, chopped
1 small green bell pepper, chopped
1 tablespoon butter
6 medium veal shoulder steaks
1 egg, beaten
1/4 cup butter
1 8-ounce can tomato sauce
1 8-ounce can mushrooms, drained
1 cup beef bouillon
4 drops of Worcestershire sauce
3 drops of Tabasco sauce
1 cup shredded mozzarella cheese

Mix cornflake crumbs, cracker meal, paprika, salt and pepper in bowl. Sauté onion and green pepper in 1 tablespoon butter in large skillet until tender-crisp; remove with slotted spoon. Dip veal steaks in egg; coat with crumb mixture. Brown on 1 side in 2 tablespoons butter in skillet. Add 2 tablespoons butter and turn steaks. Cook until brown on remaining side. Combine next 5 ingredients with sautéed vegetables. Pour over veal. Simmer, covered, for 15 to 20 minutes. Sprinkle with cheese. Simmer until cheese melts.

Dawn C. Frizzell

VEAL MARSALA

Yield:
6 servings

Approx Per Serving:
Cal 305
Prot 24 g
Carbo 5 g
Fiber <1 g
T Fat 20 g
Chol 117 mg
Sod 648 mg

1 1/2 pounds 1/2-inch thick veal
1/4 cup flour
1 teaspoon salt
1/8 teaspoon pepper
1 clove of garlic, minced
2 green onions, chopped
1/4 cup olive oil
1/4 cup butter
1/4 cup Marsala
1/4 cup water
1 cup beef consommé
1/4 teaspoon parsley
1/8 teaspoon salt
1/8 teaspoon pepper

Pound veal with meat mallet. Cut into long slices. Coat with mixture of flour, 1 teaspoon salt and 1/8 teaspoon pepper. Sauté garlic and green onions in olive oil and butter in large heavy skillet until light brown. Add veal. Brown lightly on both sides. Mix wine with remaining ingredients. Add to veal gradually. Simmer, covered, for 20 minutes or until veal is tender and sauce is slightly thickened. Serve with spaghetti.

M. Irene Richmond

Poultry
and Seafood

The Tomb of the Unknown

ANDY'S BLEU CHEESE CHICKEN

Yield:
6 servings

**Approx Per
Serving:**
*Cal 725
Prot 48 gr
Carbo 38 g
Fiber 1 g
T Fat 42 g
Chol 120 mg
Sod 1102 mg*

3 pounds chicken
  breasts
2 8-ounce bottles of
   bleu cheese salad
   dressing
1/4 cup milk
2 cups flour

1 teaspoon pepper
1/2 teaspoon seasoned
   salt
1/2 teaspoon Old Bay
   seasoning
Salt to taste

Rinse chicken; pat dry. Pour salad dressing into bowl; rinse bottles with milk and add to salad dressing. Mix flour and seasonings in shallow bowl. Coat chicken with flour; roll in salad dressing. Arrange in 9x13-inch baking dish. Pour any remaining salad dressing over chicken. Bake, uncovered, at 350 degrees for 1 hour. May substitute mixed chicken pieces or thighs for breasts. This dish is enjoyed even by those who claim not to like bleu cheese.

Nutritional information does not include Old Bay seasoning.

Bonnie Klepp-Egge

CHICKEN AND BROCCOLI CASSEROLE

Yield:
8 servings

**Approx Per
Serving:**
*Cal 234
Prot 15 gr
Carbo 7 g
Fiber 2 g
T Fat 17 g
Chol 44 mg
Sod 456 mg*

4 chicken breasts
2 10-ounce packages
   frozen broccoli
   spears
1 10-ounce can cream
   of chicken soup
1/2 cup mayonnaise
1/2 teaspoon curry
   powder

1/2 teaspoon lemon
   juice
1/2 cup water
1/2 cup shredded
   Cheddar cheese
1/4 cup fresh bread
   crumbs
1 tablespoon melted
   margarine

Rinse chicken; place in saucepan with water to cover. Simmer until tender. Drain chicken; skin and bone. Cook broccoli until almost tender using package directions; drain. Layer broccoli and chicken in 9x13-inch baking dish. Combine soup, mayonnaise, curry powder, lemon juice and water in bowl; mix well. Spoon over chicken. Sprinkle with cheese. Toss crumbs with margarine; sprinkle over top. Bake at 350 degrees for 45 minutes.

Dale N. Bradley

CHICKEN AND BISCUITS CASSEROLE

Yield:
6 servings

**Approx Per
Serving:**
*Cal 420
Prot 24 gr
Carbo 32 g
Fiber 4 g
T Fat 21 g
Chol 52 mg
Sod 393 mg*

1 cup chopped onion
2 tablespoons margarine
1/4 cup dry Sherry
1 10-ounce can low-
   sodium chicken broth
1/4 cup flour
1 teaspoon poultry
   seasoning
Salt to taste
2 1/2 cups chopped
   cooked chicken
   breasts

1 10-ounce package
   frozen peas and
   carrots, thawed
3/4 cup flour
3/4 cup oats
2 teaspoons baking
   powder
6 tablespoons margarine
1/2 cup skim milk
1 egg white

Sauté onion in 2 tablespoons margarine in skillet over medium heat for 3 minutes or until tender. Blend Sherry, broth, 1/4 cup flour, poultry seasoning and salt in small bowl. Stir into skillet. Cook until thickened, stirring constantly. Mix in chicken and vegetables. Pour into 2-quart casserole. Combine 3/4 cup flour, oats and baking powder in bowl. Cut in 6 tablespoons margarine until crumbly. Add skim milk and egg white; mix until moistened. Drop by 1/4 cupfuls over chicken mixture. Bake at 425 degrees for 38 to 42 minutes or until golden brown.

Joyce M. Michaels

CHICKEN DIVINE

Yield:
6 servings

**Approx Per
Serving:**
*Cal 480
Prot 31 gr
Carbo 17 g
Fiber 3 g
T Fat 33 g
Chol 97 mg
Sod 795 mg*

6 chicken breasts
Chopped celery to taste
Chopped carrots to taste
2 10-ounce packages
   frozen broccoli spears,
   cooked, drained
1 10-ounce can cream
   of chicken soup
2/3 cup mayonnaise

1/3 cup evaporated milk
1 cup shredded
   Cheddar cheese
1 teaspoon lemon juice
1/2 teaspoon curry
   powder
1 tablespoon melted
   butter
1/2 cup bread crumbs

Rinse chicken. Cook with celery and carrots in water to cover in large saucepan for 25 minutes or until tender; drain and discard celery and carrots. Layer broccoli and chicken in 9x13-inch baking dish. Mix next 5 ingredients in bowl. Pour over layers. Sprinkle mixture of butter and crumbs over top. Bake at 375 degrees for 30 minutes or until brown.

Donna Adams

MARINATED SLICED CHICKEN BREAST

Yield:
6 servings

Approx Per Serving:
Cal 276
Prot 21 gr
Carbo 2 g
Fiber <1 g
T Fat 20 g
Chol 52 mg
Sod 486 mg

6 chicken breasts, skinned
Minced zest of 1 lemon
1 tablespoon lemon juice
1 teaspoon salt
1/8 teaspoon pepper
1/2 teaspoon rosemary
1 or 2 cloves of garlic, minced
1/4 cup olive oil
1/2 cup fresh Italian-style bread crumbs
1/4 cup Parmesan cheese
1/4 cup olive oil

Rinse chicken; pat dry. Sprinkle with lemon zest and juice. Combine salt, pepper, rosemary, garlic and 1/4 cup olive oil in small bowl; mix well. Add chicken, coating well. Marinate in refrigerator for 30 minutes. Scrape off olive oil mixture; pat chicken dry with paper towels. Cut chicken into 3/8x2-inch slices. Coat slices with mixture of bread crumbs and cheese. Heat remaining 1/4 cup olive oil in skillet over high heat. Add chicken. Cook for 3 to 5 minutes or until cooked through, tossing frequently. Serve with Beaujolais or California Chenin Blanc.

Nutritional information includes marinade.

Suzie Carothers

MUSHROOM CHICKEN

Yield:
4 servings

Approx Per Serving:
Cal 228
Prot 21 gr
Carbo 6 g
Fiber <1 g
T Fat 12 g
Chol 65 mg
Sod 679 mg

4 chicken breasts
2 tablespoons melted butter
1   10-ounce can golden mushroom soup
1/2 cup chopped tomato
2 tablespoons dry Sherry
1/2 teaspoon dried basil leaves, crushed

Rinse chicken; pat dry. Arrange skin side down in 8x12-inch baking dish. Drizzle with butter. Bake at 375 degrees for 20 minutes. Turn chicken skin side up. Bake for 20 minutes longer. Combine soup, tomato, Sherry and basil in bowl; mix well. Pour over chicken. Bake for 20 minutes longer or until tender. Remove chicken to serving plate. Stir sauce to mix well. Serve over hot cooked rice.

Bill Caldwell

MUSHROOM AND WINE CHICKEN BREASTS

Yield:
6 servings

Approx Per Serving:
Cal 251
Prot 22 gr
Carbo 7 g
Fiber 1 g
T Fat 11 g
Chol 50 mg
Sod 667 mg

6 chicken breasts, skinned
1/2 cup chopped onion
1/2 cup chopped celery
3 tablespoons margarine
1 10-ounce can chicken broth
1 10-ounce can cream of mushroom soup
Salt and pepper to taste
2 cups sliced fresh mushrooms
1 to 1 1/2 cups white wine

Rinse chicken; pat dry. Sauté onion and celery in margarine in skillet; remove to bowl. Cook chicken in skillet for 3 to 5 minutes on each side or until golden brown. Arrange in 9x13-inch baking dish. Mix sautéed vegetables with broth, soup, salt and pepper. Pour over chicken. Add mushrooms. Bake at 350 degrees for 30 minutes. Stir in wine. Bake for 10 minutes longer. Serve with P.O.T. Rice (page 135) and green vegetable.

Elise P. Evans

CHICKEN PRIMAVERA

Yield:
4 servings

Approx Per Serving:
Cal 308
Prot 23 gr
Carbo 10 g
Fiber 1 g
T Fat 20 g
Chol 65 mg
Sod 734 mg

1 10-ounce can cream of chicken soup
1/3 cup mayonnaise
2 teaspoons paprika
4 chicken breast filets
2 cups mixed chopped celery, onion and green bell pepper

Combine soup, mayonnaise and paprika in large deep skillet; mix well. Rinse chicken; pat dry. Arrange chicken in skillet. Add vegetables. Bring to a simmer. Simmer for 20 minutes or until chicken and vegetables are tender. Serve over hot cooked rice.

June Weakley

 For *Easy Marinated Chicken Breasts*, *marinate chicken breast filets in a mixture of 1/2 cup soy sauce, minced garlic, 3/4 teaspoon ginger, 2 tablespoons sugar and 1 ounce Sherry for 4 to 6 hours. Grill for 15 minutes.*

Quick Chicken Chasseur

Yield:
6 servings

Approx Per
Serving:
Cal 347
Prot 18 gr
Carbo 36 g
Fiber 2 g
T Fat 11 g
Chol 33 mg
Sod 304 mg

1 pound chicken
  breast filets
1/3 cup cornstarch
1/4 cup oil
1/2 teaspoon tarragon
1/2 teaspoon thyme
1/4 teaspoon pepper
1 cup sliced scallions

2 cups chicken broth
3/4 cup cooking Sherry
1 cup sliced
  mushrooms
3 tomatoes, cut into
  eighths
3 cups hot cooked rice

Rinse chicken; pat dry. Cut into strips. Coat with cornstarch. Cook in oil in skillet until brown on all sides. Add tarragon, thyme, pepper and scallions. Cook for 2 minutes. Add broth and Sherry. Cook, covered, over low heat for 10 minutes. Stir in mushrooms and tomatoes gently. Simmer, covered, for 5 minutes longer. Serve over or with rice.

Marge Fritz

Tucson Hot Chicken Salad

Yield:
8 servings

Approx Per
Serving:
Cal 528
Prot 24 gr
Carbo 22 g
Fiber 3 g
T Fat 39 g
Chol 65 mg
Sod 1198 mg

6 1/2 chicken breasts
3 10-ounce cans
  cream of chicken
  soup
1 cup mayonnaise
3 tablespoons lemon
  juice

2 cups chopped celery
1 cup slivered almonds
1 cup crushed potato
  chips
1 cup herb-seasoned
  stuffing mix

Rinse chicken. Cook chicken in a small amount of water in saucepan until tender. Drain, bone and coarsely chop chicken. Combine chicken, soup, mayonnaise, lemon juice, celery and almonds in bowl; mix well. Spoon into buttered casserole. Top with mixture of potato chips and stuffing mix. Bake at 350 degrees for 45 minutes.

Pat Henning

STEWED CHICKEN CASSEROLE

Yield:
10 servings

Approx Per
Serving:
Cal 153
Prot 14 gr
Carbo 7 g
Fiber <1 g
T Fat 7 g
Chol 48 mg
Sod 300 mg

6 large chicken breasts
1 1½-ounce envelope tuna casserole mix
2 tablespoons butter
2 cups milk
1 10-ounce can cream of celery soup
1 3-ounce can French-fried onions

Rinse chicken. Cook in water to cover in saucepan until tender. Drain, bone, and chop chicken; place in oiled casserole. Combine tuna casserole mix and butter in saucepan. Stir in milk. Cook until heated through, stirring constantly. Add soup; mix well. Pour over chicken. Bake at 350 degrees for 30 minutes. Sprinkle with onions. Bake for 5 minutes longer.

Nutritional information does not include tuna mix.

Reba G. Anderson

STUFFED CHICKEN BREASTS IN PHYLLO CRUST

Yield:
8 servings

Approx Per
Serving:
Cal 369
Prot 30 gr
Carbo 25 g
Fiber 2 g
T Fat 17 g
Chol 81 mg
Sod 439 mg

1 10-ounce package frozen chopped spinach, thawed
1 cup shredded Swiss cheese
¼ cup ricotta cheese
½ teaspoon salt
½ teaspoon minced garlic
¼ cup chopped walnuts
¼ cup chopped onion
8 chicken breast filets
8 ounces phyllo dough
2 to 3 tablespoons melted butter
2 tablespoons melted margarine
2 tablespoons flour
3 tablespoons chopped green onions
1 tablespoon Brandy
1 tablespoon tomato paste
¼ cup sour cream
Salt and pepper to taste

Drain spinach well. Combine with next 6 ingredients in bowl; mix well. Rinse chicken; pat dry. Pound to even thickness. Spoon 3 tablespoons spinach mixture onto each chicken breast; roll to enclose filling. Fold phyllo sheets into halves; brush with melted butter. Wrap chicken in dough; place seam side down on greased baking sheet. Brush with melted butter. Bake at 400 degrees until golden brown. Blend 2 tablespoons melted margarine with flour in saucepan. Add next 3 ingredients. Cook until thickened, stirring constantly. Stir in sour cream, salt and pepper. Heat to serving temperature; do not boil. Serve over chicken.

Doris A. Baylor

Chicken Waikiki Beach

Yield:
4 servings

Approx Per
Serving:
Cal 884
Prot 47 gr
Carbo 98 g
Fiber 2 g
T Fat 35 g
Chol 125 mg
Sod 1210 mg

4 chicken leg quarters
4 chicken breast quarters
1/2 cup flour
1 teaspoon salt
1/4 teaspoon pepper
1/2 cup oil
1   20-ounce can sliced
    pineapple
1 cup sugar

2 tablespoons
    cornstarch
1/2 cup vinegar
1 tablespoon soy sauce
1/4 teaspoon ginger
1 chicken bouillon cube
1 large green bell
    pepper, sliced
    crosswise

Rinse chicken; pat dry. Coat with mixture of flour, salt and pepper. Fry in hot oil in skillet until brown on all sides. Arrange in 9x13-inch baking dish. Drain pineapple, reserving juice. Add enough water to reserved juice to measure 1 1/4 cups. Combine with sugar, cornstarch, vinegar, soy sauce, ginger and bouillon cube in saucepan; mix well. Bring to a boil, stirring constantly. Boil for 2 minutes. Pour over chicken. Bake, uncovered, for 30 minutes. Add pineapple and green pepper slices. Bake for 30 minutes longer. Serve with fluffy rice.

Audrey C. Rothman

Coq au Vin

Yield:
8 servings

Approx Per
Serving:
Cal 339
Prot 27 gr
Carbo 7 g
Fiber 1 g
T Fat 18 g
Chol 107 mg
Sod 597 mg

3 pounds chicken
1/2 cup butter
3 medium onions, cut
    into quarters
1 clove of garlic,
    minced
2 bay leaves
1/2 teaspoon thyme

1/4 teaspoon pepper
1 teaspoon salt
2 tablespoons flour
1   4-ounce can sliced
    mushrooms
1 cup chicken stock
2 cups white cooking
    wine

Rinse chicken. Cook chicken as desired; drain. Discard skin and bones. Melt butter in 12-inch skillet. Add chicken, onions and garlic. Sprinkle with mixture of bay leaves, thyme, pepper, salt and flour. Add mushrooms, chicken stock and wine. Simmer for 45 minutes. Refrigerate overnight. Reheat before serving; thicken sauce with additional flour if necessary. Discard bay leaves. Serve over rice or noodles with salad and crunchy bread. May add your own touches such as tomatoes, chopped ham, etc.

Fran Brosius

Deviled Chicken

Yield:
8 servings

Approx Per
Serving:
Cal 264
Prot 23 gr
Carbo 13 g
Fiber <1 g
T Fat 13 g
Chol 80 mg
Sod 780 mg

2 pounds chicken
   breasts and thighs
1 cup flour
1 teaspoon paprika
1 teaspoon salt
1/4 teaspoon pepper
1/2 cup butter
1/2 teaspoon salt

2 teaspoons prepared
   mustard
1 tablespoon
   Worcestershire sauce
1 tablespoon minced
   onion
2 cups chicken broth

Rinse chicken; pat dry. Coat with mixture of flour, paprika, 1 teaspoon salt and pepper; reserve remaining flour mixture. Brown chicken on all sides in butter in skillet; arrange in 9x13-inch baking dish. Blend 2 tablespoons reserved flour mixture into drippings in skillet. Add 1/2 teaspoon salt, mustard, Worcestershire sauce and onion; mix well. Stir in broth. Cook until thickened, stirring constantly. Pour over chicken. Bake, covered, at 350 degrees for 40 to 45 minutes or until tender.

Adelia C. Watson

Chicken and Dressing Casserole

Yield:
6 servings

Approx Per
Serving:
Cal 497
Prot 61 gr
Carbo 47 g
Fiber 2 g
T Fat 6 g
Chol 133 mg
Sod 1740 mg

1 4-pound chicken
3 cups bread crumbs
1 cup corn bread
   stuffing mix
1/4 cup chopped celery

1 tablespoon salt
1/4 teaspoon pepper
1/4 teaspoon poultry
   seasoning
2 tablespoons flour

Rinse chicken. Place in large saucepan with water to cover. Cook for 40 minutes or until tender. Drain, reserving 3 cups broth. Bone chicken; discard skin and bone. Combine bread crumbs, stuffing mix, celery, salt, pepper and poultry seasoning in bowl. Add 2 cups reserved broth; mix well. Layer chicken and dressing 1/2 at a time in 9x13-inch baking dish. Blend flour and 1/4 cup broth in saucepan. Cook until thickened, stirring constantly. Stir in remaining broth. Pour over layers. Bake at 350 degrees for 30 minutes.

Saundra Stalter

MAYCE CHICKEN CASSEROLE

Yield:
6 servings

Approx Per Serving:
Cal 419
Prot 27 gr
Carbo 44 g
Fiber 2 g
T Fat 14 g
Chol 84 mg
Sod 630 mg

1½ cups uncooked rice
½ cup (or more) chopped celery
¼ cup melted butter
½ cup chopped green bell pepper
½ cup sliced mushrooms
2½ cups chopped onions
1 envelope onion soup mix
Garlic salt to taste
3 cups chopped cooked chicken
3 cups skimmed chicken broth

Layer rice, celery, melted butter, green pepper, mushrooms, onions, soup mix, garlic salt and chicken in 1-quart baking dish. Pour broth over top. Bake, covered, at 350 degrees for 45 minutes or until rice is tender, adding a small amount of water if necessary.

Frank Stottlemyer

EASY BAKED CHICKEN

Yield:
4 servings

Approx Per Serving:
Cal 431
Prot 52 gr
Carbo 9 g
Fiber 1 g
T Fat 20 g
Chol 158 mg
Sod 755 mg

1 3-pound chicken, cut up
1 onion, chopped
2 stalks celery, chopped
1 tablespoon margarine
Salt and pepper to taste
½ cup water
1 10-ounce can cream of chicken soup

Rinse chicken; pat dry. Arrange in 9x13-inch baking dish. Layer onion and celery over chicken. Dot with margarine; sprinkle with salt and pepper. Drizzle water over top. Bake, uncovered, at 350 degrees for 20 minutes. Cover tightly with foil. Bake for 30 minutes longer. May substitute chicken breasts for whole chicken.

Jeannette Mobley

SKILLET CHICKEN

Yield:
4 servings

Approx Per Serving:
Cal 561
Prot 53 gr
Carbo 26 g
Fiber 3 g
T Fat 27 g
Chol 152 mg
Sod 961 mg

1   3-pound chicken, cut up
½ cup flour
¼ teaspoon garlic salt
¼ teaspoon pepper
¼ cup oil

1 medium onion, chopped
2   8-ounce cans tomato sauce
1 tablespoon sugar
1 teaspoon vinegar

Rinse chicken; pat dry. Shake chicken with mixture of flour, garlic salt and pepper in paper bag until coated. Brown on all sides in hot oil in skillet. Pour off oil. Combine onion, tomato sauce, sugar and vinegar in bowl; mix well. Pour over chicken in skillet. Simmer, covered, for 1 hour, basting occasionally.

Charlotte Wood

SPANISH CHICKEN

Yield:
6 servings

Approx Per Serving:
Cal 353
Prot 33 gr
Carbo 2 g
Fiber 1 g
T Fat 20 g
Chol 101 mg
Sod 103 mg

3 pounds chicken pieces
⅓ cup olive oil
1 cup white wine

1 cup chopped parsley
1 bay leaf
Minced garlic to taste
⅓ cup chopped onion

Sauté chicken in olive oil in skillet. Add wine, parsley, bay leaf, garlic and onion. Cook, covered, for 30 minutes or until chicken is tender. Discard bay leaf.

Hannah L. Spalding

*For **Easy Chicken and Rice**, layer 1 cup uncooked rice, chicken pieces and 1 envelope dry onion soup mix in baking dish and pour 4 cups chicken broth over top. Bake at 375 degrees for 1 hour.*

SPICED CHICKEN

1 cup orange juice
1½ cups undrained sliced canned peaches
2 tablespoons brown sugar
2 tablespoons tarragon vinegar
1 teaspoon nutmeg
1 teaspoon sweet basil
6 each chicken legs and thighs
½ cup flour
1 teaspoon salt
⅛ teaspoon pepper
Oil for frying

Combine first 6 ingredients in saucepan. Simmer for 10 minutes, stirring occasionally. Rinse chicken; pat dry. Coat with mixture of flour, salt and pepper. Cook in ½ inch hot oil in large skillet until brown on all sides. Pour off oil. Pour sauce over chicken in skillet. Simmer, covered, for 20 minutes or until tender. May use chicken breast filets if preferred. Serve with hot cooked rice and broccoli.

Nutritional information does not include oil for frying.

Mary Ann Davis

STEWED CHICKEN DINNER

1 4-pound chicken
1 teaspoon salt
3 medium potatoes, cut into halves
6 small onions
12 small carrots
1 head cauliflower, cut up
1 bunch broccoli, cut up
2 teaspoons flour
2 tablespoons melted shortening
1 teaspoon salt
½ teaspoon paprika
¼ cup grated horseradish
½ cup water
½ cup cream
2 egg yolks, well beaten

Rinse chicken. Combine with water to cover in stock pot. Bring to a boil; reduce heat. Simmer, covered, for 1½ to 2 hours. Add 1 teaspoon salt. Simmer for 30 minutes or until chicken is tender. Remove chicken. Cook vegetables in chicken broth until tender. Blend flour, shortening, 1 teaspoon salt and paprika in saucepan. Add horseradish, water and cream. Cook until thickened, stirring constantly. Stir a small amount of hot mixture into egg yolks; stir egg yolks into hot mixture. Cook for 1 minute, stirring constantly. Serve chicken with vegetables and horseradish sauce.

Helen A. Canter

Unbelievable Microwave Chicken

Yield:
4 servings

Approx Per Serving:
Cal 643
Prot 50 gr
Carbo 57 g
Fiber 1 g
T Fat 24 g
Chol 160 mg
Sod 389 mg

1 3-pound chicken, cut up
1 cup apricot-pineapple preserves
¼ cup mayonnaise
1 envelope onion soup mix

Rinse chicken; pat dry. Arrange in 8x12-inch baking dish with thicker pieces toward outer edge. Combine preserves, mayonnaise and soup mix in bowl; mix well. Spoon over chicken pieces, covering completely. Microwave, covered with waxed paper, on High for 18 to 22 minutes or until tender, rotating dish after 10 minutes. Let stand for 5 to 10 minutes before serving. Serve with hot cooked rice.

Robert Montgomery

Turkey Cakes

Yield:
8 servings

Approx Per Serving:
Cal 229
Prot 25 gr
Carbo 17 g
Fiber 1 g
T Fat 6 g
Chol 109 mg
Sod 128 mg

4 cups chopped cooked turkey
1 medium onion, chopped
1 teaspoon thyme
2 eggs, beaten
3 slices bread
½ cup milk
½ cup cornmeal
¼ cup flour
Oil for frying

Combine turkey, onion, thyme and eggs in bowl; mix well. Soak bread in milk in bowl. Add to turkey mixture; mix well. Shape into 3-inch patties. Coat with mixture of cornmeal and flour. Fry in oil in skillet over medium heat for 10 minutes on each side or until brown.

Nutritional information does not include oil for frying.

Colleen Campbell

 Roast a larger turkey than you need. Package leftovers in meal-sized portions and freeze for future use.

Turkey Tetrazzini

Yield:
8 servings

Approx Per
Serving:
Cal 383
Prot 20 gr
Carbo 30 g
Fiber 2 g
T Fat 19 g
Chol 73 mg
Sod 1097 mg

8 ounces uncooked
  spaghetti
1/2 cup melted butter
1/2 cup flour
2 1/2 cups chicken broth
1 cup half and half
1/4 cup cooking Sherry
1 teaspoon salt
1 teaspoon garlic
  powder
1 teaspoon thyme
1 teaspoon oregano

1 teaspoon basil
White pepper to taste
1/2 teaspoon MSG
1 6-ounce can
  mushrooms
1/4 cup chopped green
  bell pepper
2 cups chopped
  cooked turkey
1/2 cup Parmesan
  cheese

Cook spaghetti using package directions; drain and set aside. Blend butter and flour in saucepan. Stir in broth and half and half. Cook until thickened, stirring constantly. Stir in Sherry, seasonings, mushrooms, green pepper and turkey. Cook for 5 minutes, stirring constantly. Add spaghetti; mixture will be soupy. Pour into 9x13-inch baking dish. Sprinkle cheese over top. Bake at 350 degrees for 25 minutes or until brown and bubbly.

Lou Ann Maclay

Codfish Cakes

Yield:
6 servings

Approx Per
Serving:
Cal 289
Prot 16 gr
Carbo 34 g
Fiber 2 g
T Fat 10 g
Chol 118 mg
Sod 128 mg

1 pound salted codfish
6 medium potatoes,
  peeled
1/4 cup butter

1 tablespoon grated
  onion
1/8 teaspoon pepper
2 eggs

Soak codfish in cold water to cover overnight. Drain well. Cover with boiling water. Let stand for 20 minutes; drain. Cover again with boiling water. Let stand for 20 minutes; drain and flake. Cook potatoes in water to cover in saucepan until tender; drain and mash. Combine all ingredients in bowl; beat until well mixed. Shape into 18 small flat cakes; place on greased baking sheet. Bake at 350 degrees until golden brown. Serve with stewed tomatoes and a green vegetable. Cakes may be fried in hot shortening if desired.

Nutritional information is for fresh codfish. Salted codfish will have a higher level of sodium.

Tossie Wright

TUNA CASSEROLE

Yield:
8 servings

Approx Per Serving:
Cal 201
Prot 16 gr
Carbo 20 g
Fiber 3 g
T Fat 6 g
Chol 24 mg
Sod 490 mg

1 cup uncooked elbow macaroni
1 medium onion, chopped
1/2 green bell pepper, chopped
1/2 red bell pepper, chopped
1 stalk celery, chopped
2 tablespoons margarine
2 6-ounce cans water-pack tuna, drained
1 teaspoon pepper
1 10-ounce can cream of mushroom soup
1 10-ounce can mixed vegetables, drained

Cook macaroni using package directions; drain. Sauté onion, bell peppers and celery in margarine in skillet until tender. Combine macaroni, sautéed vegetables, tuna, pepper and soup in bowl; mix well. Add mixed vegetables; mix lightly. Spoon into 3-quart casserole. Bake at 350 degrees for 1 hour. May top with cheese if desired.

Alice McDonald

NO-BAKE TUNA CASSEROLE

Yield:
6 servings

Approx Per Serving:
Cal 193
Prot 15 gr
Carbo 27 g
Fiber 1 g
T Fat 4 g
Chol 21 mg
Sod 395 mg

1 medium green bell pepper, chopped
1 medium onion, chopped
1 tablespoon butter
1 7-ounce package macaroni and cheese dinner
1 6-ounce can water-pack tuna
Salt and pepper to taste

Sauté green pepper and onion in butter in skillet until light brown. Cook macaroni from dinner for 13 minutes using package directions; drain. Add sautéed vegetables, tuna and cheese mix from dinner; mix well. Season with salt and pepper.

Reneé Thompson

 Water-packed tuna has about 300 fewer calories per 6½-ounce can than tuna packed in oil.

Tuna and Noodle Skillet

Yield:
8 servings

Approx Per
Serving:
Cal 140
Prot 14 gr
Carbo 7 g
Fiber 1 g
T Fat 6 g
Chol 40 mg
Sod 261 mg

1 medium green bell
  pepper, chopped
1 cup chopped celery
2 tablespoons butter
4 cups water
2 envelopes cheese-
  flavored noodles
  and sauce mix
1/4 teaspoon pepper

2 6-ounce cans water-
  pack tuna
1 medium tomato,
  chopped
3 tablespoons minced
  parsley
1/2 cup dry bread
  crumbs
2 tablespoons butter

Sauté green pepper and celery in 2 tablespoons butter in small skillet over medium heat for 4 minutes or until tender; remove from heat. Bring 4 cups water to a boil in large skillet. Stir in noodle mix and pepper. Cook over medium heat for 7 minutes or until noodles are tender. Stir in tuna, tomato, 2 tablespoons parsley and sautéed vegetables. Sauté remaining 1 tablespoon parsley with bread crumbs in 2 tablespoons butter in small skillet until golden brown. Sprinkle over noodle mixture.

Nutritional information does not include noodles and sauce mix.

Charlene "Joy" Boyd

Hot Tuna Sandwiches

Yield:
20 servings

Approx Per
Serving:
Cal 303
Prot 13 gr
Carbo 22 g
Fiber 1 g
T Fat 18 g
Chol 85 mg
Sod 510 mg

2 6-ounce cans tuna
8 ounces Cheddar
  cheese, finely
  chopped
6 hard-boiled eggs,
  chopped
2 tablespoons chopped
  green bell pepper

1/4 cup chopped onion
1/4 cup chopped green
  olives
1/4 cup chopped sweet
  pickle
1 cup mayonnaise
20 hot dog buns

Combine tuna, cheese, eggs, green pepper, onion, olives, pickle and mayonnaise in bowl; mix well. Spoon into buns. Wrap each bun in foil, sealing tightly. Bake at 325 degrees for 20 minutes or until cheese melts.

Dale N. Bradley

DEVILED CLAMS

Yield:
6 servings

Approx Per Serving:
Cal 272
Prot 21 gr
Carbo 13 g
Fiber 1 g
T Fat 14 g
Chol 114 mg
Sod 262 mg

¼ cup minced onion
1 clove of garlic, minced
¼ cup butter
Salt and pepper to taste
1 tablespoon flour
Tabasco sauce to taste
2 tablespoons Sherry
Thyme to taste
1 15-ounce can minced clams
½ cup dry bread crumbs
1 egg, lightly beaten
2 tablespoons minced parsley
½ cup fresh bread crumbs
2 tablespoons butter

Sauté onion and garlic in butter in skillet until tender but not brown. Add salt, pepper and flour; mix well. Stir in Tabasco sauce, Sherry, thyme and undrained clams; remove from heat. Add dry bread crumbs, egg and parsley; mix well. Spoon into 6 small ramekins or baking shells. Sprinkle bread crumbs on top; dot with butter. Bake at 425 degrees for 6 to 7 minutes or until brown and bubbly.

Tossie Wright

CRAB CAKES

Yield:
6 servings

Approx Per Serving:
Cal 187
Prot 18 gr
Carbo 12 g
Fiber 1 g
T Fat 7 g
Chol 86 mg
Sod 429 mg

½ onion, grated
½ green bell pepper, chopped
2 tablespoons butter
2 tablespoons flour
1 cup milk
Salt to taste
Celery seed to taste
1 teaspoon mustard
1 16-ounce can crab meat
1 cup (about) cracker crumbs
Oil for frying

Sauté onion and green pepper in butter in skillet until tender but not brown. Sprinkle with flour. Stir in milk gradually. Cook until thickened, stirring constantly. Mix in salt, celery seed and mustard. Let stand until cool. Add crab meat; mix well. Shape into patties. Coat with crumbs. Chill for 30 minutes. Brown on both sides in a small amount of oil in skillet.

Nutritional information does not include oil for frying.

Catherine O'Malley

Smith Island Crab Cakes

Yield:
6 servings

Approx Per
Serving:
Cal 140
Prot 15 gr
Carbo 4 g
Fiber <1 g
T Fat 7 g
Chol 134 mg
Sod 264 mg

1½ slices white bread, toasted
2 eggs, beaten
2 tablespoons (heaping) mayonnaise
1 teaspoon prepared mustard
1 teaspoon Old Bay seasoning
Salt and pepper to taste
1 pound lump crab meat

Process toast in blender until fine crumbs. Combine with eggs, mayonnaise, mustard and seasonings in bowl; beat with wire whisk until smooth. Add crab meat gradually, mixing gently with hands just until mixed to avoid shredding crab meat. Shape into patties; place on lightly greased baking sheet. Bake at 350 degrees for 10 minutes on each side. May fry in 1½ inches hot oil until golden brown if preferred.

Nutritional information does not include Old Bay seasoning.

Adelia C. Watson

Seafood Cashew Casserole

Yield:
6 servings

Approx Per
Serving:
Cal 227
Prot 13 gr
Carbo 16 g
Fiber 2 g
T Fat 12 g
Chol 52 mg
Sod 669 mg

1 cup finely chopped celery
¼ cup chopped onion
1 tablespoon butter
1 8-ounce can sliced water chestnuts, drained
¼ cup Sherry
1 10-ounce can cream of mushroom soup
2 cups shredded cooked crab meat
1 cup chow mein noodles
⅓ cup cashews

Sauté celery and onion in butter in skillet. Combine with water chestnuts, Sherry, soup and crab meat in bowl; mix well. Spoon into casserole. Top with chow mein noodles and cashews. Bake at 350 degrees for 25 to 30 minutes or until bubbly. May substitute lobster or scallops for crab meat. May omit noodles and cashews and serve as hot hors d'oeuvre with firm crackers.

Marge Fritz

SEAFOOD-STUFFED GREEN PEPPERS

Yield:
6 servings

Approx Per Serving:
Cal 393
Prot 16 gr
Carbo 22 g
Fiber 3 g
T Fat 28 g
Chol 116 mg
Sod 593 mg

6 medium green bell peppers
Salt to taste
8 ounces shrimp, cooked, peeled
8 ounces crab meat
1 cup cooked rice
2 tablespoons chopped pimento
1/2 cup chopped celery
1/2 cup chopped onion
3/4 cup mayonnaise
1 teaspoon Old Bay seasoning
1/2 teaspoon salt
Pepper to taste
1/2 cup bread crumbs
2 tablespoons butter

Cut tops from peppers; discard seed and membrane. Cook in boiling salted water to cover in large pan for 5 minutes; drain well and set aside. Combine shrimp, crab meat, rice, pimento, celery and onion in bowl. Blend mayonnaise with seasonings. Add to seafood mixture; mix well. Spoon into green pepper shells. Sprinkle with crumbs; dot with butter. Place in 1 1/2-quart baking dish. Add 1/2 inch hot water. Bake at 350 degrees for 30 minutes.

Nutritional information does not include Old Bay seasoning.

Joyce Kay

SEAFOOD AND VEGETABLE QUICHE

Yield:
18 servings

Approx Per Serving:
Cal 383
Prot 15 gr
Carbo 16 g
Fiber 1 g
T Fat 29 g
Chol 131 mg
Sod 494 mg

1 cup finely chopped broccoli
1/2 cup finely chopped green onions
1 6-ounce can sliced mushrooms, drained
1/4 cup margarine
4 eggs
2 cups shredded Swiss cheese
2 cups whipping cream
1/4 teaspoon salt
1/8 teaspoon pepper
Nutmeg to taste
1 pound crab meat
1 cup cooked shrimp
3 unbaked 9-inch deep-dish pie shells
1 cup Parmesan cheese
Parsley flakes to taste

Sauté broccoli, green onions and mushrooms in margarine in skillet until tender; set aside. Combine eggs, Swiss cheese, whipping cream and seasonings in bowl; beat until well mixed. Stir in crab meat, shrimp and sautéed vegetables. Pour into pie shells. Sprinkle with Parmesan cheese and parsley flakes. Bake at 350 degrees for 40 minutes or until set. Let stand for 15 to 20 minutes before cutting. Serve with tossed salad.

Juanda H. Day

SHRIMP CASSEROLE

Yield:
8 servings

Approx Per Serving:
Cal 283
Prot 11 gr
Carbo 20 g
Fiber 2 g
T Fat 18 g
Chol 102 mg
Sod 523 mg

12 ounces fresh mushrooms, sliced
1/4 cup butter
2 cups cooked peeled shrimp
2 cups cooked rice
1 cup chopped green bell pepper
1 cup chopped onion
1/2 chopped celery
1/4 cup chopped pimento
1 20-ounce can tomatoes, drained
3/4 teaspoon salt
1/2 teaspoon chili powder
1/2 cup melted butter

Sauté mushrooms in 1/4 cup butter in skillet just until tender. Combine with shrimp, rice, green pepper, onion, celery, pimento, tomatoes, salt and chili powder in bowl; mix well. Spoon into 2-quart casserole. Pour melted butter over top. Bake at 300 degrees for 1 hour. May prepare and refrigerate for several hours before baking.

Orvylle Mae Dye

EASY SHRIMP SCAMPI

Yield:
4 servings

Approx Per Serving:
Cal 504
Prot 39 gr
Carbo 3 g
Fiber <1 g
T Fat 37 g
Chol 447 mg
Sod 698 mg

2 pounds medium shrimp
Old Bay seasoning to taste
1/4 cup finely chopped onion
4 cloves of garlic, crushed
4 sprigs of parsley, chopped
3/4 cup butter
1/4 cup dry white wine
2 tablespoons lemon juice
Salt and freshly ground pepper to taste

Steam shrimp with Old Bay seasoning until shrimp turn pink. Peel and devein. Sauté onion, garlic and parsley in butter in large skillet; reduce heat. Add shrimp, white wine, lemon juice, salt and pepper. Simmer for several minutes. Serve immediately over rice or fettucini.

Georgianne Atzrodt

Vegetables
and Side Dishes

Asparagus Casserole

Yield:
4 servings

Approx Per
Serving:
Cal 124
Prot 5 g
Carbo 12 g
Fiber 2 g
T Fat 7 g
Chol 18 mg
Sod 655 mg

1 16-ounce can
   asparagus spears
1 tablespoon butter
1 tablespoon flour

1 ounce Velveeta
   cheese, crumbled
1/2 cup cracker crumbs

Drain asparagus, reserving liquid. Melt butter in skillet over medium heat. Blend in flour. Stir in reserved asparagus liquid gradually. Cook until thickened, stirring constantly. Add cheese; stir until melted. Arrange asparagus in 1-quart casserole. Pour sauce over asparagus. Sprinkle with cracker crumbs. Bake at 350 degrees for 15 minutes or until golden brown.

Mary Johnson

Calico Beans

Yield:
20 servings

Approx Per
Serving:
Cal 181
Prot 10 g
Carbo 23 g
Fiber 6 g
T Fat 6 g
Chol 20 mg
Sod 416 mg

1 pound ground beef
1 small onion, chopped
8 ounces bacon, crisp-
   fried, crumbled
1 16-ounce can
   kidney beans
1 16-ounce can lima
   beans

1 28-ounce can pork
   and beans
1/2 cup packed brown
   sugar
1/2 cup catsup
1 tablespoon prepared
   mustard
1 tablespoon vinegar

Brown ground beef with onion in skillet, stirring until crumbly; drain. Combine ground beef mixture, bacon, kidney beans, lima beans, pork and beans, brown sugar, catsup, mustard and vinegar in Crock•Pot; mix well. Cook on Low for several hours. May bake in large casserole at 350 degrees for 45 minutes.

Trish Giles

Darn Good Beans

Yield:
20 servings

Approx Per
Serving:
Cal 168
Prot 8 g
Carbo 26 g
Fiber 6 g
T Fat 4 g
Chol 13 mg
Sod 349 mg

4 slices bacon, chopped
1 medium onion,
  chopped
1 16-ounce can
  kidney beans,
  drained
1 16-ounce can green
  lima beans, drained
1 28-ounce can pork
  and beans
1/2 cup packed brown
  sugar
1/2 cup catsup
1 1/2 cups Cheddar
  cheese cubes
2 tablespoons
  Worcestershire sauce

Brown bacon and onion in skillet; drain. Combine with kidney beans, lima beans, undrained pork and beans, brown sugar, catsup, cheese cubes and Worcestershire sauce in large baking dish; mix well. Bake at 350 degrees for 30 to 40 minutes or until hot and bubbly.

Mildred Sheldon

Hoppin' John

Yield:
4 servings

Approx Per
Serving:
Cal 182
Prot 9 g
Carbo 33 g
Fiber 7 g
T Fat 2 g
Chol 3 mg
Sod 56 mg

1 10-ounce package
  frozen black-eyed
  peas
2 slices bacon
1 small onion, chopped
1 clove of garlic,
  minced
1 cup cooked rice
2 tablespoons red
  wine vinegar
Salt and freshly ground
  pepper to taste
1/4 cup finely chopped
  green onions
2 tablespoons chopped
  parsley

Cook peas using package directions for 20 minutes or until tender. Drain, reserving 1/4 cup liquid. Cook bacon in large heavy skillet until crisp; drain and crumble, reserving drippings. Cook onion in reserved drippings for 3 minutes. Add garlic. Cook for 2 minutes longer. Add peas and rice. Cook until heated through, stirring constantly. Add vinegar and enough reserved liquid to moisten. Cook for 5 minutes. Add salt and pepper. Spoon into serving dish. Sprinkle bacon, green onions and parsley on top.

Tossie Wright

BEETS AND PINEAPPLE

Yield:
6 servings

Approx Per
Serving:
Cal 181
Prot 2 g
Carbo 45 g
Fiber 4 g
T Fat <1 g
Chol 0 mg
Sod 76 mg

1 15-ounce can
pineapple chunks
or tidbits
1/2 cup sugar
2 to 3 tablespoons
cornstarch
1/4 cup vinegar
1/2 cup water
2 pounds fresh beets,
cooked

Drain pineapple, reserving juice. Mix sugar and cornstarch in saucepan. Add reserved juice, vinegar and water; mix well. Cook until thickened, stirring constantly. Add beets and pineapple; mix well. Bring to serving temperature. May substitute two 16-ounce cans beets, cut into quarters, for fresh beets.

Audrey E. Reid

BROCCOLI CASSEROLE

Yield:
6 servings

Approx Per
Serving:
Cal 330
Prot 16 g
Carbo 19 g
Fiber 5 g
T Fat 23 g
Chol 159 mg
Sod 688 mg

3 10-ounce packages
frozen chopped
broccoli
1/2 cup chopped onion
1/4 cup butter
2 tablespoons flour
1/2 cup water
8 ounces Cheez Whiz
3 eggs, beaten
Salt and pepper to
taste
1/2 cup cracker crumbs
1 tablespoon melted
butter

Cook broccoli using package directions; drain. Sauté onion in 1/4 cup butter in skillet until tender. Add flour to water; mix well. Stir into onions. Cook until thickened, stirring constantly. Stir in Cheez Whiz until melted. Add broccoli, eggs, salt and pepper; mix well. Pour into greased 9x13-inch baking dish. Toss crumbs with melted butter. Sprinkle over top. Bake at 350 degrees for 45 minutes.

Donna Sakai

BROCCOLI-CHEESE CASSEROLE

2 10-ounce packages frozen chopped broccoli
1/2 cup chopped onion
2 tablespoons butter
2 tablespoons flour
1/2 cup water
8 ounces Cheez Whiz
Salt and pepper to taste
3 eggs, beaten
1/2 cup cracker crumbs
2 tablespoons butter

Cook broccoli using package directions; drain. Sauté onion in 2 tablespoons butter in skillet until clear. Add flour, stirring to mix. Add water. Cook until thickened, stirring constantly. Stir in Cheez Whiz until melted. Add broccoli, salt and pepper. Add eggs; mix well. Spoon into 8x8-inch baking dish. Sprinkle with cracker crumbs; dot with remaining 2 tablespoons butter. Bake at 325 degrees for 45 to 55 minutes or until hot and bubbly.

Mrs. Ashby A. Kelley

BROCCOLI AND RICE CASSEROLE

1 medium onion, chopped
1/2 cup butter
1 16-ounce package frozen broccoli
1 cup minute rice
1 10-ounce can cream of celery soup
8 ounces Cheez Whiz
1/2 cup bread crumbs

Sauté onion in butter in skillet until tender. Cook broccoli using package directions; drain. Cook rice using package directions. Combine onion, broccoli, rice, celery soup and Cheez Whiz in 1¾-quart casserole; mix well. Sprinkle top with bread crumbs. Bake at 350 degrees for 45 minutes.

Ann Holman

CHEDDAR BROCCOLI CASSEROLE

Yield:
8 servings

Approx Per Serving:
Cal 292
Prot 9 g
Carbo 16 g
Fiber 4 g
T Fat 22 g
Chol 35 mg
Sod 541 mg

3 10-ounce packages frozen broccoli spears
1 10-ounce can cream of chicken soup
1 10-ounce can cream of broccoli soup
4 ounces Cheddar cheese, shredded
1/2 cup mayonnaise
2 tablespoons melted butter
1/2 cup Italian bread crumbs

Cook broccoli using package directions; drain. Layer broccoli in 2-quart baking dish. Mix chicken soup, broccoli soup, cheese and mayonnaise in bowl. Pour over broccoli. Combine butter and bread crumbs in bowl; toss to mix. Sprinkle over top. Bake at 375 degrees for 30 to 35 minutes or until bubbly.

Lisa A. Mack

TASTY BROCCOLI CHEESE CASSEROLE

Yield:
6 servings

Approx Per Serving:
Cal 632
Prot 15 g
Carbo 39 g
Fiber 3 g
T Fat 48 g
Chol 129 mg
Sod 1275 mg

2 10-ounce packages frozen chopped broccoli
1 8-ounce package herb-seasoned stuffing mix
1/4 cup melted butter
1 10-ounce can cream of mushroom soup
1 cup mayonnaise
1 small onion, chopped
2 eggs, beaten
1 cup shredded mozzarella cheese

Cook broccoli using package directions; drain. Combine stuffing mix and butter in bowl; toss to mix. Combine soup, mayonnaise, onion and eggs in bowl; mix well. Layer half the broccoli, soup mixture, cheese and stuffing mix in 2-quart casserole. Repeat layers with remaining ingredients, ending with stuffing mix. Bake at 375 degrees for 45 minutes. May be cooked in Crock•Pot on Low for 4 to 5 hours.

Gwynne Lazure

Pennsylvania Red Cabbage

Yield:
4 servings

Approx Per Serving:
Cal 165
Prot 1 g
Carbo 26 g
Fiber 3 g
T Fat 7 g
Chol 42 mg
Sod 621 mg

2 tablespoons bacon drippings
4 cups shredded red cabbage
2 cups cubed unpeeled apples
1/4 cup vinegar

1/4 cup packed brown sugar
1 teaspoon salt
Pepper to taste
1/2 teaspoon caraway seed
1/4 cup water

Heat bacon drippings in large skillet. Add cabbage, apples, vinegar, brown sugar, salt, pepper, caraway seed and water; mix well. Cook, covered, over low heat for 15 minutes for tender-crisp cabbage or 25 minutes for very tender cabbage, stirring occasionally.

Velma L. Graham

Marinated Carrots

Yield:
12 servings

Approx Per Serving:
Cal 175
Prot 2 g
Carbo 22 g
Fiber 3 g
T Fat 10 g
Chol 0 mg
Sod 381 mg

2 pounds carrots
3 small onions, thinly sliced
1 large green bell pepper, thinly sliced
1 cup tomato soup
1/2 cup sugar
1/4 cup lemon juice

1/4 teaspoon prepared mustard
1 tablespoon barbecue sauce
1/2 cup oil
1 teaspoon salt
1 teaspoon pepper

Peel carrots; cut into julienne strips. Blanch carrots in boiling water; drain. Combine carrots, onions and green pepper in large container; mix well. Mix tomato soup, sugar, lemon juice, mustard, barbecue sauce, oil, salt and pepper in bowl. Pour over vegetables. Marinate in refrigerator for 2 hours or longer.

Ginger Sauls

GRANTS' PLANTATION CORN

Yield:
6 servings

**Approx Per
Serving:**
*Cal 127
Prot 3 g
Carbo 22 g
Fiber 4 g
T Fat 4 g
Chol 10 mg
Sod 36 mg*

8 ears of fresh corn,
shucked
1 cup cold water
3 tablespoons flour
2 tablespoons melted
butter

3 strips fat-back side
meat
Salt and pepper to
taste

Hold corn cob vertically in large bowl. Slice off tops
of kernels with sharp knife. Scrape remaining corn
on cobs to remove pulp. Combine with cold water,
flour and butter in 2-quart saucepan; mix well.
Cook over low heat until corn is tender and mixture
thickens, stirring occasionally. Fry side meat in skillet until crisp. Add meat drippings to corn; mix
well. Add salt and pepper. Serve immediately. This
recipe has been handed down for generations from
plantations in and around northern South Carolina.

Nutritional information does not include drippings.

Bobby Dean Blue

CHILI-CHEESE CORN FRITTERS

Yield:
6 servings

**Approx Per
Serving:**
*Cal 113
Prot 5 g
Carbo 5 g
Fiber <1 g
T Fat 8 g
Chol 51 mg
Sod 205 mg*

3/4 cup shredded
Cheddar cheese
1/2 cup drained whole
kernel corn
1 egg, beaten
3 tablespoons dry
bread crumbs
1/8 teaspoon garlic
powder
1/8 teaspoon onion
powder

1/8 teaspoon chili
powder
1/8 teaspoon baking
powder
Salt and cayenne
pepper to taste
1 tablespoon oil
Oil for deep frying

Combine cheese, corn, egg, bread crumbs, garlic
powder, onion powder, chili powder, baking powder, salt, cayenne pepper and 1 tablespoon oil in
bowl; mix well. Drop by spoonfuls into hot deep oil
in skillet. Cook until brown; drain.

Nutritional information does not include oil for
deep frying.

Mrs. David Sturgill

Corn Pudding

Yield:
6 servings

Approx Per
Serving:
Cal 157
Prot 5 g
Carbo 28 g
Fiber 1 g
T Fat 4 g
Chol 109 mg
Sod 294 mg

3 eggs
1/2 cup sugar
1 1/2 teaspoons nutmeg
1/2 cup milk
1/4 teaspoon salt
1 12-ounce can
    cream-style corn

Combine eggs, sugar, nutmeg, milk and salt in bowl; mix well. Stir in corn. Pour into 8-inch baking dish. Bake at 300 degrees for 1 hour or until top is golden brown.

Charlotte Wood

Italian Mushrooms and Green Beans

Yield:
4 servings

Approx Per
Serving:
Cal 443
Prot 7 g
Carbo 20 g
Fiber 6 g
T Fat 38 g
Chol 123 mg
Sod 590 mg

1 cup minced green
    onions with tops
12 ounces mushrooms,
    thinly sliced
1/3 cup butter
1/2 cup dry white wine
1 14-ounce can
    Italian tomatoes,
    drained, chopped
1 teaspoon basil
1/2 teaspoon rosemary
1 clove of garlic,
    crushed
1 cup whipping cream
1/2 teaspoon salt
1/2 teaspoon freshly
    ground pepper
1 pound green beans,
    trimmed
1 tablespoon minced
    parsley

Sauté green onions and mushrooms in butter in skillet until green onions are tender and pan juices evaporate. Add wine. Simmer until wine evaporates. Add tomatoes, basil, rosemary, garlic and cream. Simmer until consistency of heavy cream. Add salt and pepper. Cook green beans in a small amount of salted water until tender; drain. Arrange green beans on serving dish. Spoon mushroom sauce over top. Top with parsley.

Betty R. Powell

ONIONS STUFFED WITH BRAZIL NUTS

6 large Spanish or Bermuda onions
2 tablespoons butter
1 cup packed coarse dry bread crumbs
1¼ cups coarsely chopped Brazil nuts

1 egg, beaten
¼ teaspoon thyme
Salt and freshly ground pepper to taste
½ cup buttered bread crumbs

Peel onions, leaving root ends intact so onions will not separate. Cut thick slice from top of each. Boil onions and top slices in a large amount of salted water in saucepan for 30 minutes or just until tender; drain and cool. Scoop out centers to form cups, leaving ⅓ to ½-inch shell; reserve centers. Invert cups to drain. Chop tops and centers of onions. Sauté chopped onion in butter in skillet until almost dry. Add dry bread crumbs, Brazil nuts, egg, thyme, salt and pepper; mix well. Spoon stuffing into onion cups. Sprinkle tops with buttered bread crumbs. Place onion cups in baking dish. Add enough water to barely cover bottom of dish. Bake at 375 degrees for 20 to 30 minutes or until crumbs are brown. May serve with tomato, mushroom or cheese sauce. May substitute filberts, pecans or peanuts for Brazil nuts.

Marcia Dark-Ward

LEFTOVER PEAS AND RICE

Onion to taste
Butter to taste
Salt and pepper to taste
Cayenne pepper and parsley to taste

Season-All salt to taste
Leftover peas
Leftover rice
Leftover mushrooms

Sauté onion in butter in skillet until tender. Add salt, pepper, cayenne pepper, parsley and Season-All. Stir in peas, rice and mushrooms. Heat to serving temperature.

Brenda Williams

Baked Sliced Potatoes

Yield:
4 servings

Approx Per Serving:
Cal 444
Prot 5 g
Carbo 52 g
Fiber 5 g
T Fat 25 g
Chol 31 mg
Sod 380 mg

4 large baking potatoes
¼ cup melted butter
¼ cup oil
½ teaspoon salt
2 cloves of garlic, minced
½ teaspoon thyme

Scrub potatoes. Cut unpeeled potatoes into ¼-inch slices. Place overlapping slices in buttered 9x13-inch casserole. Mix butter and oil. Brush potatoes with mixture; pour remaining mixture over potatoes. Sprinkle with salt, garlic and thyme. Bake at 400 degrees for 25 to 30 minutes or until potatoes are tender and brown at edges.

Tossie Wright

Mom's Baked Hashed Browns

Yield:
8 servings

Approx Per Serving:
Cal 585
Prot 12 g
Carbo 23 g
Fiber 2 g
T Fat 51 g
Chol 56 mg
Sod 1054 mg

1 16-ounce package frozen hashed brown potatoes, thawed
½ cup melted margarine
½ cup chopped onion
1 10-ounce can cream of celery soup
1 teaspoon salt
8 ounces Cheddar cheese, shredded
2 cups sour cream
½ cup melted margarine
2 cups cornflakes, crushed

Combine hashed brown potatoes, ½ cup melted margarine, onion, soup, salt, cheese and sour cream in bowl; mix well. Spoon into greased 9x13-inch baking dish. Combine remaining ½ cup margarine and cornflakes in bowl; toss to mix. Sprinkle over potato mixture. Bake at 350 degrees for 1¼ hours or until brown. May substitute cream of mushroom soup for celery soup.

Nancy Cavanaugh

Hot Hashed Brown Potato Salad

Yield:
8 servings

Approx Per Serving:
Cal 459
Prot 8 g
Carbo 41 g
Fiber 3 g
T Fat 31 g
Chol 50 mg
Sod 955 mg

8 ounces cream cheese, softened
1 cup sour cream
1 10-ounce can cream of potato soup
1 10-ounce can cream of celery soup
1 small onion, chopped
1 teaspoon salt
1/4 teaspoon pepper
2 16-ounce packages frozen hashed brown potatoes, thawed

Blend cream cheese and sour cream in large bowl. Add potato soup, celery soup, onion, salt and pepper; mix well. Add potatoes; toss gently to mix. Spoon into greased 9x13-inch baking dish. Bake at 300 degrees for 1 1/2 hours or until brown.

Joyce Kay

Spinach Pie

Yield:
8 servings

Approx Per Serving:
Cal 600
Prot 26 g
Carbo 23 g
Fiber 4 g
T Fat 46 g
Chol 278 mg
Sod 1252 mg

4 10-ounce packages frozen chopped spinach, thawed
1/2 cup olive oil
2 teaspoons salt
1/2 cup Parmesan cheese
16 ounces light cream cheese
16 ounces part-skim ricotta cheese
1 all ready pie pastry
8 small eggs

Drain spinach; squeeze dry. Combine spinach, olive oil, salt and Parmesan cheese in bowl. Spoon into greased 10-inch pie plate. Combine cream cheese and ricotta cheese in bowl. Beat until blended. Spread over spinach mixture. Make 8 wells in cheese mixture with back of spoon. Break 1 egg into each well. Top with pie pastry; seal to edge. Bake at 350 degrees for 1 hour. This recipe is my Great-grandmother's from Italy.

Elise P. Stevens

Spinach Supreme

<table>
<tr><td>

Yield:
8 servings

Approx Per Serving:
Cal 256
Prot 6 g
Carbo 12 g
Fiber 2 g
T Fat 22 g
Chol 62 mg
Sod 418 mg

</td><td>

2   10-ounce packages frozen chopped spinach
8 ounces cream cheese
1/4 cup butter

1 cup herb-seasoned stuffing mix
1   4-ounce can mushrooms, drained
1/4 cup melted butter

</td></tr>
</table>

Cook spinach using package directions. Drain, leaving a small amount of pan juices. Add cream cheese and 1/4 cup butter; stir until butter melts. Combine stuffing mix, mushrooms and remaining 1/4 cup melted butter in bowl; mix well. Spread spinach mixture in greased 2-quart casserole. Top with stuffing mixture. Bake at 350 degrees for 20 to 25 minutes or until browned on top. May substitute onion and garlic croutons for stuffing mix.

Deborah Kulinski

Sweet Potato and Apple Casserole

<table>
<tr><td>

Yield:
6 servings

Approx Per Serving:
Cal 286
Prot 3 g
Carbo 44 g
Fiber 4 g
T Fat 12 g
Chol 21 mg
Sod 171 mg

</td><td>

1/3 cup packed brown sugar
1/4 teaspoon cinnamon
1/4 teaspoon salt
1 pound sweet potatoes, peeled

2 cups thinly sliced peeled tart apples
1/3 cup raisins
1/4 cup butter
1/3 cup slivered almonds

</td></tr>
</table>

Combine brown sugar, cinnamon and salt in bowl; mix well. Slice sweet potatoes 1 inch thick. Layer sweet potatoes, apples, raisins and brown sugar mixture 1/2 at a time in greased 2-quart baking dish. Dot with butter; sprinkle with almonds. Bake, covered, at 375 degrees for 35 to 40 minutes or until sweet potatoes are almost tender. Bake, uncovered, for 10 minutes longer.

Jean Kiger-Thompson

Sweet Potato Casserole

Yield:
10 servings

Approx Per Serving:
Cal 434
Prot 5 g
Carbo 41 g
Fiber 2 g
T Fat 48 g
Chol 67 mg
Sod 339 mg

4 large sweet potatoes
1/2 cup margarine
1/2 cup sugar
3 eggs, beaten
1 cup milk
1/2 teaspoon nutmeg
1 cup chopped pecans
1 teaspoon cinnamon
3 cups cornflakes, crushed
1/2 cup melted margarine
1/2 cup packed brown sugar

Cook sweet potatoes in water to cover in saucepan until tender; drain. Peel sweet potatoes; mash in large bowl. Add 1/2 cup margarine, sugar, eggs, milk, nutmeg and cinnamon; mix well. Spoon into 2 1/2-quart casserole. Bake at 350 degrees for 15 to 20 minutes. Combine pecans, cornflake crumbs, melted margarine and brown sugar in bowl; mix well. Sprinkle over sweet potatoes. Bake for 15 to 20 minutes longer or until topping is brown and bubbly.

Dale N. Bradley

Sweet Potato Soufflé

Yield:
10 servings

Approx Per Serving:
Cal 525
Prot 5 g
Carbo 67 g
Fiber 3 g
T Fat 28 g
Chol 94 mg
Sod 308 mg

3 cups mashed cooked sweet potatoes
2 eggs, beaten
1/2 cup melted butter
1/2 cup milk
1 teaspoon vanilla extract
1 cup sugar
1 cup packed brown sugar
1/2 cup self-rising flour
1 cup chopped pecans
1/2 cup butter

Combine sweet potatoes, eggs, melted butter, milk, vanilla and sugar in bowl; mix well. Spoon into buttered 9 1/2-inch square baking dish. Combine brown sugar, self-rising flour and pecans in bowl. Cut in remaining 1/2 cup butter until crumbly. Sprinkle over sweet potatoes. Bake at 300 degrees for 30 minutes.

Dorothy G. Davis

Sweet Potatoes and Green Peppers

Yield:
1 serving

Approx Per
Serving:
Cal 245
Prot 3 g
Carbo 33 g
Fiber 5 g
T Fat 12 g
Chol 31 mg
Sod 112 mg

1 medium sweet potato
1/4 medium onion
1/2 small green bell
  pepper

1 tablespoon butter
Garlic powder, salt
  and pepper to taste

Cook sweet potato in water to cover in saucepan until tender; drain and cool. Peel; cut into small pieces. Sauté onion and green pepper in butter in skillet. Add sweet potatoes and seasonings; mix well.

Maria A. Velez

Pineapple-Orange-Honey-Glazed Sweet Potatoes

Yield:
6 servings

Approx Per
Serving:
Cal 511
Prot 2 g
Carbo 96 g
Fiber 3 g
T Fat 16 g
Chol 41 mg
Sod 159 mg

4 medium sweet
  potatoes
1 6-ounce can
  crushed pineapple
1 cup orange juice
1 1/4 cups packed
  brown sugar

1/2 cup butter
1/2 cup honey
1 teaspoon cinnamon
1 teaspoon nutmeg
Salt to taste

Cook sweet potatoes in water to cover in saucepan until tender; drain and cool. Peel and slice diagonally. Place in greased 2-quart casserole. Combine pineapple, orange juice, brown sugar and butter in saucepan. Heat until butter melts. Add honey and spices. Bring to a boil, stirring frequently. Pour over sweet potatoes. Bake at 350 degrees for 40 to 45 minutes or until glazed, basting occasionally with pan juices. May substitute 2 cups pineapple-orange juice for crushed pineapple and orange juice.

Florence P. Perry

Stuffed Tomatoes au Gratin

Yield:
8 servings

Approx Per
Serving:
Cal 254
Prot 10 g
Carbo 21 g
Fiber 5 g
T Fat 15 g
Chol 35 mg
Sod 158 mg

4 tomatoes, cut into
    halves
1¹/2 pounds fresh peas
1 onion, finely
    chopped
2 tablespoons oil
Salt and pepper to
    taste

¹/4 cup butter
2 tablespoons flour
1 cup milk
1 cup shredded
    Cheddar cheese
1 tablespoon soft
    bread crumbs

Scoop out tomato pulp, leaving shells. Discard seed; chop tomato pulp. Shell peas. Sauté onion in oil in skillet until transparent. Add peas. Cook, covered, over low heat for 5 minutes. Add chopped tomato, salt and pepper. Cook for 10 minutes. Melt butter in saucepan. Stir in flour. Cook for 1 minute. Stir in milk gradually. Cook until mixture comes to a boil and thickens, stirring constantly. Add ³/4 cup cheese to sautéed mixture. Add cream sauce; mix gently. Spoon into tomato shells. Place in 8x12-inch baking dish. Top with mixture of remaining ¹/4 cup cheese and bread crumbs. Bake in preheated 400-degree oven for 20 minutes.

Gladys Rockenbaugh

Zucchini Squash Casserole

Yield:
20 servings

Approx Per
Serving:
Cal 130
Prot 3 g
Carbo 12 g
Fiber 1 g
T Fat 8 g
Chol 18 mg
Sod 312 mg

6 cups sliced zucchini
¹/4 cup chopped onion
1 cup sour cream
1   10-ounce can
    chicken-mushroom
    soup

1 cup shredded carrots
¹/2 cup melted butter
1   8-ounce package
    herb-seasoned
    stuffing mix

Place zucchini and onion in saucepan with water to cover. Bring to a boil; reduce heat. Simmer for 5 minutes; drain. Combine sour cream and soup in bowl; mix well. Add carrots; mix well. Fold in zucchini and onion. Combine butter and stuffing mix in bowl; mix well. Spoon half the stuffing into buttered 9x13-inch baking dish. Spoon zucchini mixture over stuffing. Top with remaining stuffing. Bake at 350 degrees for 30 to 35 minutes or until lightly browned.

Barbara Wheeler

DUMPLINGS

Yield:
12 servings

Approx Per Serving:
Cal 212
Prot 6 g
Carbo 44 g
Fiber 3 g
T Fat 2 g
Chol 36 mg
Sod 234 mg

6 medium potatoes
2 eggs, beaten
1 teaspoon salt
2 cups (or more) sifted flour
3 slices bread, trimmed

Cook potatoes in water to cover in saucepan until tender. Let stand until cool. Peel; put through food chopper. Combine potatoes, eggs, salt and flour in bowl; mix well. Cut bread into cubes. Place on baking sheet. Bake at 350 degrees until light brown. Add to potato mixture; mix well. Shape into 3-inch dumplings. Chill in refrigerator for 4 to 5 hours if desired. Bring a generous amount of salted water to a boil in large saucepan. Place dumplings in water. Cook for 30 minutes. Remove to serving dish with slotted spoon.

Helen Canter

MACARONI AND CHEESE

Yield:
8 servings

Approx Per Serving:
Cal 402
Prot 14 g
Carbo 40 g
Fiber 2 g
T Fat 21 g
Chol 34 mg
Sod 545 mg

3 cups uncooked macaroni
1½ cups shredded sharp Cheddar cheese
1 10-ounce can cream of chicken soup
1 medium onion, finely chopped
½ green bell pepper, chopped
1 cup evaporated milk
6 tablespoons melted margarine
Salt and pepper to taste

Cook macaroni using package directions. Combine macaroni, cheese, soup, onion, green pepper, evaporated milk, margarine, salt and pepper in bowl; mix well. Spoon into 2-quart casserole. Bake at 350 degrees for 30 minutes.

Mrs. David A. Sturgill

 Substitute bulgur wheat, hominy grits or kasha for rice as a side dish to spice up meals.

GRANDPA HERMAN'S POTATO LATKES

Yield:
8 servings

Approx Per Serving:
Cal 107
Prot 3 g
Carbo 23 g
Fiber 2 g
T Fat 1 g
Chol 27 mg
Sod 117 mg

5 potatoes, peeled, grated
1 onion, grated
1 egg, beaten

1 teaspoon soda
Salt and pepper to taste
Oil for frying

Place potatoes and onion in wire strainer; drain well. Combine egg, soda and seasonings in bowl; mix well. Add potatoes and onion; mix well. Drop by spoonfuls into a small amount of hot oil in skillet. Brown on both sides. Serve with applesauce, sour cream or preserves. I remember my eighty year old grandfather coming by train from Brooklyn to Newark to make these delicious crisp latkes for his grandchildren.

Nutritional information does not include oil for frying.

Heschel Falek

FRIED RICE VERMICELLI

Yield:
8 servings

Approx Per Serving:
Cal 405
Prot 22 g
Carbo 46 g
Fiber 3 g
T Fat 15 g
Chol 86 mg
Sod 1109 mg

1 16-ounce package rice vermicelli
1 pound ground turkey
1 large onion, coarsely chopped
1/2 head cabbage, sliced into 1/3-inch wide strips
4 to 5 tablespoons oil
1/2 teaspoon curry powder

1 tablespoon salt
1/4 to 1/2 teaspoon garlic powder
1/2 teaspoon seasoned salt
Cayenne pepper to taste
2 eggs, beaten
2 tablespoons soy sauce
1 tablespoon sesame oil (optional)

Place rice vermicelli in 4-quart saucepan. Add enough boiling water to cover. Let stand for 3 to 5 minutes or to desired tenderness; drain. Let stand for several minutes, shaking saucepan occasionally to prevent sticking. Stir-fry ground turkey, onion and cabbage in oil in skillet or wok. Add seasonings. Push to side of pan. Add eggs. Cook until dry, stirring constantly. Stir turkey mixture into eggs. Drain if desired. Add rice vermicelli, soy sauce and sesame oil; mix gently with wooden spoons. Buy rice vermicelli, also called rice sticks or rice noodles, in the foreign food section of the supermarket. May substitute ground beef or pork for turkey.

Eddie T. Yo

P.O.T. Rice

Yield:
5 servings

Approx Per Serving:
Cal 148
Prot 3 g
Carbo 31 g
Fiber <1 g
T Fat 1 g
Chol 0 mg
Sod 932 mg

2¹/₂ cups water
3 or 4 chicken
  bouillon cubes
1 teaspoon parsley

1 teaspoon oregano
1 teaspoon tarragon
1 teaspoon margarine
1 cup uncooked rice

Bring water with bouillon cubes to a boil in saucepan. Add parsley, oregano, tarragon and margarine. Reduce heat to low. Add rice. Cook, tightly covered, for 20 minutes or until liquid is absorbed,

Elise P. Evans

Mushroom-Rice Casserole

Yield:
8 servings

Approx Per Serving:
Cal 178
Prot 3 g
Carbo 28 g
Fiber 1 g
T Fat 6 g
Chol <1 mg
Sod 305 mg

1 medium onion,
  chopped
¹/₄ cup margarine
1¹/₃ cups uncooked rice

1 10-ounce can beef
   consommé
2 4-ounce cans
   mushrooms

Sauté onion in margarine in saucepan; remove from heat. Add rice, consommé and undrained mushrooms. Pour into greased 2-quart casserole. Bake, covered, at 400 degrees for 45 minutes. Bake, uncovered, for 15 minutes.

Lin Kogle

 For fluffy rice, place 2 layers of paper towels over the saucepan when rice is done. Cover with a tight-fitting lid and let stand for 5 to 30 minutes. The towels will absorb the excess moisture.

Stuffing Balls and Gravy

Yield:
8 servings

Approx Per
Serving:
Cal 294
Prot 11 g
Carbo 49 g
Fiber 1 g
T Fat 6 g
Chol 7 mg
Sod 1631 mg

1 10-ounce can cream of chicken soup
1 10-ounce can cream of celery soup
1 14-ounce can chicken broth
1 cup chopped onion
1 cup chopped celery
1 16-ounce package herb-seasoned stuffing mix
1 14-ounce can chicken broth

Combine chicken soup, celery soup and 1 can chicken broth in bowl; mix well. Pour half the mixture into Crock•Pot. Combine onion, celery, stuffing mix and remaining can chicken broth in bowl; mix well. Shape into balls. Place in Crock•Pot. Top with remaining soup mixture. Cook on High for 2¹/₂ hours.

Mrs. David A. Sturgill

Ham and Olive Stuffing

Yield:
12 servings

Approx Per
Serving:
Cal 272
Prot 11 g
Carbo 43 g
Fiber 3 g
T Fat 6 g
Chol 79 mg
Sod 951 mg

4 cups cooked rice
4 cups toasted bread cubes
4 eggs, lightly beaten
1 cup chopped cooked ham
2/3 cup chopped stuffed green olives
1 teaspoon salt
1 teaspoon sage
1 teaspoon marjoram
1/2 teaspoon freshly ground pepper
1/4 teaspoon garlic powder
1/2 cup chopped fresh parsley
1 cup chopped onion
1 cup chopped celery

Combine rice, bread cubes and eggs in bowl; mix lightly. Add ham and olives; mix well. Season with salt, sage, marjoram, pepper and garlic powder. Add parsley, onion and celery; mix well. Spoon into cavity of 12 to 15-pound turkey. Roast using turkey package directions.

Marcia Dark-Ward

Stuffing for Turkey

Yield:
12 servings

Approx Per Serving:
Cal 265
Prot 4 g
Carbo 24 g
Fiber 1 g
T Fat 17 g
Chol 41 mg
Sod 555 mg

¾ cup finely chopped onion
1 cup chopped celery
1 cup butter
1 teaspoon salt
1 teaspoon pepper
1 tablespoon sage

1 tablespoon thyme
1 tablespoon marjoram
1 tablespoon poultry seasoning
1 20-ounce loaf bread, torn

Sauté onion and celery in butter in skillet. Season with salt, pepper, sage, thyme, marjoram and poultry seasoning. Pour over bread in large bowl; toss lightly. Add enough water ¼ cup at a time to moisten thoroughly; do not saturate. Spoon into cavity of 13-pound turkey. Roast using turkey package directions.

Lou Ann Maclay

Pineapple Bread Stuffing

Yield:
6 servings

Approx Per Serving:
Cal 419
Prot 6 g
Carbo 55 g
Fiber 1 g
T Fat 20 g
Chol 142 mg
Sod 346 mg

1 cup sugar
½ cup margarine, softened
4 eggs

1 16-ounce can crushed pineapple, drained
5 slices day-old bread, cubed

Cream sugar and margarine in mixer bowl until light and fluffy. Add eggs 1 at a time, beating well after each addition. Add pineapple; mix well. Fold in bread cubes. Pour into 6x11-inch baking pan. Bake at 350 degrees for 45 minutes.

Rita E. Alexander

 Substitute crushed wheat germ for buttered crumbs for a delicious, nutritious and easy casserole topping.

Escalloped Pineapple

Yield:
6 servings

Approx Per Serving:
Cal 471
Prot 6 g
Carbo 71 g
Fiber 1 g
T Fat 20 g
Chol 109 mg
Sod 326 mg

4 cups bread cubes
1¹/₃ cups sugar
3 eggs, slightly beaten
¹/₂ cup milk
¹/₂ cup melted margarine
1 16-ounce can crushed pineapple

Combine bread, sugar, eggs, margarine, milk and undrained pineapple in bowl; mix well. Spoon into 9x9-inch baking dish. Bake at 350 degrees for 40 minutes. Serve warm.

June Bodmer

Pineapple Casserole

Yield:
4 servings

Approx Per Serving:
Cal 436
Prot 8 g
Carbo 44 g
Fiber 2 g
T Fat 27 g
Chol 218 mg
Sod 303 mg

3 eggs
3 tablespoons (rounded) flour
2 tablespoons sugar
1 20-ounce can juice-pack crushed pineapple
Crumbs of 3 slices bread
¹/₂ cup melted butter

Combine eggs, flour and sugar in mixer bowl. Beat until creamy. Add pineapple; mix well. Pour into small greased casserole. Sprinkle with bread crumbs; drizzle with butter. Bake at 350 degrees for 1 hour. This is good served with ham.

Leona C. Shobe

CROCK•POT APPLE BUTTER

Yield:
32 servings

Approx Per Serving:
Cal 91
Prot <1 g
Carbo 24 g
Fiber 1 g
T Fat <1 g
Chol 0 mg
Sod 1 mg

3 16-ounce cans applesauce
1 tablespoon cinnamon
3 cups sugar
1 teaspoon ground cloves
1½ teaspoons lemon juice

Combine applesauce, cinnamon, sugar, cloves and lemon juice in Crock•Pot; mix well. Cook on High for 8 to 10 hours or on Low for 16 to 20 hours. Remove cover during final hours of cooking to cook to desired thickness.

Virginia L. Barnes

CRANBERRY CHUTNEY

Yield:
24 servings

Approx Per Serving:
Cal 46
Prot <1 g
Carbo 12 g
Fiber 1 g
T Fat <1 g
Chol 0 mg
Sod 1 mg

1 cup water
1 cup sugar
1 tablespoon cider vinegar
2 cups cranberries
½ cup golden raisins
1½ teaspoons grated fresh gingerroot
½ teaspoon mustard seed
¼ teaspoon crushed red pepper

Combine water, sugar and vinegar in saucepan. Cook until sugar dissolves and mixture comes to a boil, stirring frequently. Cook for 5 minutes. Add cranberries, raisins, gingerroot, mustard seed and red pepper; mix well. Return to a boil; reduce heat. Simmer for 5 minutes, stirring occasionally. Let stand until cool. Store, tightly covered, in refrigerator for up to 2 weeks.

Marge Fritz

Green Tomato Chutney

Yield:
64 servings

**Approx Per
Serving:**
*Cal 42
Prot <1 g
Carbo 11 g
Fiber 1 g
T Fat <1 g
Chol 0 mg
Sod 109 mg*

3 pounds green
  tomatoes
2 cups chopped onions
2 cups raisins
1½ cups packed
  brown sugar

2 tablespoons
  Worcestershire sauce
1 tablespoon salt
1 teaspoon dry mustard
2 cups cider vinegar

Parboil tomatoes for 1 minute; drain and rinse with cold water. Remove skin; core and chop enough tomatoes to measure 10 cups. Combine tomatoes, onions, raisins, brown sugar, Worcestershire sauce, salt, mustard and vinegar on deep saucepan. Simmer for 45 minutes or until thickened. Spoon into hot sterilized jars, leaving ⅛-inch headspace. Seal with 2-piece lids. Process in hot water bath for 15 minutes. Let stand until cool.

Tossie Wright

Easy and Delicious Pickles

Yield:
8 servings

**Approx Per
Serving:**
*Cal 166
Prot 1 g
Carbo 43 g
Fiber 1 g
T Fat <1 g
Chol 0 mg
Sod 803 mg*

2 cucumbers, thinly
  sliced
1 onion, thinly sliced
½ green bell pepper,
  thinly sliced

1 cup white vinegar
1½ cups sugar
1½ teaspoons celery
  seed
1 tablespoon salt

Pack cucumbers, onion and green pepper into hot sterilized 1-pint jars. Combine vinegar, sugar, celery seed and salt in saucepan. Heat until sugar dissolves. Pour over cucumbers. Cover with waxed paper; seal. Let stand in refrigerator for 2 to 3 days, shaking occasionally. Store in refrigerator for several months.

Joyce Kay

Breads

CHEESE BISCUITS

Yield:
18 servings

Approx Per Serving:
Cal 94
Prot 2 g
Carbo 9 g
Fiber <1 g
T Fat 5 g
Chol 8 mg
Sod 130 mg

1½ cups flour
2¼ teaspoons baking powder
½ teaspoon salt
¼ cup shortening

1½ cups milk
¼ cup shredded Cheddar cheese
2 tablespoons butter, softened

Sift flour, baking powder and salt into bowl. Cut in shortening with pastry blender or 2 knives until mixture resembles coarse crumbs. Add milk all at once; stir quickly to form stiff dough. Knead on floured surface for 20 seconds. Roll ¼ inch thick; cut with 1½-inch biscuit cutter. Combine cheese and butter in bowl; mix well. Spread ⅔ of the cheese mixture on half the biscuits; top with remaining biscuits. Spread remaining cheese mixture on tops. Place on baking sheet. Bake at 450 degrees for 12 minutes or until golden brown. May cut cheese mixture into dry ingredients with shortening if preferred.

Deborah Morton

WHOLE WHEAT BISCUITS

Yield:
12 servings

Approx Per Serving:
Cal 130
Prot 3 g
Carbo 16 g
Fiber 2 g
T Fat 6 g
Chol <1 mg
Sod 165 mg

1 cup whole wheat flour
1 cup all-purpose flour
2½ teaspoons baking powder

½ teaspoon salt
⅔ cup skim milk
⅓ cup oil

Mix whole wheat flour, all-purpose flour, baking powder and salt in bowl; make well in center. Blend milk and oil in small bowl. Pour into well in dry ingredients. Stir with fork until mixture leaves side of bowl. Knead 18 times on lightly floured surface. Roll ½ inch thick; cut with 2-inch biscuit cutter. Place on baking sheet. Bake at 450 degrees for 12 minutes or until light brown.

Judith E. Ware

 Hot rolls or biscuits will stay hot longer if you place aluminum foil under the napkin in the basket.

Monkey Bread

Yield:
15 servings

Approx Per Serving:
Cal 300
Prot 3 g
Carbo 42 g
Fiber 1 g
T Fat 13 g
Chol 2 mg
Sod 612 mg

²/₃ cup sugar
1 teaspoon cinnamon
3 10-count cans
  Hungry Jack biscuits

³/₄ cup margarine
1 cup packed brown
  sugar
1 teaspoon cinnamon

Mix sugar with 1 teaspoon cinnamon in small bowl. Cut each biscuit into quarters. Roll in cinnamon-sugar, coating well. Place in greased bundt pan. Bring margarine, brown sugar and 1 teaspoon cinnamon to a boil in saucepan. Pour over biscuits. Bake at 375 degrees for 25 to 30 minutes or until brown. Let stand in pan for 20 minutes. Invert onto serving plate. We serve this with an egg casserole on Christmas morning.

Linda A. Leavitt

Pinwheel Coffee Cake

Yield:
20 servings

Approx Per Serving:
Cal 281
Prot 4 g
Carbo 38 g
Fiber 1 g
T Fat 13 g
Chol 46 mg
Sod 193 mg

1 cup milk
¼ cup butter
¼ cup sugar
1 teaspoon salt
2 eggs, beaten
1 envelope dry yeast
1 teaspoon sugar
¼ cup lukewarm water

3½ cups sifted flour
1¼ cups sugar
½ cup packed brown
  sugar
²/₃ cup melted butter
1 cup chopped walnuts
2 teaspoons cinnamon

Scald milk in saucepan. Add ¼ cup butter, ¼ cup sugar and salt; mix well. Cool to room temperature. Blend in eggs. Dissolve yeast with 1 teaspoon sugar in lukewarm water in bowl. Add milk mixture; mix well. Add flour; mix well. Let rise, covered with waxed paper and towel for 1 hour or until doubled in bulk. Line large pizza pan with foil, allowing foil to extend 2 to 4 inches beyond pan; grease foil. Beat dough with spoon. Shape into rolls the size of small sausage links. Arrange in spiral starting in center of pan. Combine 1¼ cups sugar, brown sugar, ²/₃ cup butter, walnuts and cinnamon in bowl; mix well. Sprinkle over dough. Let rise, covered, until doubled in bulk. Bake at 350 degrees for 25 to 30 minutes or until golden brown. This is a traditional breakfast dish for family holidays. May add raisins and candied fruit if desired.

Barbara Wheeler

SOUR CREAM COFFEE CAKE

Yield:
15 servings

Approx Per
Serving:
Cal 331
Prot 4 g
Carbo 42 g
Fiber 1 g
T Fat 17 g
Chol 72 mg
Sod 248 mg

1/2 cup butter, softened
1 cup sugar
3 eggs
2 cups flour
1 teaspoon baking
   powder
1 teaspoon soda
1/2 teaspoon salt

1 teaspoon vanilla
   extract
1 cup sour cream
1 cup packed brown
   sugar
1 teaspoon cinnamon
3 tablespoons butter
3/4 cup chopped pecans

Cream 1/2 cup butter and sugar in mixer bowl until light and fluffy. Add eggs; mix well. Combine flour, baking powder, soda, salt and vanilla in bowl; mix well. Add to creamed mixture alternately with sour cream, mixing well after each addition. Combine brown sugar, cinnamon, 3 tablespoons butter and pecans in bowl; mix well. Layer coffee cake batter and pecan mixture 1/2 at a time in greased 9x13-inch baking pan. Bake at 350 degrees for 40 minutes. May reduce amount of pecan mixture and add blueberries if desired.

Adelia C. Watson

BROCCOLI CORN BREAD

Yield:
12 servings

Approx Per
Serving:
Cal 157
Prot 5 g
Carbo 10 g
Fiber 1 g
T Fat 11 g
Chol 94 mg
Sod 236 mg

1/2 cup melted butter
1/3 cup chopped onion
3/4 cup cottage cheese
1   10-ounce package
    frozen broccoli,
    thawed, drained

4 eggs, slightly beaten
Salt to taste
1   8 1/2-ounce package
    corn muffin mix
1 teaspoon honey

Combine butter, onion, cottage cheese, broccoli, eggs and salt in bowl; mix well. Stir in corn muffin mix and honey. Spoon into greased 9x11-inch baking pan. Bake at 400 degrees for 20 to 25 minutes or until brown.

Audrey Hamm

BEST-MADE HUSH PUPPIES

Yield:
30 servings

Approx Per
Serving:
Cal 56
Prot 2 g
Carbo 10 g
Fiber 1 g
T Fat 1 g
Chol 15 mg
Sod 198 mg

1½ cups cornmeal mix
1½ cups water
⅓ cup milk
1 tablespoon oil
1 small onion, finely
  chopped
2 eggs, beaten

1 cup flour
3 tablespoons baking
  powder
2 teaspoons sugar
1 teaspoon salt
Oil for deep frying

Combine cornmeal mix and water in saucepan. Cook over medium heat for 6 minutes, stirring constantly until mixture begins to form ball; remove from heat. Stir in milk, oil and onion. Add gradually to eggs in large bowl, stirring to mix well. Add mixture of flour, baking powder, sugar and salt; mix well. Drop by teaspoonfuls into oil heated to 350 degrees. Deep-fry until brown; drain well.

Nutritional information does not include oil for deep frying.

Mrs. David A. Sturgill

GRANDMOTHER'S FLAT BREAD

Yield:
6 servings

Approx Per
Serving:
Cal 315
Prot 8 g
Carbo 47 g
Fiber 2 g
T Fat 10 g
Chol 3 mg
Sod 760 mg

3 cups sifted flour
1½ teaspoons baking
  powder
½ teaspoon soda

1½ teaspoons salt
¼ cup shortening
1¾ cups buttermilk

Sift flour, baking powder, soda and salt into bowl. Add shortening. Mix with fingers until mixture resembles coarse cornmeal. Stir in buttermilk just until moistened. Knead lightly 35 times on floured surface. Divide into 3 portions. Pat into 6-inch circles; place on lightly greased baking sheet. Bake at 450 degrees for 15 to 20 minutes or until dark golden brown. Serve hot with butter or margarine. May reheat to serve.

Regina Ann Ratliff

CHEDDAR APPLE BREAD

Yield:
12 servings

Approx Per Serving:
Cal 345
Prot 10 g
Carbo 37 g
Fiber 1 g
T Fat 18 g
Chol 57 mg
Sod 338 mg

2¹/2 cups flour
³/4 cup sugar
2 teaspoons baking powder
¹/2 teaspoon cinnamon
¹/2 teaspoon salt
2 eggs, beaten
³/4 cup milk
¹/3 cup melted margarine
2 cups shredded sharp Cheddar cheese
1¹/2 cups chopped peeled apples
³/4 cup chopped pecans

Mix flour, sugar, baking powder, cinnamon and salt in bowl. Combine eggs, milk and margarine in large bowl; mix well. Add dry ingredients; mix well. Stir in cheese, apples and pecans. Spoon into greased and floured 5x9-inch loaf pan. Bake at 350 degrees for 1 hour to 1 hour and 10 minutes or until wooden pick inserted in center comes out clean. Let stand in pan for 5 minutes. Remove to wire rack to cool completely.

Saundra Stalter

BANANA PECAN BREAD

Yield:
24 servings

Approx Per Serving:
Cal 182
Prot 2 g
Carbo 27 g
Fiber 1 g
T Fat 8 g
Chol 18 mg
Sod 145 mg

¹/2 cup sugar
1 cup packed brown sugar
¹/2 cup shortening
2 eggs
³/4 cup bran flakes
1 teaspoon soda
1 teaspoon salt
1 teaspoon vanilla extract
4 or 5 bananas, mashed
1¹/2 cups flour
1 cup chopped pecans

Cream sugar, brown sugar and shortening in mixer bowl until light and fluffy. Beat in eggs. Add bran flakes, soda, salt and vanilla; mix well. Add bananas and flour; mix well. Stir in pecans. Line bottoms of 2 loaf pans with waxed paper; grease pans. Spoon batter into pans. Bake at 350 degrees for 45 minutes or until loaves test done. Remove loaves to wire rack to cool. May substitute walnuts for pecans or omit nuts. This is Grandma Aylward's recipe and a special Christmas treat for friends and family.

Cheryl Yoder

NEW ORLEANS FRENCH BREAD

2 tablespoons
  shortening
1 tablespoon sugar
1 tablespoon salt
1 cup boiling water
1 cup cold water

1 envelope dry yeast
5½ to 6 cups flour
1 egg white
2 tablespoons cold
  water

Combine shortening, sugar, salt and boiling water in large bowl; stir until shortening melts. Add 1 cup cold water. Cool to 105 to 115 degrees. Sprinkle yeast over mixture. Let stand for 4 minutes; stir to dissolve yeast. Beat in 4 cups flour gradually. Add enough remaining flour to form stiff dough. Knead on floured surface for 5 minutes or until smooth and elastic. Place in greased bowl, turning to coat surface. Let rise in warm place for 1 to 1½ hours or until doubled in bulk. Punch dough down. Let rise for 30 minutes or until doubled in bulk. Knead lightly on floured surface to press out bubbles. Shape into 14 to 16-inch loaf on greased baking sheet. Let rise, covered, until doubled in bulk. Cut ¼-inch deep slashes in top with sharp knife. Brush with mixture of egg white and 2 tablespoons cold water. Bake at 375 degrees for 40 to 50 minutes or until loaf tests done.

Doris A. Baylor

IRISH BREAD

4 cups flour
2 teaspoons baking
  powder
1 teaspoon soda
½ cup sugar
1 teaspoon salt

2 tablespoons
  shortening
1½ cups raisins
1½ teaspoons caraway
  seed
2 cups sour milk

Sift flour, baking powder, soda, sugar and salt into large bowl. Add shortening; mix with fingers or back of spoon. Add raisins, caraway seed and sour milk; mix well. Spoon into greased and floured bundt pan. Bake at 325 degrees for 1 hour or until bread tests done. Remove to wire rack to cool. May substitute milk for sour milk, omitting soda and increasing baking powder to 4 teaspoons.

Diane Cotter

PUMPKIN NUT BREAD

Yield:
12 servings

Approx Per Serving:
Cal 372
Prot 4 g
Carbo 54 g
Fiber 2 g
T Fat 17 g
Chol 45 mg
Sod 74 mg

2 cups flour
1½ teaspoons baking powder
¼ teaspoon soda
1½ teaspoons (or more) cinnamon
½ teaspoon allspice
¼ teaspoon ginger
Nutmeg to taste
1¾ cups sugar
⅔ cup oil
2 eggs
1⅓ cups canned pumpkin
½ cup raisins
½ cup chopped pecans

Mix flour, baking powder, soda, cinnamon, allspice, ginger and nutmeg together. Combine sugar and oil in large bowl; mix well. Beat in eggs 1 at a time. Stir in pumpkin and dry ingredients. Add raisins and pecans; mix well. Spoon into greased and floured 5x9-inch loaf pan. Bake at 350 degrees for 30 minutes. Reduce oven temperature to 325 degrees. Bake for 45 minutes longer. Remove to wire rack to cool.

Terry Vieyra

SWEET POTATO BREAD

Yield:
24 servings

Approx Per Serving:
Cal 274
Prot 3 g
Carbo 43 g
Fiber 1 g
T Fat 10 g
Chol 36 mg
Sod 282 mg

3 cups sugar
1 cup oil
1   16-ounce can sweet potatoes, drained
4 eggs, beaten
3½ cups flour
1 teaspoon baking powder
2 teaspoons soda
2 teaspoons salt
1 teaspoon cinnamon
1 teaspoon allspice
1 teaspoon nutmeg
½ teaspoon cloves
⅔ cup water

Combine sugar, oil, sweet potatoes and eggs in mixer bowl; beat until light and fluffy. Sift flour, baking powder, soda, salt, cinnamon, allspice, nutmeg and cloves together. Add to sweet potato mixture alternately with water, mixing well after each addition. Spoon into 2 greased 5x9-inch loaf pans. Bake at 350 degrees for 1 hour or until center springs back when lightly pressed. Cool in pans for 10 minutes. Remove to wire rack to cool completely. May substitute pumpkin for sweet potatoes.

Horace G. Holliday

World's Easiest Bread

Yield:
12 servings

Approx Per Serving:
Cal 134
Prot 3 g
Carbo 27 g
Fiber 1 g
T Fat <1 g
Chol 0 mg
Sod 339 mg

3 cups self-rising flour   1 12-ounce can warm
3 tablespoons sugar   beer

Combine flour, sugar and beer in bowl; mix well. Spoon into greased and floured loaf pan. Bake at 350 degrees for 50 minutes. Brush top with margarine. Bake for 10 minutes longer. Remove to wire rack. Serve warm, cooled or toasted.

Justine A. Smith

Yeast Bread

Yield:
48 servings

Approx Per Serving:
Cal 104
Prot 3 g
Carbo 18 g
Fiber 1 g
T Fat 2 g
Chol 10 mg
Sod 185 mg

2 envelopes dry yeast   4 teaspoons salt
1 teaspoon sugar   2 eggs, beaten
1/4 cup lukewarm water   8 cups flour
2 cups milk   1/3 cup melted
1/3 cup sugar   shortening

Dissolve yeast with 1 teaspoon sugar in lukewarm water. Scald milk in saucepan. Combine with 1/3 cup sugar and salt in bowl. Cool to lukewarm. Add yeast mixture, eggs and half the flour; mix until smooth. Add remaining flour and melted shortening; mix well. Place in greased bowl; cover. Store in refrigerator until ready to bake. Shape into rolls; place in greased baking pan. Let rise in warm place until doubled in bulk. Bake at 425 degrees for 20 minutes or until golden brown.

Margaret E. Williams

 Reduce yeast bread rising time in half by setting to rise in microwave. Place dough in glass bowl in center of microwave. Place 1 cup hot water in microwave. Microwave on Low (10%) until doubled in bulk.

ZUCCHINI BREAD

Yield:
24 servings

Approx Per Serving:
Cal 242
Prot 3 g
Carbo 29 g
Fiber 1 g
T Fat 13 g
Chol 27 mg
Sod 120 mg

3 eggs, slightly beaten
1 cup oil
2 cups sugar
3 cups sifted flour
1/4 teaspoon baking powder
1 tablespoon cinnamon
1 teaspoon salt
1 teaspoon soda
1 tablespoon vanilla extract
2 cups grated peeled zucchini
1 cup chopped walnuts

Combine eggs and oil in large mixer bowl; beat until well mixed. Add sugar; beat until thick and lemon-colored. Add flour, baking powder, cinnamon, salt, soda and vanilla; mix well. Stir in zucchini and walnuts. Spoon into 2 greased and floured loaf pans. Bake at 325 degrees for 1 hour. Remove to wire rack to cool.

Nancy L. Rebar

ZUCCHINI RAISIN BREAD

Yield:
24 servings

Approx Per Serving:
Cal 283
Prot 4 g
Carbo 38 g
Fiber 1 g
T Fat 13 g
Chol 36 mg
Sod 216 mg

4 eggs
2 cups packed light brown sugar
1 cup oil
3 1/2 cups unbleached flour
3/4 teaspoon baking powder
1 1/2 teaspoons soda
1 1/2 teaspoons salt
1 teaspoon cinnamon
2 cups grated zucchini
1 cup raisins
1 teaspoon vanilla extract
1 cup chopped walnuts

Beat eggs in mixer bowl. Beat in brown sugar and oil gradually. Mix flour, baking powder, soda, salt and cinnamon together. Add to egg mixture alternately with zucchini, mixing well after each addition. Stir in raisins, vanilla and walnuts. Spoon into 2 greased and lightly floured 5x9-inch loaf pans. Bake at 350 degrees on lower oven rack for 55 minutes or until loaves test done. Cool in pans for 10 minutes. Remove to wire rack to cool completely. May glaze with mixture of confectioners' sugar and cream if desired.

Kathryn B. Cave

Oatmeal Apple Muffins

Yield:
12 servings

Approx Per Serving:
Cal 229
Prot 4 g
Carbo 31 g
Fiber 2 g
T Fat 11 g
Chol 20 mg
Sod 274 mg

1 egg
1/2 cup oil
3/4 cup milk
1 cup flour
1 tablespoon baking powder
1/3 cup sugar
1 teaspoon salt
1 teaspoon nutmeg
2 teaspoons cinnamon
1 cup quick-cooking oats
1 cup raisins
1 cup chopped apple

Beat egg in bowl. Stir in oil and milk. Add flour, baking powder, sugar, salt, nutmeg, cinnamon and oats; mix just until moistened. Stir in raisins and apple. Fill 12 greased muffin cups 3/4 full. Bake at 400 degrees for 15 to 20 minutes or until muffins test done. Serve hot or cool.

Joyce M. Michaels

Bran Griddle Cakes

Yield:
6 servings

Approx Per Serving:
Cal 336
Prot 9 g
Carbo 53 g
Fiber 5 g
T Fat 11 g
Chol 38 mg
Sod 717 mg

2 cups flour
1 tablespoon baking powder
1 teaspoon soda
3 1/2 tablespoons sugar
1/2 teaspoon salt
1 cup All-Bran cereal
1 cup hot water
1 egg
1 1/2 cups buttermilk
1/4 cup oil

Sift flour, baking powder, soda, sugar and salt together. Combine All-Bran and hot water in bowl. Beat egg in mixer bowl. Stir in buttermilk and oil. Add All-Bran mixture; mix well. Stir in sifted dry ingredients just until moistened. Bake on hot griddle until light brown on both sides. May store batter in refrigerator for up to 2 weeks.

Linda Bryant

 *Substitute 1/2 cup maple syrup for 1/2 cup milk in your favorite muffin recipe for **Maple Syrup Muffins**.*

Irish Pancake

Yield:
2 servings

Approx Per Serving:
Cal 434
Prot 12 g
Carbo 28 g
Fiber 1 g
T Fat 31 g
Chol 221 mg
Sod 363 mg

¼ cup margarine
2 eggs, slightly beaten

½ cup milk
½ cup flour

Heat margarine in 8 or 9-inch cast-iron skillet in 425-degree oven for 5 minutes. Combine eggs, milk and flour in bowl; mix until smooth. Pour into hot margarine in skillet. Bake at 425 degrees for 15 minutes. Garnish with confectioners' sugar. Pancake will puff like a soufflé.

Justine A. Smith

Rice Pancakes

Yield:
4 servings

Approx Per Serving:
Cal 293
Prot 9 g
Carbo 33 g
Fiber 1 g
T Fat 14 g
Chol 115 mg
Sod 404 mg

1 cup flour
1 teaspoon baking
   powder
1 tablespoon sugar
½ teaspoon salt

2 egg yolks
1 cup milk
2½ tablespoons oil
¼ cup cooked rice
2 egg whites

Mix flour, baking powder, sugar and salt in bowl. Combine egg yolks, milk and oil in large bowl; mix well. Add dry ingredients. Stir in rice. Beat egg whites until stiff peaks form. Fold gently into batter. Bake by ¼ cupfuls on hot greased griddle until light brown on both sides. Serve with syrup.

Mrs. David A. Sturgill

 Bake pancakes and cool. Freeze in serving portions in plastic bags. Reheat, wrapped in moist paper towel, at 200 degrees or microwave on High for 20 seconds per pancake.

HUNGARIAN WALNUT BUNS

Yield:
24 servings

Approx Per
Serving:
Cal 513
Prot 11 g
Carbo 60 g
Fiber 2 g
T Fat 26 g
Chol 78 mg
Sod 350 mg

10 cups flour, sifted
1¹/₂ cups sugar
2 tablespoons baking powder
1¹/₂ teaspoons salt
1 cup butter
4 eggs
1¹/₂ cups evaporated milk
2 cups sour cream
2 teaspoons vanilla extract
6 tablespoons melted butter
12 ounces walnuts, crushed
¹/₄ cup sugar
6 tablespoons evaporated milk
Vanilla extract to taste

Combine first 5 ingredients in bowl; mix well. Add eggs, 1¹/₂ cups evaporated milk, sour cream and 2 teaspoons vanilla; mix to form nonsticky dough. Divide into 3 portions. Chill for 30 minutes. Roll dough 1 portion at a time on floured surface. Brush with melted butter. Spread mixture of walnuts and ¹/₄ cup sugar over dough. Sprinkle with mixture of 6 tablespoons evaporated milk and a small amount of vanilla. Roll as for jelly roll. Cut into 1-inch slices; place in greased baking pan. Bake at 350 degrees for 30 minutes or just until buns test done; do not over-bake. Brush with additional melted butter. Garnish with frosting and walnut halves if desired.

Elizabeth Vargo Niles

DILL BREADSTICKS

Yield:
20 servings

Approx Per
Serving:
Cal 109
Prot 3 g
Carbo 18 g
Fiber 1 g
T Fat 3 g
Chol 0 mg
Sod 4 mg

2 envelopes dry yeast
1 tablespoon sugar
¹/₄ cup warm (100 to 115-degree) water
¹/₄ cup olive oil
¹/₂ cup flour
1¹/₄ cups warm water
2¹/₂ to 3 cups flour
2 tablespoons dill
1 egg white
1 tablespoon water

Dissolve yeast and sugar in ¹/₄ cup warm water in bowl. Add olive oil; beat for 3 minutes. Add ¹/₂ cup flour; mix well. Add 1¹/₄ cups water alternately with 2 to 2¹/₂ cups flour, mixing well after each addition. Mix in dill. Knead in remaining ¹/₂ cup flour on floured surface. Let rest for 5 minutes. Roll into rectangle 24 inches long. Cut into strips. Place on oiled baking sheet. Let rise for 20 minutes. Brush with egg white beaten with 1 tablespoon water. Bake at 300 degrees for 30 minutes or until light brown.

Cara Davis

Extra-Special Rolls

Yield:
48 servings

Approx Per
Serving:
Cal 86
Prot 2 g
Carbo 11 g
Fiber <1 g
T Fat 4 g
Chol 13 mg
Sod 60 mg

2 envelopes dry yeast
3 tablespoons warm
(105 to 115-degree)
water
1/2 cup sugar
1/2 cup melted
shortening

2 eggs, beaten
1 cup warm (105 to
115-degree) water
1 teaspoon salt
4 to 4 1/2 cups flour
6 tablespoons butter,
softened

Dissolve yeast in 3 tablespoons warm water in large mixer bowl; let stand for 5 minutes. Add sugar, shortening, eggs, 1 cup warm water, salt and 2 cups flour. Beat at low speed for 1 minute. Stir in enough remaining flour gradually to form soft dough. Knead on lightly floured surface for 4 minutes or until smooth and elastic. Place in greased bowl, turning to coat surface. Let rise, covered, in warm place for 1 hour or until doubled in bulk. Punch dough down; divide into 4 portions. Roll each portion into 12-inch circle on floured surface. Spread with butter. Cut each circle into 12 wedges; roll up from wide end. Place point side down on lightly greased baking sheet. Let rise, covered, for 1 hour or until doubled in bulk. Bake at 400 degrees for 10 to 12 minutes or until light brown.

Bea Souder

Garlic French Bread

Yield:
12 servings

Approx Per
Serving:
Cal 126
Prot 3 g
Carbo 18 g
Fiber 1 g
T Fat 4 g
Chol 8 mg
Sod 227 mg

3 tablespoons butter,
softened
1 teaspoon chopped
garlic

1 loaf French bread

Combine butter and garlic in small bowl; mix well. Cut bread into halves lengthwise. Spread with butter mixture. Wrap in foil. Bake at 400 degrees for 10 minutes or until heated through.

Charlene "Joy" Boyd

Desserts

© 1987 VOLK

Apple Crisp

Yield:
6 servings

Approx Per Serving:
Cal 368
Prot 2 g
Carbo 66 g
Fiber 3 g
T Fat 12 g
Chol 31 mg
Sod 187 mg

6 large baking apples, peeled, sliced
1/2 cup sugar
1/4 teaspoon cinnamon
1/2 cup orange juice
3/4 cup flour
1/2 cup sugar
6 tablespoons butter
1/4 teaspoon salt
Cinnamon and nutmeg to taste

Spread apples in buttered 6-cup baking dish. Combine 1/2 cup sugar, 1/4 teaspoon cinnamon and orange juice in small bowl. Drizzle over apples. Combine flour, 1/2 cup sugar, butter and salt in bowl; mix well. Spread over apples. Sprinkle with additional cinnamon and nutmeg. Bake at 350 degrees for 40 to 45 minutes or until brown. Serve warm with ice cream or whipped cream.

Helen C. Guilfoyle

Banana Split Dessert

Yield:
12 servings

Approx Per Serving:
Cal 629
Prot 6 g
Carbo 77 g
Fiber 3 g
T Fat 36 g
Chol 37 mg
Sod 474 mg

3 cups graham cracker crumbs
1/2 cup sugar
1/2 cup melted margarine
2 cups confectioners' sugar
2 eggs
1 cup margarine, softened
7 bananas
2 cups drained crushed pineapple
2 cups whipped topping
1 cup chopped pecans

Mix cracker crumbs, sugar and 1/2 cup melted margarine in bowl. Press into 9x13-inch dish. Combine confectioners' sugar, eggs and 1 cup margarine in mixer bowl; beat for 10 minutes. Spread in prepared dish. Cut bananas into halves lengthwise and crosswise. Arrange over confectioners' sugar layer. Layer pineapple, whipped topping and pecans over top. Garnish with maraschino cherries. Chill in refrigerator overnight.

Marie L. Zurick

AMARETTO CHEESECAKE

Yield:
12 servings

**Approx Per
Serving:**
*Cal 378
Prot 3 g
Carbo 42 g
Fiber <1 g
T Fat 21 g
Chol 88 mg
Sod 153 mg*

3 cups vanilla wafer
  crumbs
2 tablespoons sugar
1/2 cup melted butter
4 ounces cream cheese,
  softened
1 cup sugar

2 eggs
1/4 cup Amaretto
16 ounces sour cream
3/4 cup sugar
2 tablespoons
  Amaretto

Mix cookie crumbs, 2 tablespoons sugar and melted butter in bowl. Press firmly into bottom of 10-inch springform pan. Bake at 350 degrees for 5 minutes. Beat cream cheese in mixer bowl until light. Add 1 cup sugar, beating until fluffy. Beat in eggs 1 at a time. Stir in 1/4 cup Amaretto. Pour into prepared pan. Bake at 350 degrees for 30 minutes or until set. Beat sour cream at medium speed in mixer bowl for 2 minutes. Add 3/4 cup sugar and 2 tablespoons Amaretto; beat for 1 minute. Spread over cheesecake. Bake for 10 minutes longer. Cool to room temperature on wire rack. Chill for 8 hours. Place on serving plate; remove side of pan.

Sadie V. Buck

B'S CHEESECAKE

Yield:
8 servings

**Approx Per
Serving:**
*Cal 66
Prot 6 g
Carbo 6 g
Fiber <1 g
T Fat 2 g
Chol 6 mg
Sod 173 mg*

1 envelope unflavored
  gelatin
1 packet artificial
  sweetener
1 tablespoon lemon
  juice
1/2 cup unsweetened
  pineapple juice
12 ounces cottage
  cheese

1 teaspoon vanilla
  extract
1/2 cup drained
  crushed pineapple
2 packets artificial
  sweetener
Cinnamon to taste

Soften gelatin with 1 packet artificial sweetener in lemon juice in cup. Bring pineapple juice to a boil in saucepan. Combine pineapple juice and gelatin mixture in blender container; blend until gelatin is dissolved. Add cottage cheese and vanilla; blend until smooth. Stir in pineapple with spatula; blend until smooth. Pour into pie plate; sprinkle with mixture of 2 packets artificial sweetener and cinnamon. Chill until firm.

Dee Fitzpatrick

BAILEY'S CHOCOLATE CHIP CHEESECAKE

Yield:
12 servings

Approx Per Serving:
Cal 690
Prot 10 g
Carbo 54 g
Fiber 1 g
T Fat 49 g
Chol 191 mg
Sod 367 mg

1 cup graham cracker crumbs
1/4 cup packed brown sugar
1/4 cup melted butter
32 ounces cream cheese, softened
1 1/2 cups sugar
4 eggs
3/4 cup Bailey's Irish Cream
1 1/2 teaspoons vanilla extract
1 cup semisweet chocolate chips
1 cup whipping cream
1 tablespoon confectioners' sugar
2 tablespoons baking cocoa
1 1/2 teaspoons instant coffee
1 ounce semisweet chocolate, grated

Mix cracker crumbs, brown sugar and butter in 10-inch springform pan; press evenly over bottom of pan. Bake at 325 degrees for 5 to 8 minutes. Beat cream cheese in large mixer bowl until light. Add sugar gradually, beating until fluffy. Beat in eggs 1 at a time. Blend in liqueur and vanilla. Sprinkle 1/2 cup chocolate chips into prepared pan. Spoon filling over chocolate chips. Top with remaining chocolate chips. Bake for 1 hour. Turn off oven. Let cheesecake stand in oven with door slightly ajar for 30 minutes. Chill for 6 hours to overnight. Place cheesecake on serving plate; remove side of pan. Combine whipping cream, confectioners sugar, cocoa and coffee in small mixer bowl; beat at medium speed until soft peaks form. Spread over cheesecake. Top with grated chocolate.

Georgianne Atzrodt

 Allow for the variation in oven temperatures by setting the timer for the minimum time indicated in the recipe. Test by inserting a tester or toothpick into the center of the dessert. If the tester comes out clean, the dessert is done.

EXCELSIOR CHEESECAKE

Yield:
12 servings

Approx Per Serving:
Cal 626
Prot 9 g
Carbo 48 g
Fiber 1 g
T Fat 45 g
Chol 156 mg
Sod 444 mg

2 cups graham cracker crumbs
1/2 cup melted butter
32 ounces cream cheese, softened
1 cup sugar
1/2 teaspoon vanilla extract
1/2 teaspoon almond extract
2 eggs
2 cups sour cream
3/4 cup sugar
1/2 teaspoon almond extract
Juice of 1/2 lemon

Mix cracker crumbs and butter in bowl. Press over bottom and 2/3 up side of lightly greased 10-inch springform pan. Beat cream cheese in mixer bowl until light. Add 1 cup sugar, vanilla and 1/2 teaspoon almond extract, beating until fluffy. Add eggs, beating just until smooth. Spoon into prepared pan. Bake at 350 degrees for 30 to 35 minutes or until set; top may brown. Combine sour cream, 3/4 cup sugar, 1/2 teaspoon almond extract and lemon juice in bowl; whisk until smooth. Spread carefully over cheesecake. Bake for 10 minutes longer. Cool to room temperature. Chill overnight. Place on serving plate; remove side of pan. May bake in 2 pie plates if preferred.

Kathleen Kondus

MINIATURE CHEESECAKES

Yield:
60 servings

Approx Per Serving:
Cal 67
Prot 1 g
Carbo 8 g
Fiber <1 g
T Fat 4 g
Chol 18 mg
Sod 43 mg

60 vanilla wafers
16 ounces cream cheese, softened
1 tablespoon lemon juice
1 teaspoon vanilla extract
2 eggs, at room temperature
3/4 cup sugar
1 21-ounce can cherry pie filling

Place 1 vanilla wafer in each of 60 paper-lined miniature muffin cups. Beat cream cheese 8 ounces at a time in mixer bowl until light. Add lemon juice and vanilla; beat until smooth. Add eggs alternately with sugar, mixing well after each addition. Spoon into prepared muffin cups with long-handled spoon. Bake at 325 degrees for 20 minutes or until top is set; do not brown. Cool to room temperature; tops of cheesecakes will sink. Place 1 cherry on each cheesecake.

Kathleen L. Nygard

159

INDIVIDUAL CHEESECAKES

Yield:
20 servings

Approx Per Serving:
Cal 165
Prot 3 g
Carbo 19 g
Fiber <1 g
T Fat 9 g
Chol 49 mg
Sod 98 mg

20 vanilla wafers
16 ounces cream cheese, softened
3/4 cup sugar
1 tablespoon lemon juice
2 eggs
1 tablespoon vanilla extract
1　21-ounce can blueberry pie filling

Place 1 vanilla wafer in each of 20 paper-lined muffin cups. Combine cream cheese, sugar, lemon juice, eggs and vanilla in mixer bowl; mix well. Spoon into prepared muffin cups. Bake at 350 degrees for 30 minutes. Cool to room temperature. Top with pie filling.

Gina Denell

YOGURT CHEESECAKE

Yield:
12 servings

Approx Per Serving:
Cal 358
Prot 12 g
Carbo 38 g
Fiber <1 g
T Fat 18 g
Chol 96 mg
Sod 267 mg

48 ounces plain low-fat yogurt
1 cup graham cracker crumbs
1/2 cup gingersnap crumbs
1/3 cup crushed walnuts
1/3 cup canola oil
1/2 teaspoon cinnamon
1/2 teaspoon ginger
8 ounces low-fat cream cheese, softened
4 eggs, at room temperature, beaten
1 cup sugar
1 tablespoon lemon juice
1 tablespoon grated lemon rind
8 ounces plain low-fat yogurt

Line colander with double thickness cheesecloth; place in sink. Spoon 48 ounces yogurt into colander. Let drain for 15 minutes. Place colander in bowl; cover with plastic wrap. Chill for 24 hours. Pull up corners of cheesecloth; squeeze out remaining moisture. Store yogurt cheese in covered container in refrigerator for up to 1 week. Butter and chill 9-inch springform pan. Mix crumbs, walnuts, oil, cinnamon and ginger in bowl. Press over bottom and halfway up side of prepared springform pan. Chill for 15 minutes or longer. Combine next 6 ingredients in mixer bowl; beat until smooth. Stir in 8 ounces yogurt. Spoon into crust. Bake at 300 degrees for 1 hour and 20 minutes to 1 1/2 hours or until center is set. Turn off oven. Cool cheesecake in oven with door ajar for 1 hour. Chill for 3 hours. Place on serving plate; remove side of pan.

Georgianne Atzrodt

AMISH APPLE COBBLER

Yield:
8 servings

Approx Per Serving:
Cal 380
Prot 3 g
Carbo 54 g
Fiber 4 g
T Fat 19 g
Chol 51 mg
Sod 280 mg

8 baking apples, chopped
²/₃ cup sugar
2 tablespoons flour
Cinnamon to taste
6 tablespoons butter
1 cup sifted flour
2 tablespoons sugar
1¹/₂ teaspoons baking powder
¹/₂ teaspoon salt
¹/₃ cup shortening
3 tablespoons milk
1 egg

Place apples in 2 or 3-quart baking dish. Sprinkle with mixture of ²/₃ cup sugar and 2 tablespoons flour. Sprinkle with cinnamon; dot with butter. Sift 1 cup flour, 2 tablespoons sugar, baking powder and salt into bowl. Add shortening, milk and egg; mix well with fork. Drop by spoonfuls over apples. Bake at 350 degrees for 25 to 30 minutes or until or until golden brown. This is a Pennsylvania Dutch recipe from Lancaster County, Pennsylvania.

Sharon M. Willingham

DUMP-IT-IN COBBLER

Yield:
6 servings

Approx Per Serving:
Cal 390
Prot 4 g
Carbo 58 g
Fiber 1 g
T Fat 17 g
Chol 6 mg
Sod 426 mg

¹/₂ cup margarine
1 cup sugar
1 cup self-rising flour
1 cup milk
1 16-ounce can cherries, drained

Melt margarine in deep 9x9-inch baking dish. Combine sugar, flour and milk in bowl; mix well. Spoon into margarine in dish; do not mix. Spread cherries over top. Bake at 350 degrees for 1 hour. May make glaze with juice from fruit if desired. May substitute berries, peaches or apples for cherries.

Ida M. Minifee

 Prepared whipped topping has 20 fewer calories per tablespoon than sweetened whipped cream.

Fruit Cobbler

Yield:
6 servings

Approx Per Serving:
Cal 355
Prot 2 g
Carbo 58 g
Fiber 3 g
T Fat 14 g
Chol 31 mg
Sod 296 mg

2 cups fresh
   blackberries
6 tablespoons butter
1 cup water
1/2 cup sugar
3/4 cup baking mix
3/4 cup sugar

Combine blackberries with butter, water and 1/2 cup sugar in saucepan. Cook until bubbly, stirring to dissolve sugar. Spoon into 8x10-inch baking dish. Combine baking mix and 3/4 cup sugar in bowl. Sprinkle over blackberries. Bake at 350 degrees for 40 minutes or until brown. Serve with whipped topping or ice cream. May substitute other fresh or canned berries or fruit for blackberries; decrease water to 1/2 cup for canned fruit.

Brenda Prestidge

Peach Cobbler

Yield:
6 servings

Approx Per Serving:
Cal 430
Prot 3 g
Carbo 70 g
Fiber 1 g
T Fat 17 g
Chol 46 mg
Sod 431 mg

2 cups sliced fresh
   peaches
3/4 cup sugar
1/2 cup butter
3/4 cup flour
3/4 cup sugar
2 teaspoons baking
   powder
1/2 teaspoon salt
3/4 cup milk
1/2 teaspoon lemon
   juice

Mix peaches and 3/4 cup sugar in bowl; set aside. Melt butter in 1 1/2-quart baking dish. Combine flour, 3/4 cup sugar, baking powder and salt in bowl. Add milk and lemon juice; mix well. Spoon into margarine in dish. Spoon peaches over top. Bake at 350 degrees for 1 hour. May substitute other fruit or berries for peaches.

Mrs. Melvin J Griggs Jr.

CHERYL'S COCONUT DREAM

Yield:
16 servings

Approx Per Serving:
Cal 310
Prot 4 g
Carbo 32 g
Fiber <1 g
T Fat 19 g
Chol 22 mg
Sod 236 mg

1½ cups flour
¾ cup melted margarine
8 ounces cream cheese, softened
1 cup confectioners' sugar
2 3-ounce packages coconut cream instant pudding mix
3 cups milk
8 ounces whipped topping

Mix flour and margarine in bowl. Pat into 9x13-inch baking dish. Bake at 350 degrees for 15 minutes or until golden brown. Cool to room temperature. Beat cream cheese and confectioners' sugar in mixer bowl until light and fluffy. Spread in prepared dish. Combine pudding mix and milk in mixer bowl; mix for 2 minutes. Spread over cream cheese layer. Top with whipped topping. Garnish with toasted coconut. Chill until serving time.

Nancy Cavanaugh

BOILED CUSTARD

Yield:
8 servings

Approx Per Serving:
Cal 154
Prot 6 g
Carbo 19 g
Fiber 0 g
T Fat 6 g
Chol 96 mg
Sod 77 mg

1 quart milk
3 eggs
½ cup sugar
Salt to taste
1 teaspoon vanilla extract
1 teaspoon almond extract

Heat milk slightly in double boiler. Beat eggs, sugar and salt in mixer bowl until thick and smooth. Stir into warm milk. Cook for 8 to 10 minutes or until mixture coats metal spoon, stirring constantly; do not overcook. Stir in flavorings. Chill in refrigerator. Serve over ice cream with Grandma's Cream Cheese Pound Cake (page 191). This is an old family recipe. My great aunt usually serves it with homemade fruitcake or coconut cake at Christmas.

Brenda N. Crist

DUMP DESSERT

Yield:
12 servings

Approx Per
Serving:
Cal 379
Prot 2 g
Carbo 52 g
Fiber 1 g
T Fat 19 g
Chol 41 mg
Sod 402 mg

1 15-ounce can
crushed pineapple
1 15-ounce can
blueberry pie filling

1 2-layer package
white cake mix
1 cup butter, sliced

Layer undrained pineapple and pie filling in 9x13-inch baking dish. Sprinkle evenly with dry cake mix. Dot with butter. Bake at 350 degrees for 1 hour. May use pie filling and cake mix of choice.

Dennis E. Pauley Jr.

CHERRY DUMP DESSERT

Yield:
12 servings

Approx Per
Serving:
Cal 473
Prot 4 g
Carbo 57 g
Fiber 2 g
T Fat 27 g
Chol 41 mg
Sod 408 mg

1 21-ounce can cherry
pie filling
1 8-ounce can
crushed pineapple
1 2-layer package
yellow cake mix

1 cup chopped walnuts
1 cup shredded
coconut
1 cup melted butter

Layer pie filling and undrained pineapple in 9x13-inch baking dish. Sprinkle with dry cake mix, walnuts and coconut. Drizzle with butter. Bake at 325 degrees for 1 hour.

Carolyn Dade

Ice Cream Dessert

Yield:
15 servings

Approx Per
Serving:
Cal 498
Prot 6 g
Carbo 53 g
Fiber 2 g
T Fat 31 g
Chol 80 mg
Sod 183 mg

1 cup melted butter
1/2 cup packed brown
sugar
1/2 cup quick-cooking
oats
2 cups flour

1 cup chopped pecans
1 1/2 8-ounce jars
fudge sauce
1/2 gallon fudge ripple
ice cream, softened

Combine butter, brown sugar, oats, flour and pecans in bowl; mix well. Spread in 9x13-inch baking pan. Bake at 375 degrees for 10 to 15 minutes or until golden brown. Cool to room temperature. Crumble mixture. Sprinkle half the mixture into 9x13-inch dish. Spread with half the fudge sauce. Spread ice cream over fudge sauce. Top with remaining crumb mixture and fudge sauce. Freeze until firm.

Lucille H. Turner

Jell-O Sherbet Dessert

Yield:
12 servings

Approx Per
Serving:
Cal 144
Prot 2 g
Carbo 26 g
Fiber 0 g
T Fat 4 g
Chol 4 mg
Sod 73 mg

1 6-ounce package
orange gelatin
3 cups boiling water
1/2 cup milk

1 envelope whipped
topping mix
1 pint orange sherbet,
softened

Dissolve gelatin in boiling water in bowl. Cool to room temperature. Combine milk with whipped topping mix in bowl. Prepare using package directions. Fold into gelatin mixture. Fold in sherbet. Spoon into 2-quart dish. Chill until set. May use flavors of gelatin and sherbet you prefer.

June C. Williams

OREO COOKIE DESSERT

Yield:
15 servings

Approx Per
Serving:
Cal 423
Prot 4 g
Carbo 48 g
Fiber <1 g
T Fat 24 g
Chol 34 mg
Sod 316 mg

1 15-ounce package
Oreo cookies,
crushed
6 tablespoons melted
butter
8 ounces cream cheese,
softened
1 cup confectioners'
sugar

16 ounces whipped
topping
1 large package
chocolate instant
pudding mix
2¼ cups milk

Mix cookie crumbs with butter in bowl. Reserve ½ cup crumb mixture. Press remaining crumbs into 9x13-inch dish. Combine cream cheese and confectioners' sugar in mixer bowl; beat until smooth. Fold in half the whipped topping. Spread over crust. Chill for 20 minutes. Prepare pudding mix with milk in bowl, using package directions. Spread over cream cheese layer. Top with remaining whipped topping and reserved crumb mixture. Chill for 8 hours to overnight.

Jean Emer

BREAD PUDDING

Yield:
8 servings

Approx Per
Serving:
Cal 237
Prot 7 g
Carbo 34 g
Fiber 1 g
T Fat 9 g
Chol 100 mg
Sod 246 mg

5 slices bread
2 tablespoons butter,
softened
½ cup plumped raisins
3 eggs, beaten

6 tablespoons sugar
¼ teaspoon salt
3 cups milk, scalded
¼ teaspoon cinnamon
2 tablespoons sugar

Toast bread; spread with butter while still hot. Arrange in buttered baking dish. Sprinkle with raisins. Combine eggs, 6 tablespoons sugar and salt in bowl; mix well. Add scalded milk gradually, stirring constantly. Pour into prepared dish. Let stand for 10 minutes. Sprinkle with mixture of cinnamon and 2 tablespoons sugar. Bake at 350 degrees for 25 minutes.

Margaret E. Williams

FRUIT PUDDING

Yield:
6 servings

Approx Per Serving:
Cal 111
Prot 2 g
Carbo 25 g
Fiber 1 g
T Fat 1 g
Chol 2 mg
Sod 124 mg

1 4-ounce package vanilla instant pudding mix
1 10-ounce can fruit cocktail

8 ounces plain low-fat yogurt

Combine pudding mix and undrained fruit cocktail in 1½-quart bowl; mix well. Fold in yogurt. Chill until serving time.

Esther S. Moreland

RICE PUDDING

Yield:
8 servings

Approx Per Serving:
Cal 142
Prot 5 g
Carbo 22 g
Fiber <1 g
T Fat 4 g
Chol 17 mg
Sod 52 mg

1 quart milk
6 tablespoons sugar

6 tablespoons uncooked rice

Combine milk, sugar and rice in 1-quart baking dish; mix well. Bake at 250 degrees for 3 hours. May remove whey which forms on top if desired. My mother always made this on "wash day" because it was so easy.

Mary L. Cowden

 *For a delicious **Pudding Topping**, mix 1 cup sour cream and ½ cup packed brown sugar. Chill for 1 hour or longer and mix well before serving.*

PUMPKIN ICE CREAM DESSERT

¾ cup graham cracker
   crumbs
¼ cup sugar
¼ cup melted
   margarine
1 cup pumpkin purée

1 pint vanilla ice
   cream, softened
½ teaspoon each
   ginger, cinnamon
   and nutmeg
Salt to taste

Mix cracker crumbs, sugar and margarine in bowl. Spread in 8x8-inch dish. Combine pumpkin, ice cream, ginger, cinnamon, nutmeg and salt in bowl; mix well. Spread in prepared pan. Freeze for 2 to 4 hours. May omit sugar or substitute frozen yogurt for ice cream if preferred.

Elise P. Evans

SIN

1 cup flour
½ cup margarine,
   softened
¾ cup chopped pecans
1½ cups whipped
   topping
8 ounces cream cheese,
   softened
1 cup sugar
2 cups skim milk

1 4-ounce package
   chocolate instant
   pudding mix
1 4-ounce package
   vanilla instant
   pudding mix
½ cup whipped
   topping
¼ cup chopped pecans

Combine flour, margarine and ¾ cup pecans in bowl; mix well. Pat into 9x13-inch baking dish. Bake at 350 degrees for 15 minutes or until golden brown. Cool to room temperature. Combine 1½ cups whipped topping, cream cheese and sugar in mixer bowl; mix until smooth. Spread in prepared dish. Combine milk and pudding mixes in mixer bowl; mix until thickened and smooth. Let stand for 5 minutes. Spread over cream cheese layer. Top with remaining ½ cup whipped topping and ¼ cup pecans. Chill until serving time.

Jan Blackford

Cakes

© 1986 VOLK

HAPPINESS CAKE

2 cups (heaping) patience
1 handful love
2 handfuls generosity
1 handful understanding
A dash of laughter
A sprinkle (generous) of kindness
Plenty of faith

Combine patience, love and generosity with understanding. Add a dash of laughter; sprinkle generously with kindness. Add plenty of faith; mix well. Spread over a period of a lifetime. Serve to everyone you meet. Sit back, relax and enjoy a slice or two every day of the year.

Jewel C. Lacek

ALMOND CAKE WITH RASPBERRIES

Yield:
16 servings

Approx Per Serving:
Cal 223
Prot 5 g
Carbo 29 g
Fiber 2 g
T Fat 11 g
Chol 16 mg
Sod 92 mg

1 10-ounce package frozen raspberries
1 cup blanched almonds
1 cup sugar
1 cup flour
8 egg whites
Salt to taste
1/3 cup sugar
1/2 cup melted butter
1 1/2 teaspoons confectioners' sugar

Butter 9-inch springform pan. Line bottom with waxed paper; butter paper. Thaw raspberries; drain well. Process almonds with 1 cup sugar to a powder. Combine with flour in bowl. Beat egg whites and salt in large bowl until soft peaks form. Add 1/3 cup sugar gradually, beating until stiff peaks form. Fold almond mixture and butter alternately 1/4 at a time into egg whites. Pour into prepared pan. Press raspberries gently into cake batter. Bake at 350 degrees for 45 to 50 minutes or until cake tests done. Cool in pan for several minutes. Invert onto serving plate. Dust with confectioners' sugar.

Karen Springfield

APPLE CAKE

Yield:
16 servings

Approx Per Serving:
Cal 332
Prot 3 g
Carbo 50 g
Fiber 1 g
T Fat 14 g
Chol 0 mg
Sod 63 mg

2 teaspoons cinnamon
5 teaspoons sugar
3 cups flour
2 cups sugar
1 tablespoon baking powder
1 cup oil
1/2 cup orange juice
2 1/2 teaspoons vanilla extract
3 or 4 large apples, peeled, sliced

Mix cinnamon and 5 teaspoons sugar in small bowl. Combine flour, 2 cups sugar, baking powder, oil, orange juice and vanilla in mixer bowl; beat until smooth. Layer batter, apples and cinnamon-sugar 1/3 at a time in greased and floured 10-inch tube pan. Bake at 350 degrees for 1 hour and 15 minutes or until cake tests done.

Beverly Kaub

JUDY'S APPLE CAKE

5 large cooking
   apples, peeled,
   sliced
5 tablespoons sugar
1 cup oil
1/3 cup thawed frozen
   orange juice
   concentrate

4 eggs
3 cups flour
1 tablespoon baking
   powder
1/2 teaspoon salt
2 1/2 cups sugar
1 tablespoon cinnamon

Combine apples and 5 tablespoons sugar in bowl; toss gently to mix. Let stand while preparing batter. Combine oil, orange juice concentrate and eggs in mixer bowl; beat well. Mix flour, baking powder, salt, remaining 2 1/2 cups sugar and cinnamon in bowl. Add to oil mixture, mixing well. Layer batter and apples 1/3 at a time in greased and floured tube pan. Bake at 350 degrees for 1 hour and 45 minutes or until cake tests done. Loosen cake with knife. Cool in pan. Invert onto serving plate. Store in airtight container. This is a very moist cake. I received this recipe from a good friend of the family 10 years ago. It always sells well at bake sales.

Judith M. Lindsay

KNOBBY APPLE CAKE

3 tablespoons butter
1 cup sugar
1 egg, beaten
1 cup flour
1/2 teaspoon cinnamon
1/2 teaspoon nutmeg
1 teaspoon soda

1/2 teaspoon salt
3 cups chopped
   Granny Smith
   apples
1/2 cup chopped pecans
1 teaspoon vanilla
   extract

Cream butter and sugar in mixer bowl until light and fluffy. Add egg; beat well. Mix flour, cinnamon, nutmeg, soda and salt. Add to creamed mixture gradually, beating well after each addition. Stir in apples, pecans and vanilla. Pour into greased 8x10-inch cake pan. Bake at 350 degrees for 45 minutes or until cake tests done. Serve warm with whipped cream or ice cream. This cake will keep, well wrapped, for 10 days.

Pearl M. Sykes

APPLESAUCE CAKE

Yield:
16 servings

Approx Per Serving:
Cal 397
Prot 5 g
Carbo 58 g
Fiber 2 g
T Fat 17 g
Chol 40 mg
Sod 256 mg

1 cup margarine
1¹/₂ cups sugar
¹/₂ cup packed brown sugar
3 eggs
3 cups flour
2 teaspoons soda
1¹/₂ teaspoons nutmeg
2¹/₂ teaspoons cinnamon
¹/₂ to 1 teaspoon allspice
¹/₄ teaspoon ginger
2 cups applesauce
1 cup finely chopped apple
1 cup raisins
1 cup chopped English walnuts

Grease and flour 10-inch tube pan; line bottom with waxed paper. Cream margarine, sugar and brown sugar in mixer bowl until light. Add eggs; beat until fluffy. Reserve ¹/₄ cup flour. Sift remaining flour, soda, nutmeg, cinnamon, allspice and ginger together. Add 1 cup flour mixture at a time to creamed mixture alternately with applesauce and apples. Toss reserved ¹/₄ cup flour, raisins and English walnuts. Fold into batter. Pour into prepared pan. Bake at 350 degrees for 15 minutes. Reduce oven temperature to 325 degrees. Bake for 45 to 50 minutes longer or until cake tests done. Cool in pan for 20 minutes. Loosen cake with knife. Invert onto cake rack to cool completely. May decorate with sprinkles before baking or top with confectioners' sugar or orange glaze. I use homemade applesauce.

Mary E. Cornell

SPICY APPLESAUCE CAKE

Yield:
16 servings

Approx Per Serving:
Cal 243
Prot 3 g
Carbo 36 g
Fiber 2 g
T Fat 11 g
Chol 16 mg
Sod 102 mg

¹/₂ cup butter, softened
1 cup sugar
1 teaspoon cinnamon
1 teaspoon cloves
1 teaspoon nutmeg
2 cups flour
1 cup raisins
1 cup chopped pecans
1 cup applesauce
1 teaspoon soda

Cream butter and sugar in mixer bowl until light and fluffy. Add cinnamon, cloves and nutmeg; mix well. Mix flour, raisins and pecans together. Add to creamed mixture, mixing well. Add applesauce and soda; mix well. Pour into greased and floured 7-inch tube pan. Bake at 350 degrees for 1 hour or until cake tests done. This is an old family recipe which travels well. It was sent to Turkey during the war.

Robert Mayer

TASTY APPLESAUCE CAKE

1 16-ounce can
   applesauce
2 teaspoons soda
1 cup butter, softened
2 cups sugar
2 eggs, beaten

3 cups flour
1 cup raisins
1/2 teaspoon nutmeg
1/2 teaspoon allspice or
   cloves
1 cup chopped pecans

Combine applesauce and soda in bowl; mix well. Let stand until applesauce turns dark. Cream butter and sugar in mixer bowl until light and fluffy. Add applesauce and eggs; beat well. Add 2 cups flour; mix well. Mix remaining 1 cup flour with raisins. Stir into batter. Add nutmeg, allspice and pecans; mix well. Pour into greased and floured tube pan. Bake at 350 degrees for 1 hour or until cake tests done. Cool in pan. Invert onto serving plate.

Dawn C. Frizzell

BLUEBERRY PUDDING CAKE WITH SAUCE

1 cup shortening
2 cups sugar
3 cups sifted flour
1 tablespoon baking
   powder
4 eggs, beaten
1 cup milk

1 quart blueberries
1/2 cup sugar
2 tablespoons flour
1/4 cup butter
1 egg yolk
1 cup (about) water

Cream shortening and 2 cups sugar in mixer bowl until light and fluffy. Sift 3 cups flour and baking powder together. Beat eggs and milk in bowl. Add flour mixture and egg mixture alternately to batter, mixing well after each addition. Rinse and dry blueberries. Fold gently into batter. Spoon into greased 10-inch tube pan. Bake at 350 degrees for 45 minutes or until cake tests done. Cool in pan on rack until bottom is cool to touch. Invert onto serving plate, tapping gently on bottom of pan to loosen. Cream remaining 1/2 cup sugar, 2 tablespoons flour and butter in double boiler. Add egg yolk and enough water to make of thick syrup consistency. Cook until smooth and thickened; do not boil. Serve sauce over cake. Store sauce and cake, covered, in refrigerator. May flavor with rum if desired.

David L. Trubey

MOOSE MOUNTAIN CARROT CAKE

Yield:
16 servings

Approx Per Serving:
Cal 213
Prot 4 g
Carbo 25 g
Fiber 1 g
T Fat 11 g
Chol 25 mg
Sod 118 mg

1 egg, at room temperature
1/4 cup olive oil
1 cup packed dark brown sugar
1/2 cup low-fat sour cream
1 1/2 cups flour
1/2 teaspoon ginger
1/2 teaspoon cloves
3/4 teaspoon soda

1 cup grated carrots
1/2 cup chopped walnuts
8 ounces low-fat cream cheese, softened
1 tablespoon confectioners' sugar
1/4 cup low-fat yogurt
1 teaspoon vanilla extract

Whisk egg and olive oil in large bowl. Add brown sugar; beat until smooth. Stir in sour cream. Mix flour, ginger, cloves and soda in bowl. Fold gently into batter. Stir in carrots and walnuts. Spoon into 2 greased and floured 8-inch cake pans. Bake at 350 degrees for 40 minutes or until cake tests done. Cool in pans for 10 minutes. Remove to wire rack to cool completely. Combine cream cheese and confectioners' sugar in bowl; beat until well blended. Add yogurt and vanilla; mix well. Spread between layers and over top and side of cooled cake.

Joyce M. Michaels

CHOCOLATE CAKE

Yield:
16 servings

Approx Per Serving:
Cal 268
Prot 3 g
Carbo 38 g
Fiber 1 g
T Fat 12 g
Chol 43 mg
Sod 315 mg

2/3 cup margarine
2 1/4 cups sifted cake flour
2 cups sugar
1 teaspoon salt
1 teaspoon baking powder

1 teaspoon soda
1 1/4 cups milk
3 eggs
3 ounces chocolate, melted
1 teaspoon vanilla extract

Cream margarine in mixer bowl until light and fluffy. Sift in flour, sugar, salt, baking powder and soda. Add 1/2 cup milk; mix well. Add remaining milk and eggs; mix well. Add chocolate and vanilla. Beat for 2 minutes. Pour into 2 greased and floured 9-inch cake pans. Bake at 350 degrees for 30 to 35 minutes or until cake tests done. Remove to wire rack to cool. Frost with favorite frosting.

Mrs. Melvin J. Griggs Jr.

CHERRY CHOCOLATE CAKE

Yield:
12 servings

Approx Per Serving:
Cal 425
Prot 4 g
Carbo 73 g
Fiber 1 g
T Fat 15 g
Chol 36 mg
Sod 349 mg

1   2-layer package chocolate cake mix
1   21-ounce can cherry pie filling
2 eggs
1 teaspoon almond extract
1 cup sugar
1/3 cup milk
5 tablespoons margarine
1 cup chocolate chips

Combine cake mix, cherry pie filling, eggs and almond extract in mixer bowl; beat well. Spoon into greased and floured 5x9-inch loaf pan. Bake at 350 degrees for 35 minutes or until cake tests done. Cool in pan for several minutes. Remove to wire rack to cool. Combine sugar, milk and margarine in saucepan. Bring to a boil. Boil for 1 minute, stirring frequently. Remove from heat. Add chocolate chips, stirring until melted. Spread over cake.

Christina J. Wolfe

CHOCOLATE CHIP CAKE

Yield:
16 servings

Approx Per Serving:
Cal 352
Prot 4 g
Carbo 39 g
Fiber <1 g
T Fat 21 g
Chol 60 mg
Sod 258 mg

1   2-layer package yellow cake mix
1   3-ounce package chocolate instant pudding mix
1 cup sour cream
3/4 cup oil
1 teaspoon vanilla extract
4 eggs
1 cup chocolate chips

Combine cake mix, pudding mix, sour cream, oil, vanilla and eggs in mixer bowl; mix well. Stir in chocolate chips. Pour into greased and floured 10-inch tube pan. Bake at 350 degrees for 50 to 60 minutes or until cake tests done. Cool in pan for several minutes. Remove to wire rack to cool.

Carolyn Dade

 An apple cut in half and placed in the cake container will keep the cake fresh for several days longer.

FAT-FREE CHOCOLATE CAKE

Yield:
16 servings

Approx Per Serving:
Cal 177
Prot 3 g
Carbo 39 g
Fiber 2 g
T Fat 2 g
Chol 27 mg
Sod 259 mg

2 cups sugar
1³/4 cups flour
³/4 cup baking cocoa
1¹/2 teaspoons soda
1¹/2 teaspoons baking powder
1 teaspoon salt
2 eggs
1 cup skim milk
¹/2 cup applesauce
2 teaspoons vanilla extract
1 cup boiling water

Combine sugar, flour, cocoa, soda, baking powder and salt in large mixer bowl. Add eggs, milk, applesauce and vanilla. Beat at medium speed for 2 minutes. Stir in boiling water. Pour into 2 greased and floured 9-inch cake pans. Bake at 350 degrees for 35 to 40 minutes or until cake tests done. Remove to wire rack to cool. Frost as desired.

Betty Hainke

GLAZED CHOCOLATE ORANGE TORTE

Yield:
8 servings

Approx Per Serving:
Cal 512
Prot 8 g
Carbo 39 g
Fiber 4 g
T Fat 40 g
Chol 127 mg
Sod 200 mg

¹/2 cup butter, softened
²/3 cup sugar
3 eggs
³/4 cup melted semisweet chocolate
1 cup almonds, finely ground
Grated rind of 1 large orange
¹/4 cup very fine bread crumbs
2 ounces unsweetened chocolate
2 ounces semisweet chocolate
¹/4 cup butter
2 teaspoons honey

Butter one 8-inch cake pan; line bottom with waxed paper. Cream ¹/2 cup butter in mixer bowl until light and fluffy. Add ²/3 cup sugar gradually, mixing well. Add eggs 1 at a time, beating well after each addition. Stir in ³/4 cup melted semisweet chocolate, almonds, orange rind and bread crumbs; mix well. Spoon into prepared pan. Bake at 375 degrees for 25 minutes or until cake tests done. Cake will be soft in center. Cool in pan for 30 minutes. Remove to wire rack to cool completely. Combine unsweetened chocolate, 2 ounces semisweet chocolate, ¹/2 cup butter and honey in double boiler. Cook until chocolate is melted, stirring frequently. Remove from heat. Beat until cool but of pouring consistency. Pour over cooled cake on waxed paper. Garnish with nuts. Do not refrigerate.

Shirley Jackson

GERMAN SWEET CHOCOLATE CAKE

1   4-ounce package
    German's sweet
    chocolate
1/2 cup boiling water
1 cup butter, softened
2 cups sugar
4 egg yolks
1 teaspoon vanilla
    extract
2 cups flour
1 teaspoon soda
1/2 teaspoon salt

1 cup buttermilk
4 egg whites, stiffly
    beaten
1 cup evaporated milk
1 cup sugar
3 egg yolks, beaten
1/2 cup butter
1 teaspoon vanilla
    extract
1 1/3 cups coconut
1 cup chopped pecans

Grease and flour 3 round 9-inch cake pans. Line with waxed paper. Combine chocolate and boiling water in bowl, stirring until chocolate is melted. Cream 1 cup butter and 2 cups sugar in mixer bowl until light and fluffy. Add 4 egg yolks, 1 at a time, beating well after each addition. Add 1 teaspoon vanilla and chocolate; mix well. Sift flour, soda and salt together. Add to batter alternately with buttermilk, beating well after each addition. Fold in beaten egg whites. Pour into prepared cake pans. Bake at 350 degrees for 30 to 35 minutes or until cake tests done. Cool in pan for several minutes. Remove to wire rack to cool completely. Combine evaporated milk, 1 cup sugar, 3 egg yolks, 1/2 cup butter and 1 teaspoon vanilla in saucepan. Cook over medium heat for 12 minutes or until thickened, stirring constantly. Stir in coconut and pecans. Cool until thick enough to spread. Spread between cake layers.

Kathleen Kondus

The top layer of a layer cake won't slip as you ice it if you hold it in place with a wire cake-tester or thin skewers inserted through all layers. Remove the tester just before completing the job.

INSIDE-OUT CHOCOLATE CAKE

Yield:
16 servings

Approx Per Serving:
Cal 264
Prot 4 g
Carbo 42 g
Fiber 1 g
T Fat 10 g
Chol 30 mg
Sod 254 mg

1   3-ounce package chocolate instant pudding mix
1   2-layer package devil's food cake mix
2 eggs
1³/₄ cups milk
1¹/₂ cups chocolate chips

Combine pudding mix, cake mix, eggs and milk in mixer bowl; beat until well mixed. Stir in chocolate chips. Pour into greased and floured 12-cup bundt cake pan. Bake at 350 degrees for 60 minutes or until cake tests done. Do not overbake. Cool in pan for 15 minutes. Remove to wire rack to cool completely. May garnish with confectioner's sugar.

Pat Henning

TEXAS HOT COCOA CAKE

Yield:
15 servings

Approx Per Serving:
Cal 452
Prot 4 g
Carbo 56 g
Fiber 1 g
T Fat 24 g
Chol 46 mg
Sod 323 mg

¹/₂ cup butter
3 tablespoons baking cocoa
¹/₂ cup oil
1 cup water
2 cups self-rising flour
2 cups sugar
¹/₂ cup buttermilk
¹/₂ teaspoon cinnamon
1 teaspoon vanilla extract
2 eggs, beaten
¹/₂ cup margarine
2 tablespoons baking cocoa
3 tablespoons milk
¹/₂ teaspoon vanilla extract
2 cups confectioners' sugar
¹/₂ cup chopped pecans

Combine ¹/₂ cup butter, 3 tablespoons cocoa, oil and water in saucepan. Bring to a boil. Remove from heat. Stir in flour and sugar. Add buttermilk, cinnamon, vanilla and eggs; mix well. Add chocolate mixture; mix well. Pour into greased and floured 9x13-inch cake pan. Bake at 400 degrees for 25 minutes or until cake tests done. Cool for 10 minutes. Combine ¹/₂ cup margarine, 2 tablespoons cocoa, milk, 1 teaspoon vanilla and confectioners' sugar in saucepan. Bring to a boil, stirring constantly. Stir in pecans. Spread over cake.

Adelia C. Watson

CHOCOLATE ZUCCHINI CAKE

3 ounces semisweet
chocolate
1/2 cup oil
3 cups grated zucchini
3 cups sugar
4 eggs

1 cup oil
3 cups sifted flour
1 1/2 teaspoons baking
powder
1 teaspoon salt
1 teaspoon soda

Combine chocolate and 1/2 cup oil in saucepan. Cook over low heat until chocolate is melted, stirring constantly. Combine chocolate, zucchini, sugar, eggs and remaining 1 cup oil in large bowl; mix well. Mix flour, baking powder, salt and soda together. Add to chocolate batter a small amount at a time, mixing well after each addition. Pour into 2 greased and floured 8- or 9-inch cake pans. Bake at 350 degrees for 1 hour. Cool in pans for several minutes. Remove to wire rack to cool completely.

Jane Stipe

TUNNEL OF FUDGE CAKE

1 1/2 cups softened
butter
6 eggs
1 1/2 cups sugar
2 cups flour

1 package double-Dutch
fudge buttercream
frosting mix
2 cups chopped
walnuts

Cream butter in mixer bowl until light and fluffy. Add eggs 1 at a time, beating well after each addition. Add sugar gradually, mixing at high speed until smooth. Stir in flour, frosting mix and walnuts. Pour into greased bundt pan. Bake at 350 degrees for 60 to 65 minutes or until crust is dry and shiny like brownies; center will be soft and fudgy. Cool in pan for 2 hours. Invert onto serving plate. Do not substitute for frosting mix and walnuts in this recipe.

Deborah J. Morton

RING OF COCONUT FUDGE CAKE

Yield:
16 servings

Approx Per Serving:
Cal 390
Prot 5 g
Carbo 60 g
Fiber 2 g
T Fat 16 g
Chol 29 mg
Sod 374 mg

1/4 cup sugar
1 teaspoon vanilla extract
8 ounces cream cheese, softened
1 egg
1/2 cup coconut
1/2 cup miniature chocolate chips
1/2 cup margarine
2 teaspoons vanilla extract
2 teaspoons vinegar
2 cups water
3 cups flour

2 cups sugar
6 tablespoons baking cocoa
2 teaspoons soda
1 teaspoon salt
1 cup confectioners' sugar
2 tablespoons baking cocoa
2 tablespoons melted margarine
2 teaspoons vanilla extract
1 to 3 tablespoons hot water

Combine 1/4 cup sugar, 1 teaspoon vanilla, cream cheese and egg in bowl; beat well. Stir in coconut and chocolate chips. Melt 1/2 cup margarine in large saucepan; remove from heat. Add 2 teaspoons vanilla, vinegar and water; mix well. Mix flour, remaining 2 cups sugar, 6 tablespoons cocoa, soda and salt in large bowl. Add vinegar mixture; mix well. Pour half the batter into greased and floured 10-inch tube pan. Spoon cream cheese filling over top. Add remaining batter. Bake at 350 degrees for 50 to 60 minutes or until cake tests done. Cool in pan for 15 minutes. Remove to wire rack to cool. Combine confectioners' sugar, remaining 2 tablespoons cocoa, 2 tablespoons margarine and 2 teaspoons vanilla in bowl; mix well. Add 1 to 3 tablespoons hot water to make of glaze consistency. Drizzle over cooled cake.

Deborah L. Bean

Red Velvet Cake

Yield:
16 servings

Approx Per Serving:
Cal 372
Prot 4 g
Carbo 47 g
Fiber 1 g
T Fat 19 g
Chol 89 mg
Sod 392 mg

1/2 cup butter, softened
1 1/2 cups sugar
3 eggs
2 tablespoons baking cocoa
2 ounces red food coloring
1 teaspoon salt
1 teaspoon vanilla extract

1 cup buttermilk
2 cups flour
1 1/2 teaspoons soda
1 tablespoon vinegar
5 tablespoons flour
1 cup milk
1 cup butter, softened
1 cup sugar
1 teaspoon vanilla extract

Cream 1/2 cup butter and 1 1/2 cups sugar in mixer bowl until light and fluffy. Add eggs 1 at a time, beating well after each addition. Add 2 tablespoons cocoa and food coloring; mix well. Mix salt and 1 teaspoon vanilla with buttermilk. Add to batter alternately with 2 cups flour, mixing well after each addition. Mix soda and vinegar. Fold into batter. Pour into 2 greased and floured round cake pans. Bake at 350 degrees for 30 minutes. Cool in pan for several minutes. Remove to wire rack to cool completely. Combine remaining 5 tablespoons flour and 1 cup milk in saucepan. Cook until smooth and thick, stirring constantly. Let stand at room temperature to cool. Cream 1 cup butter and 1 cup sugar in mixer bowl until light and fluffy. Add remaining 1 teaspoon vanilla and flour mixture; beat well. Spread between layers and on top and side of cooled cake. Do not substitute margarine for butter in this recipe.

Margaret E. Williams

For a delicious **Chocolate Chocolate Chip Torte**, split 2 chocolate cake layers and fill with mixture of 16 ounces whipped topping, 8 ounces softened cream cheese, 4 cups confectioners' sugar, 2 cups miniature chocolate chips and 1/2 cup nuts.

Mama's Christmas Cake

½ cup shortening
½ cup butter, softened
3 cups sugar
5 eggs
3 cups flour
1 teaspoon vanilla extract
1 tablespoon rum flavoring
1 cup milk
1 cup coconut
½ cup green candied cherries, cut into quarters
½ cup red candied cherries, cut into quarters
1 cup chopped black walnuts

Cream shortening, butter and sugar in mixer bowl until light and fluffy. Add eggs 1 at a time, beating well after each addition. Add flour alternately with vanilla, rum flavoring and milk, beginning and ending with flour and mixing well after each addition. Fold in coconut, green cherries, red cherries and black walnuts. Pour into greased and floured tube pan. Bake at 325 degrees for 1½ hours or until cake tests done. Do not open oven door until cake has baked for 1 hour. Flavor is enhanced by storing, wrapped in foil, for several days before slicing.

MaryAlice Thomas

Fruitcake

2½ cups sifted flour
1 teaspoon soda
1 14-ounce can sweetened condensed milk
2 eggs, beaten
1 28-ounce jar mincemeat
16 ounces mixed candied fruit
1 cup chopped walnuts

Sift flour and soda together. Combine condensed milk, eggs, mincemeat, candied fruit and walnuts in large bowl; mix well. Fold in flour mixture. Pour into greased 9-inch tube pan. Bake at 300 degrees for 2 hours or until cake tests done and is golden brown. Cool in pan for 5 minutes. Remove to wire rack to cool completely.

Nutritional information does not include mincemeat.

Charlotte Wood

Yes Virginia Fruitcake

Yield:
12 servings

Approx Per Serving:
Cal 336
Prot 4 g
Carbo 49 g
Fiber 2 g
T Fat 15 g
Chol 55 mg
Sod 188 mg

2 eggs, beaten
1 16-ounce roll refrigerator cookie dough, softened
1 cup raisins
1 cup coarsely chopped walnuts
1 cup whole candied cherries

Greased 5x9-inch loaf pan; line with waxed paper. Combine eggs and crumbled cookie dough in large bowl; mix well. Add raisins, walnuts and cherries; mix well. Spread in prepared pan. Bake at 325 degrees for 1 hour and 10 minutes or until cake tests done. Cool in pan for 15 minutes. Remove to wire rack to cool completely. Flavor will be enhanced by storing, tightly wrapped, for several days.

Margaret E. Williams

Fruit Cocktail Cake

Yield:
16 servings

Approx Per Serving:
Cal 141
Prot 2 g
Carbo 28 g
Fiber 1 g
T Fat 3 g
Chol 13 mg
Sod 77 mg

1 cup flour
1 cup sugar
1 teaspoon soda
Salt to taste
1 egg, beaten
1 cup drained fruit cocktail
1/2 cup packed brown sugar
1/2 cup chopped pecans

Combine flour, sugar, soda and salt in mixer bowl; mix well. Add egg and fruit cocktail. Beat for 3 minutes. Spoon into greased and floured 8x8-inch cake pan. Sprinkle brown sugar and pecans over top. Bake at 350 degrees for 45 minutes or until cake tests done. Cool on wire rack.

Marge Fritz

 Holiday fruitcakes can be stored indefinitely. Wrap them in Brandy or wine-soaked cloths and then in foil. Store in an airtight container in a cool place.

HUMMINGBIRD CAKE

Yield:
16 servings

Approx Per Serving:
Cal 672
Prot 5 g
Carbo 87 g
Fiber 2 g
T Fat 35 g
Chol 71 mg
Sod 290 mg

3 cups flour
2 cups sugar
1½ teaspoons vanilla extract
1½ cups oil
3 eggs
2 cups mashed bananas
1 teaspoon salt
1 teaspoon soda
1 teaspoon cinnamon
½ cup chopped pecans
1 8-ounce can crushed pineapple
8 ounces cream cheese, softened
½ cup butter, softened
1 1-pound package confectioners' sugar
1 teaspoon vanilla extract

Combine flour, sugar, 1½ teaspoons vanilla, oil, eggs, bananas, salt, soda and cinnamon in mixer bowl; beat well. Stir in pecans and pineapple. Pour into greased tube pan. Bake at 300 degrees for 1½ hours. Cool in pan for 1 hour. Invert onto serving plate. Combine remaining ingredients in mixer bowl; beat until smooth and creamy. Spread over cake.

Kathleen Kondus

ITALIAN CREAM CAKE

Yield:
16 servings

Approx Per Serving:
Cal 560
Prot 6 g
Carbo 77 g
Fiber 2 g
T Fat 27 g
Chol 83 mg
Sod 228 mg

½ cup margarine, softened
½ cup oil
2 cups sugar
5 egg yolks
2 cups flour
1 teaspoon soda
1 cup buttermilk
1 teaspoon vanilla extract
1 7-ounce can coconut
1 cup chopped pecans
5 egg whites, stiffly beaten
8 ounces cream cheese, softened
¼ cup margarine, softened
1 1-pound package confectioners' sugar
1 teaspoon vanilla extract

Cream ½ cup margarine, oil and sugar in mixer bowl until light. Blend in egg yolks. Add flour and soda alternately with buttermilk, mixing well after each addition. Stir in 1 teaspoon vanilla, coconut and pecans. Fold in egg whites. Pour into 3 greased and floured 8-inch cake pans. Bake at 350 degrees for 25 to 30 minutes or until cake tests done. Cool in pan for several minutes. Remove to wire rack to cool completely. Combine remaining ingredients in mixer bowl; beat until smooth. Spread between layers and over top and side of cake.

Jean S. Ward

Mexican Wedding Cake

2 cups sugar
2 cups flour
1/2 teaspoon salt
1 teaspoon soda
2 teaspoons vanilla
extract
2 eggs
1 20-ounce can
crushed pineapple
1 cup chopped pecans
8 ounces cream cheese,
softened
1 1/2 cups
confectioners' sugar
1/2 cup margarine,
softened
2 teaspoons vanilla
extract

Mix first 4 ingredients in mixer bowl. Add 2 teaspoons vanilla and eggs; beat until smooth. Stir in undrained pineapple and pecans. Pour into greased 9x13-inch cake pan. Bake at 350 degrees for 50 minutes. Cool on wire rack. Combine remaining ingredients in mixer bowl. Beat until smooth and creamy. Spread over cooled cake.

Bea Souder

Milky Way Wonder Cake

15 bite-size Milky
Way candy bars
1/2 cup butter
2 cups sugar
1/2 cup butter
4 eggs, beaten
2 1/2 cups flour
1/2 teaspoon soda
1 1/4 cups buttermilk
1 teaspoon vanilla
extract
1 cup chopped walnuts
1 16-ounce can cream
cheese frosting
2 or 3 drops of yellow
food coloring
1/2 teaspoon lemon
extract

Melt candy bars and 1/2 cup butter in saucepan, stirring frequently. Cream sugar and remaining 1/2 cup butter in mixer bowl until light and fluffy. Add eggs; beat well. Sift flour and soda together. Add to batter alternately with buttermilk, mixing well after each addition. Add melted candy mixture and vanilla; mix well. Stir in walnuts. Pour into greased and floured bundt pan. Bake at 350 degrees for 50 minutes or until cake tests done. Cool in pan for several minutes. Invert onto wire rack to cool for 1 hour. Combine cream cheese frosting, food coloring and lemon extract in mixer bowl; mix well. Spread over cooled cake.

Juanda H. Day

Frosted Oatmeal Cake

Yield:
16 servings

Approx Per
Serving:
Cal 547
Prot 5 g
Carbo 57 g
Fiber 2 g
T Fat 35 g
Chol 102 mg
Sod 264 mg

1½ cups boiling water
1 cup oats
1 cup shortening
1 cup packed brown
 sugar
1 cup sugar
2 eggs
1 teaspoon cinnamon
¼ teaspoon nutmeg
½ teaspoon salt

1 teaspoon soda
1½ cups flour
1 cup evaporated milk
3 egg yolks
1 teaspoon vanilla extract
1 cup sugar
1 cup butter
1⅓ cups coconut
1 cup chopped pecans

Pour boiling water over oats in bowl, stirring to mix. Let stand until cool. Cream shortening, brown sugar and 1 cup sugar in mixer bowl until light and fluffy. Add eggs; beat well. Mix cinnamon, nutmeg, salt, soda and flour together. Stir flour mixture and oats into batter. Pour into greased and floured cake pan. Bake at 350 degrees for 35 to 45 minutes or until cake tests done. Cool in pan for several minutes. Remove to wire rack to cool completely. Combine next 5 ingredients in saucepan. Cook over medium heat until thickened, stirring constantly. Stir in coconut and pecans. Spread over cake.

Marge Fritz

Pig Picking Cake

Yield:
16 servings

Approx Per
Serving:
Cal 334
Prot 4 g
Carbo 41 g
Fiber 1 g
T Fat 18 g
Chol 55 mg
Sod 261 mg

1 2-layer package
 yellow cake mix
4 eggs
⅔ cup oil
1 8-ounce can
 mandarin oranges
9 ounces whipped
 topping

1 16-ounce can
 crushed pineapple,
 drained
1 3-ounce package
 vanilla instant
 pudding mix
½ cup chopped pecans

Combine cake mix, eggs, oil and undrained oranges in mixer bowl; beat well. Pour into 3 greased and floured cake pans. Bake at 350 degrees for 25 minutes or until cakes test done. Cool in pans for several minutes. Remove to wire rack to cool completely. Combine whipped topping, pineapple and pudding mix in bowl; mix well. Stir in pecans. Spread between layers and over top and side of cake.

Deborah Poncheri

Pineapple Skillet Cake

¼ cup shortening
1 cup packed brown sugar
1 20-ounce can sliced pineapple, drained
4 eggs
1 cup sugar
1 cup flour
1 teaspoon baking powder
½ teaspoon salt
2 tablespoons water
1 teaspoon vanilla extract

Heat shortening and brown sugar in large heavy iron skillet until sugar is melted, stirring frequently. Cool in skillet. Arrange pineapple slices in mixture. Beat eggs and sugar in mixer bowl until thick and lemon-colored. Sift flour, baking powder and salt together. Add to batter alternately with water and vanilla, mixing well after each addition. Pour into prepared pan. Bake at 350 degrees for 40 minutes or until cake tests done. Invert onto serving plate while hot. Garnish with whipped cream and cherries.

Helen Bell

Any Flavor Pound Cake

1 2-layer package any flavor cake mix
1 3-ounce package any flavor instant pudding mix
½ cup oil
1 cup water
4 eggs
1 cup confectioners' sugar
2 tablespoons milk

Combine cake mix, pudding mix, oil, water and eggs in mixer bowl; beat well. Pour into greased and floured tube pan. Bake at 350 degrees for 45 to 55 minutes or until cake tests done. Cool in pan for several minutes. Remove to wire rack to cool completely. Combine confectioners' sugar and milk in mixer bowl; beat until sugar is dissolved. Pour over cake. May combine chocolate cake mix with chocolate pudding mix or white cake mix and vanilla pudding mix. May substitute lemon juice for milk in glaze.

Adelia C. Watson

CHOCOLATE POUND CAKE

Yield:
16 servings

Approx Per Serving:
Cal 428
Prot 5 g
Carbo 57 g
Fiber 1 g
T Fat 21 g
Chol 100 mg
Sod 203 mg

1 cup butter, softened
1/2 cup shortening
3 cups sugar
5 eggs
3 cups flour
1/2 teaspoon baking powder

1/2 teaspoon salt
4 to 5 tablespoons (heaping) baking cocoa
1 cup milk
2 teaspoons vanilla extract

Cream butter, shortening and sugar in mixer bowl until light and fluffy. Add eggs 1 at a time, beating well after each addition. Mix flour, baking powder, salt and cocoa together. Add to batter alternately with milk and vanilla, mixing well after each addition. Pour into greased and floured tube pan. Bake at 275 degrees for 1 1/2 to 2 hours or until cake tests done. Remove to wire rack to cool.

Rita Adams

COLD-OVEN BUTTERNUT POUND CAKE

Yield:
16 servings

Approx Per Serving:
Cal 473
Prot 5 g
Carbo 56 g
Fiber 1 g
T Fat 26 g
Chol 144 mg
Sod 248 mg

2 cups butter, softened
3 cups sugar
6 eggs
3 cups flour
1 teaspoon baking powder

1 cup milk
1 teaspoon vanilla extract
1 teaspoon butternut flavoring

Cream butter and sugar in mixer bowl until light and fluffy. Add eggs 1 at a time, beating well after each addition. Add flour and baking powder with milk, beginning and ending with dry ingredients and mixing well after each addition. Add flavorings; beat for 2 minutes. Pour into greased and floured tube pan. Place in cold oven. Set oven temperature at 350 degrees. Bake for 1 1/2 hours or until cake tests done. Remove to wire rack to cool. May substitute lemon flavoring for butternut if preferred.

Margaret E. Williams

COLD-OVEN LEMON POUND CAKE

Yield:
16 servings

Approx Per Serving:
Cal 367
Prot 5 g
Carbo 56 g
Fiber 1 g
T Fat 14 g
Chol 100 mg
Sod 126 mg

1 cup butter, softened
1/2 cup shortening
3 cups sugar
5 eggs
3 cups flour

1 cup milk
1 teaspoon vanilla
  extract
1 teaspoon lemon
  flavoring

Cream butter, shortening and sugar in mixer bowl until light and fluffy. Add eggs 1 at a time, beating well after addition. Add flour alternately with milk, vanilla and lemon flavoring, mixing well after each addition. Pour into greased and floured tube pan. Place in cold oven. Set oven temperature at 325 degrees. Bake for 1 1/2 hours or until cake tests done. Remove to wire rack to cool.

Florine W. Mooring

CREAM CHEESE POUND CAKE

Yield:
16 servings

Approx Per Serving:
Cal 394
Prot 6 g
Carbo 58 g
Fiber 1 g
T Fat 16 g
Chol 95 mg
Sod 203 mg

3/4 cup margarine,
  softened
8 ounces cream cheese,
  softened
3 cups sugar
6 eggs

1 1/2 teaspoons vanilla
  extract
3 cups flour
1/4 teaspoon salt
1/4 cup confectioners'
  sugar

Cream butter, cream cheese and sugar in mixer bowl until light and fluffy. Add eggs 1 at a time, beating well after each addition. Add vanilla. Sift in flour and salt, mixing well. Pour into greased and floured tube pan. Bake at 325 degrees for 1 hour and 15 minutes or until cake tests done. Cool in pan for 10 minutes. Remove to wire rack. Sift confectioners' sugar over hot cake. Cool completely.

Mrs. David A. Sturgill

GRANDMA'S CREAM CHEESE POUND CAKE

Yield:
16 servings

Approx Per Serving:
Cal 463
Prot 6 g
Carbo 56 g
Fiber 1 g
T Fat 25 g
Chol 142 mg
Sod 214 mg

1½ cups butter, softened
8 ounces cream cheese, softened
3 cups sugar

6 eggs
3 cups flour
2 teaspoons vanilla extract

Cream butter, cream cheese and sugar in mixer bowl until light and fluffy. Add eggs 1 at a time, beating well after each addition. Add flour and vanilla; mix well. Pour into greased and floured tube pan. Bake at 325 degrees for 1½ hours or until cake tests done. Cool in pan for several minutes. Remove to wire rack to cool completely. This is good served with fresh fruit, homemade jam or boiled custard.

Brenda N. Crist

ELEGANT POUND CAKE

Yield:
16 servings

Approx Per Serving:
Cal 481
Prot 6 g
Carbo 55 g
Fiber 1 g
T Fat 27 g
Chol 171 mg
Sod 227 mg

8 egg whites
2⅔ cups sugar
2 cups butter, softened
8 egg yolks, beaten

3½ cups sifted flour
½ cup half and half
1 teaspoon vanilla extract

Beat egg whites until soft peaks form. Add 6 tablespoons sugar gradually, beating constantly until stiff peaks form. Chill in refrigerator. Cream remaining sugar and butter in mixer bowl until light and fluffy. Add egg yolks; mix well. Sift flour 3 times. Add to batter alternately with half and half and vanilla, beating well after each addition. Add 1 heaping tablespoon egg whites, stirring into batter vigorously. Fold in remaining egg whites. Pour into greased and floured 10-inch tube pan. Bake at 300 degrees for 1 hour and 45 minutes or until cake tests done. Invert cake pan onto wire rack to cool. Loosen edge with spatula. Remove to serving plate.

Doris A. Baylor

Lemon Pound Cake

Yield:
16 servings

Approx Per Serving:
Cal 422
Prot 5 g
Carbo 56 g
Fiber 1 g
T Fat 20 g
Chol 129 mg
Sod 199 mg

1½ cups butter, softened
3 cups sugar
6 eggs
2 tablespoons lemon extract
1 tablespoon vanilla extract
3 cups flour
1 teaspoon baking powder
1 cup milk

Cream butter and sugar in mixer bowl until light and fluffy. Add eggs 1 at a time, beating well after each addition. Add lemon and vanilla flavorings. Mix flour and baking powder together. Add to batter alternately with milk, beating well after each addition. Pour into greased and floured tube pan. Bake at 350 degrees for 1 hour or until cake tests done; do not overbake. Cool in pan for several minutes. Remove to wire rack to cool completely.

Margaret E. Williams

Million Dollar Almond Pound Cake

Yield:
16 servings

Approx Per Serving:
Cal 499
Prot 6 g
Carbo 62 g
Fiber 1 g
T Fat 26 g
Chol 144 mg
Sod 226 mg

2 cups butter, softened
3 cups sugar
6 eggs, at room temperature
4 cups flour
¾ cup milk
1 teaspoon almond extract
1 teaspoon vanilla extract

Cream butter and sugar in mixer bowl until light and fluffy. Add eggs 1 at a time, beating well after each addition. Add flour alternately with milk, beating well after each addition. Add flavorings; mix well. Pour into greased and floured pan. Bake at 300 degrees for 1 hour and 40 minutes or until cake tests done. Cool in pan for several minutes. Remove to wire rack to cool.

Clarise B. Witcher

Million Dollar Pound Cake

Yield:
16 servings

**Approx Per
Serving:**
*Cal 498
Prot 7 g
Carbo 62 g
Fiber 1 g
T Fat 25 g
Chol 143 mg
Sod 219 mg*

1¹/₂ cups butter,
  softened
8 ounces cream cheese,
  softened
3 cups sugar
6 eggs, at room
  temperature

4 cups flour
³/₄ cup milk
1 teaspoon lemon
  extract
1 teaspoon vanilla
  extract

Cream butter, cream cheese and sugar in mixer bowl until light and fluffy. Add eggs 1 at a time, beating well after each addition. Add flour alternately with milk and flavorings, beating well after each addition. Pour into greased and floured 10-inch tube pan. Bake at 325 degrees for 1¹/₂ hours or until cake tests done. Cool in pan for 15 minutes. Remove to wire rack to cool completely. May sprinkle with confectioners' sugar.

Mary M. Hines

Old-Fashioned Pound Cake

Yield:
16 servings

**Approx Per
Serving:**
*Cal 399
Prot 5 g
Carbo 51 g
Fiber 1 g
T Fat 20 g
Chol 153 mg
Sod 181 mg*

1¹/₂ cups butter,
  softened
2³/₄ cups sugar

8 eggs
3 cups cake flour

Cream butter and sugar in mixer bowl until light and fluffy. Add eggs 2 at a time, beating well after each addition. Add flour gradually, beating well after each addition. Spoon into greased and floured 10-inch tube pan. Bake at 325 degrees for 1 hour and 15 minutes or until cake tests done. Cool completely in pan. Invert onto serving plate. Serve with fresh strawberries and whipped topping.

Deborah J. Morton

Seven-Up Pound Cake

Yield:
16 servings

Approx Per Serving:
Cal 418
Prot 4 g
Carbo 57 g
Fiber 1 g
T Fat 20 g
Chol 98 mg
Sod 121 mg

1 cup butter, softened
1/2 cup shortening
3 cups sugar
5 eggs
3 cups flour
8 ounces 7-Up
1 teaspoon lemon extract

Cream butter, shortening and sugar in mixer bowl until light and fluffy. Add eggs 1 at a time, beating well after each addition. Add flour alternately with 7-Up and lemon extract, beating well after each addition. Pour into greased and floured tube pan. Bake at 350 degrees for 1 1/2 hours or until cake tests done. Cool in pan for several minutes. Remove to wire rack to cool completely. May bake in 2 loaf pans. May substitute Mountain Dew for 7-Up.

Jan K. Schmalz

Sour Cream Pound Cake

Yield:
16 servings

Approx Per Serving:
Cal 392
Prot 5 g
Carbo 56 g
Fiber 1 g
T Fat 17 g
Chol 117 mg
Sod 174 mg

1 cup butter, softened
3 cups sugar
3 cups flour
1/4 teaspoon salt
1/4 teaspoon soda
8 ounces sour cream
1 teaspoon vanilla extract
6 egg yolks, beaten
6 egg whites

Cream butter and sugar in mixer bowl until light and fluffy. Sift flour, salt and soda together. Add to batter alternately with sour cream and vanilla, beating well after each addition. Add egg yolks; mix well. Beat egg whites until foamy. Add to batter. Beat for 3 minutes. Pour into greased and floured tube pan. Bake at 350 degrees for 1 hour or until cake tests done. Cool in pan for several minutes. Remove to wire rack to cool completely.

V. Emily Lewis

Pumpkin Cake with Cream Cheese Icing

4 eggs
2 cups flour, sifted
2 teaspoons soda
1/2 teaspoon salt
1 teaspoon cloves
2 teaspoons cinnamon
1/2 teaspoon ginger
1/4 teaspoon nutmeg
2 cups sugar

1 cup oil
1   16-ounce can
   pumpkin
6 ounces cream cheese,
   softened
1 tablespoon vanilla
   extract
3 cups confectioners'
   sugar

Place eggs in large mixer bowl. Let stand, covered, for 30 minutes. Sift flour, soda, salt, cloves, cinnamon, ginger and nutmeg together. Beat eggs thoroughly. Add sugar; beat until lemon-colored. Add oil and pumpkin gradually, beating well after each addition. Add flour mixture gradually, beating well after each addition. Pour into ungreased tube pan. Bake at 350 degrees for 1 hour or until cake tests done. Cool in pan. Beat cream cheese and vanilla in bowl until smooth. Add confectioners' sugar gradually, beating until light and fluffy. Invert cake onto serving plate. Spread frosting over top and side of cake. Garnish with pecan halves. Store, tightly covered, in refrigerator. Let stand at room temperature for 30 minutes before serving.

Lisa R. Washington

 For **Quick Confectioners' Sugar Icing**, *blend 2 tablespoons softened margarine, 2 cups confectioners' sugar and enough milk to make of spreading consistency. Flavor and tint as desired.*

Pumpkin Roll

Yield:
8 servings

*Approx Per
Serving:*
Cal 422
Prot 6 g
Carbo 57 g
Fiber 1 g
T Fat 20 g
Chol 103 mg
Sod 333 mg

3 eggs
1 cup sugar
2/3 cup canned
  pumpkin
1 teaspoon lemon juice
3/4 cup flour
1 teaspoon baking
  powder
2 teaspoons cinnamon
1/2 teaspoon ginger
1/2 teaspoon nutmeg
1/2 teaspoon salt

1/2 cup chopped
  walnuts
1/4 cup confectioners'
  sugar
6 ounces cream cheese,
  softened
1 cup confectioners'
  sugar
1/4 cup margarine,
  softened
1/2 teaspoon vanilla
  extract

Grease and flour 10x15-inch jelly roll pan; line with waxed paper. Beat eggs for 5 minutes in mixer bowl. Add sugar gradually, beating constantly. Add pumpkin and lemon juice; mix well. Mix flour, baking powder, cinnamon, ginger, nutmeg and salt together. Add to batter gradually, beating well after each addition. Spread in prepared pan. Sprinkle with walnuts. Bake at 375 degrees for 15 minutes or until golden brown and cake tests done. Spread tea towel on flat surface; sprinkle with 1/4 cup confectioners' sugar. Invert jelly roll onto towel; roll from short side, including towel. Allow to cool. Combine cream cheese, 1 cup confectioners' sugar, margarine and vanilla in mixer bowl; beat until smooth and creamy. Unroll cake carefully. Spread with filling. Roll as for jelly roll to enclose filling. Store, wrapped in waxed paper, in refrigerator. May wrap in foil and freeze.

Gale Graney

MATT'S FAVORITE RUM CAKE

Yield:
16 servings

Approx Per
Serving:
Cal 367
Prot 3 g
Carbo 44 g
Fiber <1 g
T Fat 17 g
Chol 69 mg
Sod 298 mg

1 2-layer package
   yellow cake mix
1 3-ounce package
   vanilla instant
   pudding mix
4 eggs
1/2 cup cold water

1/2 cup oil
1/2 cup golden rum
1 cup sugar
1/2 cup butter
1/4 cup water
1/2 cup golden rum

Combine cake mix, pudding mix, eggs, cold water and oil in mixer bowl; mix well. Add 1/2 cup rum; mix well. Pour into greased and floured 10-inch tube pan. Bake at 325 degrees for 60 minutes or until cake tests done. Invert pan onto wire rack; cool for 20 minutes. Remove to wire rack to cool completely. Combine sugar, butter and 1/4 cup water in saucepan. Simmer for 15 minutes, stirring constantly; remove from heat. Stir in remaining 1/2 cup rum. Pierce holes in top of cooled cake. Spoon glaze over cake until all glaze is absorbed.

Justine A. Smith

RUM CAKE

Yield:
16 servings

Approx Per
Serving:
Cal 304
Prot 3 g
Carbo 45 g
Fiber <1 g
T Fat 10 g
Chol 67 mg
Sod 321 mg

1 2-layer package
   yellow butter cake
   mix
1 3-ounce package
   lemon instant
   pudding mix
1/2 cup water

1/2 cup rum
5 eggs
1/2 cup margarine
1 cup sugar
1/4 cup water
1/4 cup rum

Combine cake mix, pudding mix, 1/2 cup water, 1/2 cup rum and eggs in mixer bowl; mix well. Pour into greased bundt pan. Bake at 350 degrees for 35 to 40 minutes or until cake tests done. Cool in pan for several minutes. Invert onto serving plate. Combine margarine, sugar and 1/4 cup water in saucepan. Bring to a boil. Boil for 1 minute, stirring constantly. Remove from heat. Stir in 1/4 cup rum. Pour hot sauce over hot cake.

Lin Kogle

Strawberry Cake

1 2-layer package strawberry cake mix
1 pint fresh strawberries, sliced
1/4 cup sugar
16 ounces whipped topping
1 cup sour cream
1/2 cup sugar

Prepare and bake cake mix using package directions for two 9-inch round cake pans. Remove to wire rack to cool. Sprinkle strawberries with 1/4 cup sugar in bowl. Combine whipped topping and sour cream in bowl; mix well. Add remaining 1/2 cup sugar; mix well. Reserve several strawberries. Layer 1/3 of the whipped topping mixture and all of the strawberries between layers of cake. Spread remaining whipped topping over top and side of cake. Top with reserved strawberries.

Eunice Booker

Black Walnut Cake

1 2-layer package white cake mix
1 cup chopped black walnuts
1 cup packed dark brown sugar
1/2 cup butter
1/4 cup milk
2 1/2 cups confectioners' sugar
3/4 cup chopped black walnuts

Prepare and bake cake mix with 1 cup chopped walnuts using package directions for 9-inch cake pans. Cool in pans for several minutes. Remove to wire rack to cool completely. Combine brown sugar and butter in saucepan. Boil for 2 minutes, stirring constantly. Add milk. Bring to a boil, stirring constantly. Remove from heat. Cool completely. Add confectioners' sugar; beat until smooth and creamy. Stir in remaining 3/4 cup chopped walnuts. Spread between layers and over top and side of cooled cake. This is Grandmother's recipe from the Shenandoah Valley of Virginia.

Daisy L. Shallcross

Yum-Yum Cake

Yield:
16 servings

Approx Per Serving:
Cal 310
Prot 3 g
Carbo 52 g
Fiber 1 g
T Fat 11 g
Chol 3 mg
Sod 285 mg

1   2-layer package yellow cake mix
1   6-ounce package vanilla instant pudding mix
1½ cups milk
16 ounces whipped topping
2   16-ounce cans crushed pineapple, drained

Prepare cake mix using package directions for 12x18-inch cake pan. Bake at 350 degrees for 20 minutes. Cool in pan. Mix pudding mix and milk in bowl. Fold in whipped topping. Spread over cooled cake. Spoon pineapple over top. Store in refrigerator.

Joanne B. Colt

Black Bottom Cupcakes

Yield:
24 servings

Approx Per Serving:
Cal 173
Prot 2 g
Carbo 22 g
Fiber 1 g
T Fat 9 g
Chol 19 mg
Sod 89 mg

⅓ cup sugar
8 ounces cream cheese, softened
1 egg
¼ teaspoon salt
1 cup chocolate chips
1½ cups flour
1 cup sugar
¼ cup baking cocoa
1 teaspoon soda
1 cup water
⅓ cup oil
1 tablespoon vinegar
1 teaspoon vanilla extract

Line miniature muffin cups with paper liners. Cream ⅓ cup sugar and cream cheese in mixer bowl. Add egg and salt; mix well. Stir in chocolate chips. Combine flour, remaining 1 cup sugar, cocoa and soda in bowl; mix well. Add water, oil, vinegar and vanilla; mix well. Spoon into prepared muffin cups. Top with cream cheese mixture. Bake at 350 degrees for 20 to 25 minutes or until cupcakes test done. Remove to wire rack to cool.

Deborah Kulinski

CHOCOLATE CHEESE CUPCAKES

Yield:
24 servings

Approx Per Serving:
Cal 179
Prot 2 g
Carbo 27 g
Fiber <1 g
T Fat 7 g
Chol 19 mg
Sod 163 mg

1 2-layer package devil's food cake mix
1 egg

8 ounces cream cheese, softened
3/4 cup sugar
3/4 cup chocolate chips

Prepare cake mix using package directions. Fill paper-lined muffin cups 2/3 full. Combine egg, cream cheese and sugar in mixer bowl; mix well. Stir in chocolate chips. Drop 1 teaspoonful into each muffin cup. Bake using package directions or until cupcakes test done. Remove to wire rack to cool.

Linda A. Leavitt

FUDGE MUFFINS

Yield:
12 servings

Approx Per Serving:
Cal 428
Prot 4 g
Carbo 45 g
Fiber 1 g
T Fat 27 g
Chol 71 mg
Sod 226 mg

4 ounces semisweet chocolate
1 cup margarine
13/4 cups sugar
Salt to taste

1 cup flour
4 eggs
1 teaspoon vanilla extract
1 cup chopped pecans

Melt chocolate with margarine in saucepan. Combine with sugar, salt and flour in mixer bowl; mix well. Add eggs 1 at a time, beating well after each addition. Stir in vanilla and pecans. Fill 12 paper-lined muffin cups 2/3 full. Bake at 325 degrees for 25 minutes or until muffins test done. Remove to wire rack to cool.

Dorothy Mason

CRANBERRY APPLESAUCE CUPCAKES

Yield:
12 servings

Approx Per Serving:
Cal 406
Prot 5 g
Carbo 63 g
Fiber 2 g
T Fat 16 g
Chol 92 mg
Sod 114 mg

½ cup melted butter
⅓ cup shortening
1½ cups sugar
4 eggs
2½ cups flour
1 teaspoon cinnamon
½ teaspoon baking powder
1 16-ounce can cranberry sauce
1½ cups applesauce

Cream butter, shortening and sugar in mixer bowl until light and fluffy. Add eggs, 1 at a time, beating well after each addition. Add flour, cinnamon, baking powder, cranberry sauce and applesauce; mix well. Fill 12 paper-lined muffin cups ⅔ full. Bake at 350 degrees for 35 minutes or until muffins test done. Remove to wire rack to cool. May frost with vanilla frosting.

Tonya Gibbs

OLD-FASHIONED CUPCAKES

Yield:
30 servings

Approx Per Serving:
Cal 153
Prot 3 g
Carbo 24 g
Fiber <1 g
T Fat 5 g
Chol 40 mg
Sod 91 mg

⅔ cup butter, softened
2 cups sugar
4 eggs, beaten
1 cup milk
3¼ cups flour
4 teaspoons baking powder
¼ teaspoon mace

Cream butter and sugar in mixer bowl until light and fluffy. Add eggs and milk; mix well. Sift flour, baking powder and mace together. Add to batter; mix well. Fill paper-lined muffin cups ¾ full. Bake at 350 degrees for 15 to 18 minutes or until cupcakes test done. Remove to wire rack to cool. These are nice for grandchildren to frost and decorate.

Barbara Kuzniewski

BUTTER CREAM ICING

Yield:
16 servings

Approx Per
Serving:
Cal 240
Prot <1 g
Carbo 34 g
Fiber 0 g
T Fat 12 g
Chol <1 mg
Sod 68 mg

¹/₂ cup shortening
¹/₂ cup softened
　margarine
1　1-pound package
　confectioners' sugar

1 teaspoon vanilla
　extract
1 tablespoon milk

Cream shortening, margarine and sugar in mixer bowl until light and fluffy. Add confectioners' sugar, a small amount at a time, beating well after each addition. Add vanilla and milk; mix well. Store in refrigerator.

Nancy L. Rebar

CHOCOLATE ICING

Yield:
16 servings

Approx Per
Serving:
Cal 185
Prot <1 g
Carbo 34 g
Fiber <1 g
T Fat 6 g
Chol 16 mg
Sod 66 mg

3 tablespoons baking
　cocoa
¹/₂ cup butter, softened
1 teaspoon vanilla
　extract

Salt to taste
1　1-pound package
　confectioners' sugar
3 tablespoons cold
　coffee

Cream cocoa and butter in mixer bowl until light and fluffy. Add vanilla and salt. Add confectioners' sugar alternately with 1 tablespoon coffee at a time, beating well after each addition. Beat at high speed until smooth and creamy. May make coffee with instant granules.

Adelia C. Watson

Candies
and Cookies

The Capitol

Marshmallow Fudge

Yield:
60 servings

*Approx Per
Serving:*
Cal 110
Prot 1 g
Carbo 16 g
Fiber <1 g
T Fat 5 g
Chol 1 mg
Sod 33 mg

3 cups sugar
3/4 cup margarine
2/3 cup evaporated milk
10 1-ounce squares
    semisweet chocolate

1 7-ounce jar
    marshmallow creme
1 cup chopped walnuts
1 teaspoon vanilla
    extract

Combine sugar, margarine and evaporated milk in 2 1/2-quart saucepan. Bring to a boil, stirring constantly. Cook over medium heat for 5 minutes, stirring constantly; remove from heat. Stir in chocolate until melted. Add marshmallow creme, walnuts and vanilla; beat until smooth. Pour into buttered 9x13-inch dish. Cool to room temperature; cut into squares.

Nancy Rebar

Peanut Butter Fudge

Yield:
60 servings

*Approx Per
Serving:*
Cal 65
Prot 1 g
Carbo 11 g
Fiber <1 g
T Fat 2 g
Chol 5 mg
Sod 21 mg

3 cups sugar
1 cup evaporated milk
1/2 cup water
3 tablespoons peanut
    butter

1/2 cup butter
3 tablespoons
    marshmallow creme
1 teaspoon vanilla
    extract

Combine sugar, evaporated milk and water in large heavy saucepan. Cook over medium heat to 250 to 268 degrees on candy thermometer, hard-ball stage; remove from heat. Add peanut butter, butter, marshmallow creme and vanilla in order listed, mixing well after each addition. Beat until mixture begins to thicken. Spoon into buttered dish. Let stand until cool; cut into squares.

Jean Sorrell

CREAMY PEANUT BUTTER FUDGE

Yield:
60 servings

Approx Per Serving:
Cal 152
Prot 2 g
Carbo 22 g
Fiber <1 g
T Fat 7 g
Chol 2 mg
Sod 62 mg

5 cups sugar
1 13-ounce can evaporated milk
1 cup margarine
9 ounces marshmallow creme
1 cup peanut butter
1 teaspoon vanilla extract
1 cup finely chopped pecans

Combine sugar, evaporated milk and margarine in large saucepan. Bring to a boil over medium heat, stirring constantly. Cook for 10 minutes, stirring constantly; remove from heat. Add marshmallow creme, peanut butter and vanilla; mix well. Beat until mixture begins to thicken. Beat in pecans. Pour into buttered 9x13-inch dish. Let stand until partially cooled; cut into squares. May reduce recipe by half and pour into 9x9-inch dish.

Mary Cornell

PEANUT BUTTER ROLL

Yield:
20 servings

Approx Per Serving:
Cal 95
Prot 2 g
Carbo 13 g
Fiber <1 g
T Fat 4 g
Chol 4 mg
Sod 27 mg

2 cups confectioners' sugar
1/4 cup cream
1 teaspoon vanilla extract
Salt to taste
1/2 cup creamy or chunky peanut butter

Combine confectioners' sugar, cream, vanilla and salt in bowl; mix to form a smooth dough. Roll 1/4 inch thick on surface sprinkled lightly with additional confectioners' sugar. Spread thinly with peanut butter. Roll as for jelly roll. Roll to 1-inch diameter. Cut into 1/2 to 1-inch slices. Store in airtight container.

Irene Craig

SEAFOAM

Yield:
60 servings

Approx Per
Serving:
Cal 55
Prot <1 g
Carbo 11 g
Fiber <1 g
T Fat 1 g
Chol 0 mg
Sod 7 mg

3 cups packed brown
  sugar
1 cup water
1 tablespoon vinegar
2 egg whites, stiffly
  beaten

1 cup chopped pecans
1 teaspoon vanilla
  extract

Combine brown sugar, water and vinegar in saucepan. Cook to 250 to 268 degrees on candy thermometer, hard-ball stage; remove from heat. Pour in fine stream over stiffly beaten egg whites, beating constantly until stiff peaks form. Add pecans and vanilla, beating until very stiff and creamy. Drop by spoonfuls onto waxed paper. Let stand until firm. May spoon into buttered dish if preferred.

June Jenkins

SPICED PECANS

Yield:
16 servings

Approx Per
Serving:
Cal 238
Prot 2 g
Carbo 18 g
Fiber 2 g
T Fat 19 g
Chol 0 mg
Sod 137 mg

1 egg white
1 tablespoon water
1 pound pecan halves

1 cup sugar
1 tablespoon cinnamon
1 teaspoon salt

Combine egg white and water in bowl; beat until fluffy. Add pecans; mix well. Add mixture of sugar, cinnamon and salt; mix until well coated. Spread in single layer on baking sheet. Bake at 325 degrees for 30 minutes, stirring every 5 minutes. Remove to waxed paper to cool.

Joyce Kay

CHOW MEIN NO-BAKE NUGGETS

Yield:
36 servings

Approx Per Serving:
Cal 92
Prot 3 g
Carbo 7 g
Fiber 1 g
T Fat 7 g
Chol 1 mg
Sod 63 mg

1 cup butterscotch chips
1/2 cup peanut butter
1 6-ounce can chow mein noodles
1 cup peanuts

Melt butterscotch chips and peanut butter in saucepan over low heat, stirring to mix well. Pour over noodles and peanuts in bowl; mix to coat well. Drop by teaspoonfuls onto waxed paper. Chill until firm.

Jan K. Schmalz

EMILIE'S PRIZE WINNERS

Yield:
36 servings

Approx Per Serving:
Cal 156
Prot 3 g
Carbo 23 g
Fiber 1 g
T Fat 7 g
Chol 0 mg
Sod 91 mg

1 cup sugar
1 cup light corn syrup
1 cup peanut butter
6 cups crisp rice cereal
1 cup butterscotch chips
1 cup semisweet chocolate chips

Combine sugar, corn syrup, peanut butter and cereal in bowl; mix well. Press into buttered 9x13-inch dish. Melt butterscotch chips and chocolate chips in double boiler, stirring to mix well. Spread evenly over cereal mixture. Let stand for 1 hour. Cut into bars. Our niece won a regional Girl Scout cooking contest with these no-bake treats.

Bennie Cavanaugh

GRAHAM CRACKER NO-BAKE DELIGHTS

1 cup margarine,
softened
8 ounces cream cheese,
softened
1 tablespoon vanilla
extract
1   1-pound package
confectioners' sugar

2 cups graham cracker
crumbs
1 cup shredded
coconut
1 cup chopped pecans
2 cups semisweet
chocolate chips
1/3 bar paraffin

Cream margarine and cream cheese in mixer bowl until fluffy. Add vanilla, confectioners' sugar, cracker crumbs, coconut and pecans; mix well. Shape into 1-inch balls. Chill for 1 hour or until easy to handle. Melt chocolate chips with half the paraffin in double boiler. Dip half the balls into chocolate mixture with toothpick. Place on waxed paper. Let stand until firm. Add remaining paraffin to chocolate mixture. Heat until melted and well mixed. Dip remaining balls into chocolate mixture. Serve chilled or at room temperature.

Elise P. Evans

LOVE TREATS

2 cups Captain Crunch
peanut butter cereal
2 cups crisp rice cereal
2 cups lightly salted
peanuts

2 cups miniature
marshmallows
16 ounces almond bark

Mix cereals, peanuts and marshmallows in bowl. Microwave almond bark in glass dish on High for 3 minutes, stirring after 2 minutes. Pour over cereal mixture; mix well. Drop by teaspoonfuls onto waxed paper. Chill until firm. May substitute white chocolate for almond bark.

Trish Giles

No-Bake Peanut Butter Cookies

Yield:
72 servings

Approx Per Serving:
Cal 104
Prot 2 g
Carbo 16 g
Fiber 1 g
T Fat 4 g
Chol <1 mg
Sod 31 mg

4 cups sugar
1 cup milk
1/2 cup margarine
2 teaspoons vanilla extract
1 cup (rounded) extra-crunchy peanut butter
6 cups quick-cooking oats

Bring sugar, milk and margarine to a rolling boil in large saucepan. Boil for 1 minute; remove from heat. Add vanilla, peanut butter and oats; mix well. Drop by spoonfuls onto waxed paper. Let stand until cool.

Mildred Sheldon

No-Bake Rum Mocha Balls

Yield:
30 servings

Approx Per Serving:
Cal 79
Prot 1 g
Carbo 11 g
Fiber <1 g
T Fat 4 g
Chol 4 mg
Sod 24 mg

1/4 cup instant freeze-dried coffee
1/4 cup rum
1 tablespoon water
2 teaspoons baking cocoa
1 cup chopped walnuts
2 cups vanilla wafer crumbs
3 tablespoons light corn syrup
Salt to taste
1 cup confectioners' sugar

Dissolve coffee in rum and water in large bowl. Add cocoa, walnuts, cookie crumbs, corn syrup and salt; mix well with spoon. Shape into 1-inch balls. Roll in confectioners' sugar, coating well. Store in airtight container.

Irene Craig

 *For **Easy No-Bake Orange Balls**, combine 1/2 cup softened margarine, 4 cups confectioners' sugar, 1/2 cup chopped pecans, 6 ounces orange juice concentrate and 4 cups vanilla wafer crumbs. Shape into balls and coat with additional crumbs.*

BRANDY SNAPS

Yield:
80 servings

Approx Per
Serving:
Cal 27
Prot <1 g
Carbo 4 g
Fiber <1 g
T Fat 1 g
Chol 3 mg
Sod 11 mg

¼ cup light corn syrup
¼ cup molasses
½ cup butter
1 cup sifted flour

⅔ cup sugar
Ginger to taste
2 teaspoons Brandy

Bring corn syrup and molasses to a boil in saucepan; remove from heat. Add butter. Sift flour, sugar and ginger together. Add to corn syrup mixture gradually, mixing constantly. Stir in Brandy. Drop by ½ teaspoonfuls 3 inches apart onto greased cookie sheet. Bake at 300 degrees for 10 minutes. Loosen 1 cookie at a time and roll over handle of wooden spoon; remove carefully. Fill with whipped cream to serve.

Marcia Dark-Ward

BEST-EVER BROWNIES

Yield:
32 servings

Approx Per
Serving:
Cal 202
Prot 2 g
Carbo 31 g
Fiber 1 g
T Fat 9 g
Chol 27 mg
Sod 81 mg

½ cup margarine,
  softened
1 cup sugar
4 eggs
1 teaspoon vanilla
  extract
1½ cups flour, sifted
1   16-ounce can
  chocolate syrup

¾ cup chopped
  walnuts
6 tablespoons
  margarine
6 tablespoons milk
1½ cups sugar
½ cup chocolate chips
1 teaspoon vanilla
  extract

Cream ½ cup margarine and 1 cup sugar in mixer bowl until light and fluffy. Beat in eggs. Add 1 teaspoon vanilla, flour, chocolate syrup and walnuts; mix well. Spoon into greased 9x13-inch baking pan. Bake at 350 degrees for 20 to 25 minutes or until brownies test done. Bring 6 tablespoons margarine, milk and 1½ cups sugar to a boil in saucepan. Boil for 30 to 60 seconds; remove from heat. Stir in chocolate chips and 1 teaspoon vanilla. Place pan in larger pan of cold water. Beat until of desired consistency. Spread on brownies. Let stand until cool. Cut into squares.

Jeanne Trapani

BETTIE'S MINT BROWNIES

Yield:
60 servings

Approx Per Serving:
Cal 131
Prot 1 g
Carbo 16 g
Fiber 1 g
T Fat 8 g
Chol 26 mg
Sod 65 mg

1 cup sugar
1/2 cup butter, softened
4 eggs, beaten
1 cup flour
1/2 teaspoon salt
1   16-ounce can chocolate syrup
1 teaspoon vanilla extract
1 1/2 cups chopped pecans
2 cups confectioners' sugar
1/2 cup butter, softened
1 tablespoon (or more) Crème de Menthe
1 cup chocolate chips
6 tablespoons butter

Cream sugar and 1/2 cup butter in mixer bowl until light and fluffy. Beat in eggs. Add flour, salt, chocolate syrup and vanilla; mix well. Stir in pecans. Spoon into greased 9x13-inch baking pan. Bake at 350 degrees for 30 minutes; do not overbake. Cool to room temperature. Combine confectioners' sugar, 1/2 cup butter and Crème de Menthe in bowl; mix until smooth. Spread over brownies. Melt chocolate chips with 6 tablespoons butter in saucepan. Cool slightly. Spread evenly over mint layer. Chill until firm. Cut into squares.

Karen Springfield

SUSI'S CHERRY BROWNIES

Yield:
36 servings

Approx Per Serving:
Cal 150
Prot 1 g
Carbo 25 g
Fiber <1 g
T Fat 5 g
Chol 17 mg
Sod 111 mg

1   2-layer package chocolate fudge cake mix
2 eggs
1   21-ounce can cherry pie filling
1 cup sugar
1/3 cup milk
5 tablespoons butter
1 1/4 cups chocolate chips

Combine cake mix, eggs and pie filling in bowl; mix until smooth. Spoon into greased 9x13-inch baking pan. Bake at 350 degrees for 20 to 25 minutes or until brownies test done. Bring sugar, milk and butter to a boil in saucepan; remove from heat. Stir in chocolate chips until melted. Pour over warm brownies. Let stand until cool. Cut into squares.

Robert W. Campbell

COLONIAL BITTERSWEET BROWNIES

Yield:
24 servings

Approx Per Serving:
Cal 237
Prot 3 g
Carbo 25 g
Fiber 1 g
T Fat 15 g
Chol 36 mg
Sod 101 mg

5 ounces unsweetened chocolate
1 cup margarine
4 eggs
2 cups sugar

1½ cups flour
1 cup chopped pecans
1 teaspoon almond extract

Melt chocolate with margarine in small saucepan; mix well. Beat eggs and sugar in small bowl. Add chocolate mixture; mix well. Stir in flour, pecans and almond extract. Spoon into lightly greased 9x13-inch baking dish. Bake at 325 degrees for 25 to 30 minutes or just until brownies test done; do not overbake.

Elise P. Evans

LUSCIOUS BROWNIES WITH FUDGE FROSTING

Yield:
24 servings

Approx Per Serving:
Cal 149
Prot 2 g
Carbo 19 g
Fiber 1 g
T Fat 8 g
Chol 32 mg
Sod 103 mg

½ cup butter, softened
1 cup sugar
2 teaspoons vanilla extract
2 eggs
⅔ cup flour
⅓ cup baking cocoa
½ teaspoon baking powder
½ teaspoon salt
½ cup chopped walnuts

3 tablespoons butter, softened
¼ cup baking cocoa
1 tablespoon light corn syrup
1 teaspoon vanilla extract
1 cup confectioners' sugar
1 to 2 tablespoons milk
3 tablespoons chopped walnuts

Cream ½ cup butter, sugar and 2 teaspoons vanilla in mixer bowl until light and fluffy. Blend in eggs with wooden spoon. Add flour, ⅓ cup cocoa, baking powder and salt. Stir in ½ cup walnuts. Spread in greased 9x9-inch baking pan. Bake at 350 degrees for 25 to 30 minutes or until brownies begin to pull away from sides of pan. Cool to room temperature. Combine 3 tablespoons butter, ¼ cup cocoa, corn syrup and 1 teaspoon vanilla in mixer bowl; mix well. Add confectioners' sugar and milk. Beat until of spreading consistency. Spread over cool brownies. Sprinkle with 3 tablespoons walnuts. Cut into squares.

Kimberly P. Hines

Peanut Butter and Chocolate Chip Brownies

Yield:
24 servings

Approx Per Serving:
Cal 248
Prot 5 g
Carbo 34 g
Fiber 1 g
T Fat 12 g
Chol 32 mg
Sod 126 mg

2 cups packed brown sugar
1/4 cup butter, softened
3/4 cup creamy or chunky peanut butter
3 eggs
1 teaspoon vanilla extract
1 teaspoon baking powder
1/2 teaspoon salt
1 3/4 cups flour
2 cups chocolate chips

Cream brown sugar and butter in mixer bowl until light and fluffy. Blend in peanut butter. Beat in eggs. Add vanilla, baking powder, salt and flour in order listed, mixing well after each addition. Spoon into greased 9x13-inch baking pan. Sprinkle with chocolate chips. Bake at 350 degrees for 20 to 30 minutes or until brownies test done and top is golden brown. May substitute Reese's Pieces or pecans for chocolate chips.

Ginger Sauls

Praline Brownies

Yield:
48 servings

Approx Per Serving:
Cal 116
Prot 1 g
Carbo 13 g
Fiber <1 g
T Fat 8 g
Chol 18 mg
Sod 58 mg

1 22-ounce package brownie mix
1/2 cup packed brown sugar
1/2 cup chopped pecans
2 tablespoons melted margarine

Grease bottom of 9x13-inch baking pan. Prepare brownies using package directions. Spread in prepared pan. Combine brown sugar, pecans and margarine in bowl; mix well. Sprinkle over batter. Bake at 350 degrees for 30 minutes. Cool on wire rack. Cut into squares. Frost with fudge frosting if desired.

Patti Maxwell

 Use shiny cookie sheets and baking pans. Dark pans absorb more heat and cause overbrowning.

SWEDISH BROWNIES

Yield:
12 servings

Approx Per Serving:
Cal 249
Prot 3 g
Carbo 26 g
Fiber 1 g
T Fat 15 g
Chol 56 mg
Sod 77 mg

½ cup melted butter
1 cup sugar
1 cup flour
2 eggs
1 teaspoon almond extract
1 cup chopped pecans

Combine butter with sugar, flour, eggs and almond extract in mixer bowl; mix well. Stir in pecans. Spoon into lightly greased 9x9-inch baking pan. Bake at 350 degrees for 20 to 25 minutes or until firm to touch. Cut into squares. Garnish with sprinkle of confectioners' sugar if desired.

Ruth D. Darby

TURTLE BROWNIES

Yield:
32 servings

Approx Per Serving:
Cal 218
Prot 2 g
Carbo 30 g
Fiber <1 g
T Fat 11 g
Chol 2 mg
Sod 183 mg

1 14-ounce package caramels
⅓ cup evaporated milk
1 2-layer package German chocolate cake mix
¾ cup melted margarine
⅓ cup evaporated milk
2 cups chocolate chips

Melt caramels with ⅓ cup evaporated milk in saucepan, stirring to mix well. Combine cake mix, margarine and ⅓ cup evaporated milk in bowl; mix well by hand. Spread half the batter in greased 9x13-inch baking pan. Bake at 350 degrees for 6 minutes. Sprinkle with chocolate chips. Spread caramel mixture over top. Top with remaining brownie batter. Bake for 25 minutes longer; do not overbake. Cool on wire rack. Cut into squares. May add 1 cup chopped pecans with chocolate chips.

Kathleen Kondus

CAKE-LIKE CHOCOLATE COOKIES

Yield:
36 servings

Approx Per Serving:
Cal 116
Prot 2 g
Carbo 16 g
Fiber <1 g
T Fat 8 g
Chol 22 mg
Sod 74 mg

1/2 cup butter, softened
1 1/2 cups sugar
2 eggs
2 ounces baking chocolate, melted
1 teaspoon vanilla extract
1 cup sour cream
2 3/4 cups flour
1/2 teaspoon baking powder
1/2 teaspoon soda
1/2 teaspoon salt

Cream butter and sugar in mixer bowl until light and fluffy. Blend in eggs and chocolate. Stir in vanilla and sour cream. Sift in flour, baking powder, soda and salt; mix well. Chill for 1 hour or longer. Drop by teaspoonfuls onto cookie sheet. Bake at 400 degrees for 8 to 10 minutes or until set. Remove to wire rack to cool. Frost with chocolate or other favorite frosting.

Patti Rabuck

MRS. CAMPBELL'S CHOCOLATE CHIP COOKIES

Yield:
72 servings

Approx Per Serving:
Cal 238
Prot 3 g
Carbo 29 g
Fiber 2 g
T Fat 14 g
Chol 26 mg
Sod 115 mg

2 cups butter, softened
2 cups sugar
2 cups packed brown sugar
4 eggs
2 teaspoons vanilla extract
4 cups flour
5 cups oats
2 teaspoons baking powder
2 teaspoons soda
1 teaspoon salt
4 cups chocolate chips
8 ounces milk chocolate, grated
3 cups chopped pecans

Cream butter, sugar and brown sugar in mixer bowl until light and fluffy. Blend in eggs and vanilla. Add mixture of flour, oats, baking powder, soda and salt; mix well. Stir in chocolate chips, grated chocolate and pecans. Shape into golf ball-sized balls; place 2 inches apart on ungreased cookie sheet. Bake at 375 degrees for 6 minutes or until cookies test done but are still soft. Remove to wire rack to cool.

Sandra Campbell

Chocolate Nut Squares

Yield:
30 servings

Approx Per
Serving:
Cal 188
Prot 2 g
Carbo 24 g
Fiber 1 g
T Fat 10 g
Chol 14 mg
Sod 102 mg

2/3 cup oil
2 cups packed light
brown sugar
2 teaspoons vanilla
extract

2 eggs, beaten
2 cups self-rising flour
1 cup semisweet
chocolate chips
1 cup chopped pecans

Combine oil and brown sugar in mixer bowl; beat until thick and smooth. Beat in vanilla and eggs. Add flour; mix well. Stir in chocolate chips and pecans. Spoon into greased 9x13-inch baking pan. Bake at 350 degrees for 25 to 30 minutes or until firm to touch. Cool on wire rack. Cut into squares.

Sheila Levine

Chocolate Oatmeal Cookies

Yield:
56 servings

Approx Per
Serving:
Cal 127
Prot 2 g
Carbo 16 g
Fiber 1 g
T Fat 7 g
Chol 17 mg
Sod 74 mg

1 cup butter, softened
1 cup sugar
1 cup packed brown
sugar
2 eggs
1 teaspoon vanilla
extract
2 1/2 cups oats
1 teaspoon baking
powder

2 cups flour
1 teaspoon soda
1/2 teaspoon salt
2 ounces chocolate
chips
4 ounces milk
chocolate, chilled,
grated
1 1/2 cups chopped
pecans

Cream butter, sugar and brown sugar in mixer bowl until light and fluffy. Beat in eggs and vanilla. Process oats in blender until fine. Mix with baking powder, flour, soda and salt in bowl. Add to creamed mixture gradually, mixing well after each addition. Stir in chocolate chips, grated chocolate and pecans. Shape into balls; place 2 inches apart on cookie sheet. Bake at 375 degrees for 6 minutes. Remove to wire rack to cool.

Kathy Kondus

CHOCOLATE AND PEANUT BUTTER CHIP COOKIES

Yield:
36 servings

Approx Per Serving:
Cal 144
Prot 1 g
Carbo 16 g
Fiber 1 g
T Fat 9 g
Chol 6 mg
Sod 106 mg

1 cup margarine, softened
1/2 cup sugar
3/4 cup packed brown sugar
1 teaspoon vanilla extract
1 tablespoon cold water
1 egg
1 cup flour
1/2 teaspoon soda
1/2 teaspoon salt
1 cup oats
1 cup chocolate chips
1/2 cup peanut butter chips
1/2 cup chopped pecans

Cream margarine, sugar and brown sugar in mixer bowl until light and fluffy. Add vanilla and water; mix well. Beat in egg. Add mixture of flour, soda and salt; mix well. Stir in oats, chocolate chips, peanut butter chips and pecans. Drop by teaspoonfuls onto cookie sheet. Bake at 350 degrees for 8 minutes. Remove to wire rack to cool. May add coconut if desired.

Fran Brosius

HOLIDAY CHOCOLATE CHIP SQUARES

Yield:
30 servings

Approx Per Serving:
Cal 214
Prot 2 g
Carbo 24 g
Fiber 1 g
T Fat 13 g
Chol 24 mg
Sod 88 mg

2 1/4 cups flour
1 1/4 teaspoons baking powder
1/4 teaspoon salt
1 cup butter, softened
1 1/4 cups sugar
1 teaspoon vanilla extract
1 egg
2 cups chocolate chips
1 cup chopped pecans
30 maraschino cherries
15 candy spearmint leaves

Mix flour, baking powder and salt in bowl. Cream butter and sugar in mixer bowl until light and fluffy. Add vanilla and egg; mix well. Blend in flour mixture gradually. Stir in chocolate chips and pecans. Spread in greased 9x13-inch glass baking dish. Press maraschino cherries into top in 5 rows of 6 cherries. Cut candies into halves lengthwise. Place 1 candy half at base of each cherry. Bake at 350 degrees for 25 to 30 minutes or until edges pull from sides of pan. Cool on wire rack. Cut into squares centered with cherries.

Dorothy Mason

GRAND PRIZE CARAMEL CHEWS

Yield:
24 servings

Approx Per Serving:
Cal 210
Prot 2 g
Carbo 26 g
Fiber 1 g
T Fat 12 g
Chol 39 mg
Sod 113 mg

1 cup butter, softened
1 1-pound package brown sugar
2 tablespoons vanilla extract
2 eggs
1½ cups flour
2½ teaspoons baking powder
1 cup chopped pecans

Combine butter, brown sugar, vanilla and eggs in mixer bowl; mix until smooth. Add flour and baking powder; mix well. Stir in pecans. Spoon into greased and floured 9x13-inch baking pan. Bake at 350 degrees for 30 minutes. Cool on wire rack. Cut into squares.

Marge Fritz

CLAIRE'S 1930s COOKIES

Yield:
60 servings

Approx Per Serving:
Cal 109
Prot 1 g
Carbo 11 g
Fiber <1 g
T Fat 7 g
Chol 27 mg
Sod 53 mg

5 cups flour
2 cups butter, softened
1 cup sugar
Juice of 1 lemon
3 egg yolks, slightly beaten
3 tablespoons milk

Combine flour, butter and sugar in bowl; mix well. Add lemon juice, egg yolks and milk; mix well. Chill, covered, for 4 hours to overnight. Knead lightly on floured surface. Roll very thin; cut as desired. Place on cookie sheet. Bake at 350 degrees for 12 minutes. Remove to wire rack to cool. May decorate with colored sprinkles or nuts before baking if desired. This recipe came from my grandmother, Claire Daiak. She mixed the flour, butter and sugar with her hands.

C. Lucinda Carr

AMY'S CHRISTMAS COOKIES

Yield:
60 servings

Approx Per Serving:
Cal 108
Prot 1 g
Carbo 18 g
Fiber <1 g
T Fat 3 g
Chol 19 mg
Sod 58 mg

5 cups flour
2 teaspoons baking powder
1/2 teaspoon mace
1/2 teaspoon salt
1 cup butter
3 eggs, slightly beaten
3 cups sugar
1 tablespoon vanilla or lemon extract

Sift flour, baking powder, mace and salt into bowl. Cut in butter until crumbly. Combine eggs, sugar and vanilla in bowl; mix well. Add to crumb mixture; mix well. Roll thin on floured surface. Cut as desired; place on cookie sheet. Bake at 375 degrees for 8 to 10 minutes or until light brown. Remove to wire rack to cool. Decorate as desired before or after baking.

Justine A. Smith

CHRISTMAS FRUITCAKE COOKIES

Yield:
72 servings

Approx Per Serving:
Cal 94
Prot 1 g
Carbo 17 g
Fiber 1 g
T Fat 3 g
Chol 13 mg
Sod 35 mg

1 1/2 cups sugar
1 cup butter, softened
2 eggs
2 1/2 cups flour
1 teaspoon soda
1 teaspoon cinnamon
Salt to taste
2 8-ounce packages dates, chopped
8 ounces candied pineapple, chopped
8 ounces candied cherries, cut into quarters

Cream sugar and butter in mixer bowl until light and fluffy. Blend in eggs. Add flour, soda, cinnamon and salt; mix well. Stir in dates, pineapple and cherries. Drop by spoonfuls onto cookie sheet. Bake at 375 degrees for 10 to 13 minutes or until golden brown. Remove to wire rack to cool.

Brenda Prestidge

JEWELED SPICE BARS

Yield:
50 servings

Approx Per Serving:
Cal 129
Prot 1 g
Carbo 20 g
Fiber <1 g
T Fat 5 g
Chol 9 mg
Sod 50 mg

1/2 cup margarine, softened
1 1/2 cups packed brown sugar
8 ounces cream cheese, softened
1 egg
1/4 cup honey
2 1/4 cups sifted flour
1 1/2 teaspoons baking powder

1 teaspoon cinnamon
1 teaspoon nutmeg
1 cup chopped pecans
1 cup chopped mixed candied fruit
1/2 cup raisins
1 1/3 cups sifted confectioners' sugar
2 tablespoons milk
1/4 teaspoon vanilla extract

Cream margarine, brown sugar and cream cheese in mixer bowl until light and fluffy. Blend in egg and honey. Add flour, baking powder, cinnamon and nutmeg; mix well. Stir in pecans, candied fruit and raisins. Spoon into greased 9x13-inch baking dish. Bake at 350 degrees for 30 minutes. Cool on wire rack. Combine confectioners' sugar, milk and vanilla in bowl; mix until smooth. Spread over baked layer. Cut diagonally into bars.

Pauline F. Simmons

FRUIT BARS

Yield:
33 servings

Approx Per Serving:
Cal 79
Prot 1 g
Carbo 9 g
Fiber 1 g
T Fat 4 g
Chol 13 mg
Sod 78 mg

1/2 cup chopped dates
1/2 cup raisins
1/2 cup chopped prunes
1 cup water
1/2 cup margarine
2 eggs
1 cup flour

1 teaspoon soda
1/4 teaspoon salt
1 teaspoon vanilla extract
1/2 teaspoon cinnamon
1/4 teaspoon nutmeg
1/2 cup chopped pecans

Bring dates, raisins, prunes and water to a boil in saucepan, stirring constantly. Boil for 5 minutes, stirring frequently; remove from heat. Stir in margarine until melted. Cool to room temperature. Add eggs, flour, soda, salt, vanilla, cinnamon and nutmeg; mix well. Stir in pecans. Spoon into 7x11-inch baking pan sprayed with nonstick cooking spray. Bake at 350 degrees for 25 to 30 minutes or until set. Cool on wire rack. Cut into bars. May substitute 1/4 cup oats for 1/4 cup flour if preferred.

Tammy Hill

CORNFLAKE COOKIES

Yield:
24 servings

Approx Per Serving:
Cal 203
Prot 2 g
Carbo 28 g
Fiber 2 g
T Fat 10 g
Chol 33 mg
Sod 124 mg

2 eggs, beaten
³/4 cup melted butter
1 cup sugar
1 teaspoon vanilla
  extract
2 cups flour

1 teaspoon soda
Salt to taste
1 cup chopped pecans
1¹/2 cups chopped
  dates
3 cups cornflakes

Combine eggs, butter, sugar and vanilla in mixer bowl; beat until smooth. Sift in flour, soda and salt; mix well. Stir in pecans, dates and cereal. Drop by spoonfuls onto cookie sheet. Bake at 350 degrees for 15 to 20 minutes or until light brown. Remove to wire rack to cool.

Marge Fritz

CREAM WAFERS

Yield:
24 servings

Approx Per Serving:
Cal 165
Prot 1 g
Carbo 16 g
Fiber <1 g
T Fat 11 g
Chol 30 mg
Sod 82 mg

1 cup butter, softened
¹/3 cup whipping cream
2 cups flour
¹/2 cup sugar
¹/4 cup butter, softened

³/4 cup confectioners'
  sugar
1 teaspoon vanilla
  extract

Combine 1 cup butter, cream and flour in bowl; mix until smooth. Chill, covered, in refrigerator. Roll dough ¹/3 at a time to ¹/8-inch thickness on cloth-covered surface. Cut with 1¹/2-inch cutter. Sprinkle waxed paper generously with additional sugar. Place cookies in sugar turning with spatula to coat well. Place on ungreased cookie sheet; prick each cookie 4 times with fork. Bake at 375 degrees for 7 to 9 minutes or just until set but not brown. Remove to wire rack to cool. Cream ¹/4 cup butter, confectioners' sugar and vanilla in mixer bowl until light and fluffy. Add several drops of water if necessary for desired consistency. Tint with food coloring if desired. Spread on half the cooled cookies; top with remaining cookies.

Nutritional information does not include additional sugar for coating cookies.

Joyce Kay

FORGOTTEN COOKIES

2 egg whites
2/3 cup sugar
Salt to taste
1 cup chocolate chips

1 cup chopped pecans
1 teaspoon vanilla
    extract

Beat egg whites with sugar and salt in mixer bowl until stiff peaks form. Fold in chocolate chips, pecans and vanilla. Drop by teaspoonfuls onto cookie sheet covered with foil. Place in oven preheated to 350 degrees. Turn off oven. Let stand in closed oven for 5 hours to overnight; do not open oven door. Store in airtight container.

Patty Peacock

CHOCOLATE FORGOTTEN COOKIES

2 egg whites
1/8 teaspoon salt
2/3 cup sugar
1/2 teaspoon vanilla
    extract
1 1/2 teaspoons water

2 tablespoons baking
    cocoa
1/3 cup chopped pecans
1/4 cup miniature
    chocolate chips

Beat egg whites in mixer bowl until stiff but not dry peaks form. Add salt and half the sugar gradually, beating constantly. Add remaining sugar alternately with mixture of vanilla and water, beating constantly. Fold in cocoa, pecans and chocolate chips. Drop by teaspoonfuls onto lightly greased cookie sheet. Place in oven preheated to 275 degrees. Turn off oven. Let stand in closed oven for 6 hours to overnight; do not open oven door. Store in airtight container.

Sal D'Adamo

Granola Bars

Yield:
36 servings

Approx Per
Serving:
Cal 160
Prot 3 g
Carbo 16 g
Fiber 1 g
T Fat 10 g
Chol 29 mg
Sod 143 mg

1¼ cups melted butter
⅔ cup packed brown
  sugar
¼ cup honey
2 eggs, beaten
¼ cup milk
1 teaspoon vanilla
  extract
1½ cups flour

1 teaspoon soda
¼ teaspoon cinnamon
¼ teaspoon nutmeg
1 teaspoon salt
3 cups oats
½ cup sunflower seed
¼ cup sesame seed
¼ cup wheat germ
½ cup chopped pecans

Combine butter, brown sugar, honey, eggs, milk and vanilla in large mixer bowl; beat until smooth. Combine flour, soda, cinnamon, nutmeg and salt in bowl. Add to batter; mix well. Combine oats, sunflower seed, sesame seed, wheat germ and pecans in bowl; mix well. Add to batter; mix well. Press into greased 9x13-inch baking pan. Bake at 350 degrees for 15 to 20 minutes or until golden brown. Cool on wire rack. Cut into bars; bars will be slightly crumbly. May add coconut, ¼ cup raisins and/or ¼ cup chocolate chips if desired.

Dawn C. Frizzell

Lemon Cheese Bars

Yield:
32 servings

Approx Per
Serving:
Cal 126
Prot 2 g
Carbo 16 g
Fiber <1 g
T Fat 6 g
Chol 21 mg
Sod 124 mg

1 2-layer package
   yellow cake mix
1 egg
⅓ cup oil
⅓ cup sugar

8 ounces cream cheese,
  softened
1 teaspoon lemon juice
1 egg

Combine cake mix, 1 egg and oil in bowl; mix until crumbly. Reserve 1 cup mixture. Pat remaining mixture lightly into 9x13-inch baking pan. Bake at 350 degrees for 15 minutes. Combine sugar, cream cheese, lemon juice and 1 egg in mixer bowl; mix until smooth. Spread over baked layer. Sprinkle with reserved crumb mixture. Bake for 15 minutes. Cool on wire rack. Cut into bars.

Adelia C. Watson

Lemon Sour Cookies

Yield:
32 servings

Approx Per
Serving:
Cal 88
Prot 1 g
Carbo 13 g
Fiber <1 g
T Fat 4 g
Chol 18 mg
Sod 25 mg

1/3 cup butter
3/4 cup flour, sifted
2 eggs
1 cup packed brown
  sugar
1/8 teaspoon baking
  powder
3/4 cup shredded
  coconut

1/2 cup chopped pecans
1/2 teaspoon vanilla
  extract
1 teaspoon grated
  lemon rind
1 1/2 tablespoons lemon
  juice
2/3 cup confectioners'
  sugar

Cut butter into flour in bowl until crumbly. Sprinkle into 7x11-inch baking pan. Bake at 350 degrees for 10 minutes. Beat eggs in mixer bowl. Add brown sugar, baking powder, coconut, pecans and vanilla; mix well. Spread over baked layer. Bake for 20 minutes. Mix lemon rind, lemon juice and enough confectioners' sugar to make of desired consistency in small bowl. Spread over hot baked layer. Cool on wire rack. Cut into squares.

Marge Fritz

Magic Cookies

Yield:
24 servings

Approx Per
Serving:
Cal 209
Prot 3 g
Carbo 22 g
Fiber 1 g
T Fat 13 g
Chol 6 mg
Sod 114 mg

1 1/2 cups graham
  cracker crumbs
1/2 cup melted
  margarine
1 cup chopped pecans
1 cup semisweet
  chocolate chips

1 1/2 cups shredded
  coconut
1   14-ounce can
  sweetened
  condensed milk

Mix cracker crumbs and margarine in bowl. Press into 9x13-inch baking dish. Layer pecans, chocolate chips and coconut in prepared pan. Pour condensed milk over layers. Bake at 350 degrees for 25 minutes or until light brown. Cool on wire rack. Cut into 2-inch squares.

Elise P. Evans

 Use a pizza cutter to slice bar cookies.

Marble Squares

Yield:
36 servings

Approx Per
Serving:
Cal 163
Prot 2 g
Carbo 22 g
Fiber 1 g
T Fat 8 g
Chol 26 mg
Sod 109 mg

½ cup margarine
1½ ounces
  unsweetened
  chocolate
¾ cup water
2 cups flour
2 cups sugar
1 teaspoon soda

½ teaspoon salt
2 eggs, beaten
½ cup sour cream
8 ounces cream cheese,
  softened
⅓ cup sugar
1 egg
1 cup chocolate chips

Melt margarine and chocolate with water and chocolate in saucepan, stirring to mix well; remove from heat. Mix flour, 2 cups sugar, soda and salt in bowl. Add chocolate mixture; mix well. Add 2 eggs and sour cream; mix well. Spoon into greased and floured 10x15-inch baking pan. Combine cream cheese and ⅓ cup sugar in mixer bowl; beat until smooth. Blend in 1 egg. Spread evenly over chocolate layer; cut through with knife to marbleize. Sprinkle with chocolate chips. Bake at 375 degrees for 25 to 30 minutes or until wooden pick inserted in center comes out clean. Cool on wire rack. Cut into squares.

Jan K. Schmalz

Matrimonial Bars

Yield:
30 servings

Approx Per
Serving:
Cal 159
Prot 2 g
Carbo 27 g
Fiber 2 g
T Fat 6 g
Chol 5 mg
Sod 89 mg

1½ cups chopped
  dates
1½ cups chopped
  apricots
¼ cup sugar
1½ cups water
½ cup margarine,
  softened

¼ cup butter, softened
1 cup packed brown
  sugar
1¾ cups sifted flour
½ teaspoon soda
1 teaspoon salt
1½ cups oats

Combine dates, apricots, sugar and water in saucepan. Cook over low heat for 10 minutes or until thickened, stirring constantly. Cool to room temperature. Cream margarine, butter and brown sugar in mixer bowl until light and fluffy. Sift in flour, soda and salt; mix well. Stir in oats. Press half the mixture into greased 9x13-inch baking pan. Spread with fruit filling. Pat remaining oats mixture lightly over top. Bake at 400 degrees for 25 to 30 minutes or until light brown. Cut into bars and remove from pan while warm.

Judith E. Ware

Peanut Butter-Chocolate Squares

Yield:
48 servings

Approx Per Serving:
Cal 122
Prot 3 g
Carbo 17 g
Fiber 1 g
T Fat 5 g
Chol 20 mg
Sod 49 mg

4 eggs
2 cups sugar
1 tablespoon vanilla extract
2 cups flour
1 tablespoon baking powder
1 cup low-fat milk, scalded
2 tablespoons butter
3/4 cup creamy peanut butter
2 cups chocolate chips

Beat eggs in mixer bowl. Add sugar, vanilla, flour and baking powder; mix well. Add hot milk and butter; mix well. Spoon into greased 12x18-inch baking pan. Bake at 350 degrees for 25 minutes. Spread peanut butter evenly over hot baked layer. Chill for 30 minutes. Melt chocolate chips in double boiler. Spread evenly over peanut butter. Cool for 30 minutes. Cut into squares.

Denise Zeidler

Peanut Butter Kiss Cookies

Yield:
60 servings

Approx Per Serving:
Cal 78
Prot 1 g
Carbo 9 g
Fiber 1 g
T Fat 4 g
Chol 6 mg
Sod 44 mg

1/4 cup butter, softened
1/4 cup shortening
1/2 cup sugar
1/2 cup packed brown sugar
1/2 teaspoon vanilla extract
1 egg
1/2 cup chunky peanut butter
1 1/3 cups flour
1 teaspoon soda
1/4 teaspoon salt
60 milk chocolate kisses

Cream butter, shortening, sugar, brown sugar and vanilla in mixer bowl until light and fluffy. Beat in egg. Add peanut butter; mix well. Stir in flour, soda and salt. Shape into two 8-inch logs; wrap with foil. Freeze until baking time. Cut frozen logs into 1/4-inch slices; arrange slices on cookie sheet. Bake at 350 degrees for 8 minutes. Press 1 candy kiss gently into center of each cookie. Bake for 2 to 4 minutes longer or until light brown. Remove to wire rack to cool.

Patricia Austin

 Grease cookie sheets with the wrapper from butter or margarine.

PECAN PIE BARS

Yield:
48 servings

**Approx Per
Serving:**
Cal 185
Prot 2 g
Carbo 23 g
Fiber 1 g
T Fat 10 g
Chol 18 mg
Sod 44 mg

3 cups flour
1/2 cup sugar
1 cup corn oil
  margarine, softened
1/2 teaspoon salt
4 eggs, slightly beaten
1 1/2 cups dark corn
  syrup

1 1/2 cups sugar
3 tablespoons melted
  margarine
1 1/2 teaspoons vanilla
  extract
2 1/2 cups chopped
  pecans

Combine flour, 1/2 cup sugar, 1 cup margarine and salt in mixer bowl; beat until mixture resembles coarse crumbs. Press firmly over bottom of greased 10x15-inch baking pan. Bake at 350 degrees for 20 minutes. Combine eggs, corn syrup, 1 1/2 cups sugar, melted margarine and vanilla in mixer bowl; mix well. Stir in pecans. Spread evenly over baked layer. Bake for 25 minutes or until set. Cool on wire rack. Cut into bars.

June Weakley

PUMPKIN GOBS

Yield:
30 servings

**Approx Per
Serving:**
Cal 275
Prot 2 g
Carbo 34 g
Fiber 1 g
T Fat 15 g
Chol 15 mg
Sod 67 mg

2 cups sugar
2 eggs
1 cup oil
2 cups pumpkin
1 teaspoon vanilla
  extract
3 cups flour
1 teaspoon baking
  powder
1 teaspoon soda
1 teaspoon cinnamon

1 teaspoon ginger
1 teaspoon cloves
1 teaspoon salt
1 3-ounce package
  French vanilla
  instant pudding mix
1 cup sugar
1 cup milk
1 cup shortening
1 teaspoon vanilla
  extract

Combine 2 cups sugar and eggs in mixer bowl; beat until thick and lemon-colored. Add oil, pumpkin and 1 teaspoon vanilla; mix well. Add flour, baking powder, soda, cinnamon, ginger, cloves and salt; mix well. Drop by tablespoonfuls onto lightly greased cookie sheet. Bake at 350 degrees for 12 to 15 minutes or until light brown. Remove to wire rack to cool. Combine pudding mix, 1 cup sugar, milk, shortening and 1 teaspoon vanilla in mixer bowl. Beat until of spreading consistency. Spread on half the cookies; top with remaining cookies.

Shirley Jackson

GRANDMOTHER RICE'S RAISIN PUFF COOKIES

Yield:
36 servings

Approx Per Serving:
Cal 171
Prot 2 g
Carbo 29 g
Fiber 1 g
T Fat 6 g
Chol 26 mg
Sod 101 mg

½ cup golden seedless raisins
1 cup dark seedless raisins
1 cup water
1 cup butter, softened
½ teaspoon salt

1 teaspoon vanilla extract
1 teaspoon soda
4 cups sifted flour
1½ cups sugar
2 eggs
1 cup sugar

Combine raisins with water in saucepan. Cook until raisins are plump and water is absorbed; do not burn. Cream butter and salt in mixer bowl until light. Add vanilla and soda; mix well. Add flour, 1½ cups sugar and eggs; mix well. Stir in raisins. Shape into 1-inch balls. Roll in 1 cup sugar, coating well. Place on cookie sheet. Bake at 325 degrees for 12 to 15 minutes or just until set and very light brown. This is a recipe from my husband's grandmother.

Brenda Eskildson

WHEATIES COOKIES

Yield:
48 servings

Approx Per Serving:
Cal 108
Prot 1 g
Carbo 15 g
Fiber 1 g
T Fat 5 g
Chol 19 mg
Sod 89 mg

1 cup butter, softened
1 cup sugar
1 cup packed brown sugar
1 teaspoon vanilla extract
2 eggs

2 cups flour
1 teaspoon baking powder
½ teaspoon salt
2 cups (rounded) Wheaties
2 cups coconut

Cream butter, sugar and brown sugar in mixer bowl until light and fluffy. Beat in vanilla and eggs. Add flour, baking powder and salt; mix well. Stir in cereal and coconut. Drop by spoonfuls onto cookie sheet. Bake at 375 degrees for 12 minutes or until cookies puff and then fall. Remove to wire rack to cool.

Marge Fritz

Always leave 1 to 2 inches between cookies dropped onto baking sheet to allow room to spread. Thin doughs will spread more than thicker doughs.

German Schnecken Cookies (Snails)

Yield:
64 servings

Approx Per Serving:
Cal 95
Prot 2 g
Carbo 7 g
Fiber <1 g
T Fat 7 g
Chol 12 mg
Sod 55 mg

1½ cups margarine
4 cups flour
3 egg yolks, slightly beaten
1 cup sour cream
1 tablespoon fruit sugar (dextrose)

3 egg whites, slightly beaten
Fruit sugar (dextrose)
Cinnamon to taste
1¼ cups ground walnuts

Cut margarine into flour in bowl until crumbly. Add egg yolks, sour cream and 1 tablespoon fruit sugar; mix well. Shape into 2 logs. Chill for several hours to overnight. Divide each log into 4 equal portions. Roll 1 portion at a time into circle on surface sprinkled generously with additional fruit sugar. Brush with egg whites; sprinkle with fruit sugar and cinnamon. Cut into 8 wedges. Place about 1 teaspoon ground walnuts on wide end of each wedge. Roll up from wide end to enclose walnuts. Place on ungreased cookie sheet. Bake at 350 degrees for 15 to 20 minutes or until light brown. Remove to wire rack to cool.

Nutritional information does not include additional fruit sugar used in rolling.

Marlene Bartus

Scottish Oat Cakes

Yield:
36 servings

Approx Per Serving:
Cal 139
Prot 2 g
Carbo 17 g
Fiber 1 g
T Fat 8 g
Chol 0 mg
Sod 123 mg

1½ teaspoons soda
½ cup boiling water
2 cups flour
1 teaspoon baking powder

2 cups bran flakes
2 cups oats
1¼ cups sugar
1 teaspoon salt
1¼ cups shortening

Dissolve soda in boiling water in small bowl. Let stand until cool. Combine flour, baking powder, bran flakes, oats, sugar and salt in bowl. Cut in shortening until crumbly. Add soda mixture; mix well. Roll thin on floured surface. Cut as desired; place on cookie sheet. Bake at 400 degrees until golden brown. This recipe comes from the Telegraph House Restaurant, Cape Breton, Nova Scotia. Alexander Graham Bell was a frequent visitor for oat cakes and coffee.

Fran Brosius

Good Sugar Cookies

Yield:
24 servings

Approx Per Serving:
Cal 169
Prot 2 g
Carbo 22 g
Fiber <1 g
T Fat 8 g
Chol 39 mg
Sod 66 mg

1 cup butter, softened
1 cup sugar
2 egg yolks
1 teaspoon vanilla extract
2½ cups sifted flour
1 cup confectioners' sugar
5 to 6 teaspoons water

Cream butter and sugar in mixer bowl until light and fluffy. Beat in egg yolks and vanilla. Add flour gradually, mixing well after each addition. Roll on floured surface; cut with cookie cutter. Place on greased cookie sheet. Bake at 350 degrees for 6 to 10 minutes or until light brown. Remove to wire rack to cool. Blend confectioners' sugar and water in small bowl. Add food coloring if desired. Brush over warm cookies. May substitute margarine for butter and add ½ teaspoon butter flavoring.

Jan K. Schmalz

Soft Sugar Cookies

Yield:
48 servings

Approx Per Serving:
Cal 119
Prot 2 g
Carbo 18 g
Fiber <1 g
T Fat 5 g
Chol 10 mg
Sod 23 mg

2 cups sugar
1 cup shortening
2 eggs
1 teaspoon vanilla extract
½ teaspoon cream of tartar
1 teaspoon soda
4½ cups flour
1 cup sour milk

Cream 2 cups sugar and shortening in mixer bowl until light and fluffy. Beat in eggs and vanilla. Combine cream of tartar, soda and flour in bowl. Add to creamed mixture alternately with sour milk, mixing well after each addition. Drop by teaspoonfuls onto lightly greased cookie sheet; sprinkle with additional sugar. Bake at 350 degrees for 10 to 12 minutes or until light brown. May add chocolate chips, raisins and nuts if desired. Do not substitute butter for shortening.

Donna Hurdle Adams

Pies

The Washington Monument

CHILLY CHERRY PIE

Yield:
8 servings

Approx Per
Serving:
Cal 381
Prot 3 gr
Carbo 64 g
Fiber 2 g
T Fat 14 g
Chol 20 mg
Sod 240 mg

1½ cups graham
  cracker crumbs
¼ cup confectioners'
  sugar
¼ cup melted
  margarine
1 envelope unflavored
  gelatin
¼ cup cold water
½ cup drained red
  sour cherries

¾ cup cherry juice
½ cup sugar
Salt to taste
1 tablespoon cherry
  gelatin
½ cup whipping cream
¼ cup sugar
1 21-ounce can cherry
  pie filling

Combine cracker crumbs, confectioners' sugar and margarine in bowl; mix well. Press into 10-inch pie plate. Bake at 350 degrees for 7 minutes. Cool. Soften unflavored gelatin in cold water for 5 minutes. Combine cherries, cherry juice, ½ cup sugar and salt in saucepan. Bring to a boil; remove from heat. Add unflavored and cherry gelatins; stir until dissolved. Chill until thickened to consistency of syrup. Whip cream with ¼ cup sugar until soft peaks form. Fold whipped cream into gelatin mixture. Pour into prepared pie plate. Chill for 30 minutes or until firm. Top with pie filling. Chill until serving time.

Lin Kogle

CHOCOLATE FUDGE PIE

Yield:
8 servings

Approx Per
Serving:
Cal 327
Prot 4 gr
Carbo 33 g
Fiber 1 g
T Fat 21 g
Chol 80 mg
Sod 162 mg

½ cup margarine
2 large squares
  German's sweet
  chocolate
1 cup sugar
3 eggs, slightly beaten

3 tablespoons
  (heaping) flour
1 teaspoon vanilla
  extract
½ cup pecans

Melt margarine and chocolate in saucepan over low heat. Combine sugar, eggs, flour and vanilla in mixer bowl. Beat at high speed for 3 minutes. Stir in chocolate mixture and pecans. Pour into greased 9-inch pie plate. Bake at 325 degrees for 30 minutes. Let stand until cool. Chill until serving time. Garnish with whipped cream.

Lin Kogle

Amaretto Chocolate Chip Pie

Yield:
8 servings

Approx Per Serving:
Cal 608
Prot 7 gr
Carbo 64 g
Fiber 3 g
T Fat 38 g
Chol 53 mg
Sod 293 mg

½ cup melted margarine
1 cup sugar
2 eggs, slightly beaten
1 cup flour

2 tablespoons Amaretto
1 cup chocolate chips
1 cup chopped pecans
1 unbaked 8-inch pie shell

Blend margarine and sugar in bowl. Beat in eggs. Add flour and Amaretto; mix well. Stir in chocolate chips and pecans. Pour into pie shell. Bake at 375 degrees for 30 minutes or until set. May substitute rum for Amaretto. This pie is a favorite on Kentucky Derby day.

Cara L. Davis

Coconut Pies

Yield:
16 servings

Approx Per Serving:
Cal 364
Prot 3 gr
Carbo 27 g
Fiber 1 g
T Fat 28 g
Chol 96 mg
Sod 208 mg

2 cups whipping cream
1 cup sugar
1½ cups coconut
2 tablespoons flour
2 eggs
1 egg yolk
½ cup melted butter
1 teaspoon lemon extract

⅛ teaspoon almond extract
⅛ teaspoon vanilla extract
2 unbaked 9-inch deep dish pie shells

Combine cream and sugar in mixer bowl; beat until mixture begins to thicken. Stir in coconut and flour. Beat eggs and egg yolk in small bowl. Add to coconut mixture. Add butter and flavorings; beat just until mixed. Pour into pie shells. Bake at 350 degrees for 35 to 40 minutes or until golden brown.

Georgia Bracy

 Prevent a soggy lower pie crust by brushing it with egg white or melted butter before adding the filling.

CRAZY PIE

Yield:
8 servings

Approx Per
Serving:
Cal 294
Prot 3 gr
Carbo 32 g
Fiber 1 g
T Fat 18 g
Chol 27 mg
Sod 206 mg

1 cup flour
1 teaspoon baking
  powder
1/2 teaspoon salt
1 tablespoon sugar
1 egg
2/3 cup shortening
3/4 cup water
1 21-ounce can apple
   pie filling
1 tablespoon lemon
  juice
1/2 teaspoon cinnamon

Combine flour, baking powder, salt, sugar, egg, shortening and water in mixer bowl; mix until smooth. Spoon into 9-inch pie plate. Combine pie filling, lemon juice and cinnamon in bowl. Pour into center of batter in pie plate; do not mix. Bake at 425 degrees for 40 to 45 minutes or until brown. This makes a cobbler-like pie. May substitute peach pie filling for apple pie filling.

Catherine O'Malley

EASY LEMON PIE

Yield:
8 servings

Approx Per
Serving:
Cal 383
Prot 6 gr
Carbo 54 g
Fiber 1 g
T Fat 17 g
Chol 70 mg
Sod 304 mg

1 14-ounce can
   sweetened
   condensed milk
1 teaspoon grated
  lemon rind
1/2 cup lemon juice
2 egg yolks, beaten
1 8-inch graham
   cracker pie shell

Combine condensed milk, lemon rind and lemon juice in bowl; mix well. Blend in egg yolks. Pour into pie shell. Chill until serving time.

Charlotte Wood

LEMON MERINGUE PIE

Yield:
8 servings

Approx Per
Serving:
Cal 579
Prot 6 gr
Carbo 102 g
Fiber 1 g
T Fat 18 g
Chol 175 mg
Sod 365 mg

⅔ cup cornstarch
2½ cups sugar
½ teaspoon salt
3 cups boiling water
6 egg yolks, beaten
⅔ cup lemon juice
¼ cup butter

1 teaspoon grated
  lemon rind
1 baked 9-inch pie
  shell
6 egg whites
¾ cup sugar

Combine cornstarch, 2½ cups sugar and salt in top of double boiler. Stir in boiling water. Cook over hot water until thickened and clear, stirring frequently. Stir a small amount of hot mixture into beaten egg yolks; stir egg yolks into hot mixture. Cook for 2 minutes longer, stirring frequently; remove from heat. Add lemon juice, butter and lemon rind; mix well. Let stand until cool. Pour into pie shell. Beat egg whites in mixer bowl until barely stiff. Add ¾ cup sugar gradually, beating constantly until stiff peaks form. Swirl over filling, sealing to edge. Bake at 350 degrees until golden brown.

Margaret E. Williams

PEANUT BUTTER PIES

Yield:
16 servings

Approx Per
Serving:
Cal 497
Prot 8 gr
Carbo 50 g
Fiber 2 g
T Fat 31 g
Chol 16 mg
Sod 353 mg

16 ounces whipped
  topping
8 ounces cream cheese,
  softened
1 cup peanut butter

2 cups confectioners'
  sugar
2 8-inch graham
   cracker pie shells

Combine whipped topping, cream cheese, peanut butter and confectioners' sugar in bowl; blend well. Spoon into pie shells. Chill until serving time.

Mrs. David A. Sturgill

FROZEN CHOCOLATE AND PEANUT BUTTER PIE

Yield:
8 servings

**Approx Per
Serving:**
*Cal 458
Prot 9 gr
Carbo 49 g
Fiber 2 g
T Fat 27 g
Chol 17 mg
Sod 360 mg*

3 ounces cream cheese,
  softened
1/2 cup creamy peanut
  butter
1 cup confectioners'
  sugar
1/2 cup milk
8 ounces whipped
  topping
1 8-inch chocolate
  crumb pie shell

Combine cream cheese, peanut butter, confec-
tioners' sugar and milk in bowl; beat until smooth.
Blend in whipped topping. Spoon into pie shell.
Garnish with chocolate shavings. Freeze overnight.

Ginny Ricciuti

SOUTHERN PECAN PIE

Yield:
8 servings

**Approx Per
Serving:**
*Cal 578
Prot 6 gr
Carbo 77 g
Fiber 2 g
T Fat 30 g
Chol 122 mg
Sod 244 mg*

1 cup sugar
1 1/4 cups light corn
  syrup
4 eggs, slightly beaten
1/4 cup butter
1 teaspoon vanilla
  extract
1 1/2 cups pecan halves
1 unbaked 9-inch pie
  shell

Combine sugar and corn syrup in saucepan. Bring
to a boil. Boil for 2 to 3 minutes. Beat hot syrup
gradually into eggs. Add butter, vanilla and pecans.
Pour into pie shell. Bake at 350 degrees for 45
minutes or until set. Filling is generous for one pie;
may double filling and bake in 3 pie shells.

Terri Vieyra

MASHED POTATO PIE

Yield:
8 servings

Approx Per
Serving:
Cal 344
Prot 6 gr
Carbo 57 g
Fiber 2 g
T Fat 11 g
Chol 86 mg
Sod 411 mg

3 cups mashed
potatoes
1¼ cups sugar
3 egg yolks, beaten
¼ teaspoon nutmeg
1 cup milk

1 teaspoon vanilla
extract
3 egg whites, stiffly
beaten
1 unbaked 9-inch pie
shell

Combine potatoes, sugar and egg yolks in bowl; mix well. Add nutmeg, milk and vanilla; mix well. Fold in stiffly beaten egg whites. Spoon into pie shell. Bake at 425 degrees for 15 minutes. Reduce heat to 350 degrees. Bake for 30 minutes longer.

Nancy S. Vance

PARADISE PUMPKIN PIE

Yield:
8 servings

Approx Per
Serving:
Cal 370
Prot 8 gr
Carbo 36 g
Fiber 1 g
T Fat 22 g
Chol 120 mg
Sod 283 mg

8 ounces cream cheese,
softened
¼ cup sugar
1 egg, beaten
½ teaspoon vanilla
extract
1 unbaked 9-inch pie
shell

1¼ cups mashed
cooked pumpkin
½ cup sugar
1 teaspoon cinnamon
¼ teaspoon ginger
¼ teaspoon nutmeg
1 cup evaporated milk
2 eggs, beaten

Combine cream cheese ¼ cup sugar, 1 egg and vanilla in bowl; mix well. Spread in pie shell. Combine pumpkin, ½ cup sugar, spices, evaporated milk and 2 eggs in bowl; mix well. Spread carefully over cream cheese layer. Bake at 350 degrees for 1 hour and 5 minutes. Let stand until cool. May brush with maple syrup and garnish with nuts if desired.

Mrs. David A. Sturgill

Fresh Strawberry Pie

Yield:
8 servings

Approx Per Serving:
Cal 290
Prot 3 gr
Carbo 46 g
Fiber 3 g
T Fat 12 g
Chol 12 mg
Sod 171 mg

6 cups strawberries
1 cup sugar
3 tablespoons cornstarch
1/2 cup water
3 ounces cream cheese, softened
1 baked 9-inch pie shell

Mash enough strawberries to measure 1 cup. Mix sugar and cornstarch in saucepan. Stir in crushed berries and water gradually. Bring to a boil over medium heat, stirring constantly. Boil for 1 minute, stirring constantly. Add desired amount of red food coloring. Let stand until cool. Beat cream cheese until smooth. Spread over bottom of pie shell. Slice enough strawberries to arrange around side of pie shell with slices touching. Fill shell with remaining strawberries. Pour cooked mixture over berries, shaking pie gently to allow mixture to flow between berries. Chill for 3 hours or until set.

Florine W. Mooring

Southern Sweet Potato Pie

Yield:
8 servings

Approx Per Serving:
Cal 434
Prot 5 gr
Carbo 58 g
Fiber 2 g
T Fat 21 g
Chol 86 mg
Sod 382 mg

2 cups mashed cooked sweet potatoes
1/2 cup butter, softened
2 egg yolks, beaten
1 cup packed brown sugar
1/4 teaspoon salt
1/4 teaspoon ginger
1/2 teaspoon cinnamon
1/2 teaspoon nutmeg
1/2 cup milk
2 egg whites
1/4 cup sugar
1 unbaked 9-inch pie shell

Combine sweet potatoes, butter, egg yolks, brown sugar, salt and spices in bowl; mix well. Blend in milk. Beat egg whites in mixer bowl until frothy. Add sugar gradually, beating constantly until stiff peaks form. Fold into sweet potato mixture. Pour into pie shell. Bake at 400 degrees for 10 minutes. Reduce temperature to 350 degrees. Bake for 30 minutes longer.

Margaret E. Williams

SUBSTITUTION CHART

	Instead of	Use
Baking	1 teaspoon baking powder 1 tablespoon cornstarch (for thickening) 1 cup sifted all-purpose flour 1 cup sifted cake flour	1/4 teaspoon soda plus 1/2 teaspoon cream of tartar 2 tablespoons flour or 1 tablespoon tapioca 1 cup plus 2 tablespoons sifted cake flour 1 cup minus 2 tablespoons sifted all-purpose flour
	1 cup dry bread crumbs	3/4 cup cracker crumbs
Dairy	1 cup buttermilk 1 cup heavy cream 1 cup light cream 1 cup sour cream 1 cup sour milk	1 cup sour milk or 1 cup yogurt 3/4 cup skim milk plus 1/3 cup butter 7/8 cup skim milk plus 3 tablespoons butter 7/8 cup sour milk plus 3 tablespoons butter 1 cup milk plus 1 tablespoon vinegar or lemon juice or 1 cup buttermilk
Seasoning	1 teaspoon allspice 1 cup catsup 1 clove of garlic 1 teaspoon Italian spice 1 teaspoon lemon juice 1 tablespoon mustard 1 medium onion	1/2 teaspoon cinnamon plus 1/8 teaspoon cloves 1 cup tomato sauce plus 1/2 cup sugar plus 2 tablespoons vinegar 1/8 teaspoon garlic powder or 1/8 teaspoon instant minced garlic or 3/4 teaspoon garlic salt or 5 drops of liquid garlic 1/4 teaspoon each oregano, basil, thyme, rosemary plus dash of cayenne 1/2 teaspoon vinegar 1 teaspoon dry mustard 1 tablespoon dried minced onion or 1 teaspoon onion powder
Sweet	1 1-ounce square chocolate 1 2/3 ounces semisweet chocolate 1 cup honey 1 cup granulated sugar	1/4 cup cocoa plus 1 teaspoon shortening 1 ounce unsweetened chocolate plus 4 teaspoons granulated sugar 1 to 1 1/4 cups sugar plus 1/4 cup liquid or 1 cup corn syrup or molasses 1 cup packed brown sugar or 1 cup corn syrup, molasses or honey minus 1/4 cup liquid

EQUIVALENT CHART

	When the recipe calls for	Use
Baking	1/2 cup butter	4 ounces
	2 cups butter	1 pound
	4 cups all-purpose flour	1 pound
	4 1/2 to 5 cups sifted cake flour	1 pound
	1 square chocolate	1 ounce
	1 cup semisweet chocolate chips	6 ounces
	4 cups marshmallows	1 pound
	2 1/4 cups packed brown sugar	1 pound
	4 cups confectioners' sugar	1 pound
	2 cups granulated sugar	1 pound
Cereal – Bread	1 cup fine dry bread crumbs	4 to 5 slices
	1 cup soft bread crumbs	2 slices
	1 cup small bread cubes	2 slices
	1 cup fine cracker crumbs	28 saltines
	1 cup fine graham cracker crumbs	15 crackers
	1 cup vanilla wafer crumbs	22 wafers
	1 cup crushed cornflakes	3 cups uncrushed
	4 cups cooked macaroni	8 ounces uncooked
	3 1/2 cups cooked rice	1 cup uncooked
Dairy	1 cup shredded cheese	4 ounces
	1 cup cottage cheese	8 ounces
	1 cup sour cream	8 ounces
	1 cup whipped cream	1/2 cup heavy cream
	2/3 cup evaporated milk	1 small can
	1 2/3 cups evaporated milk	1 13-ounce can
Fruit	4 cups sliced or chopped apples	4 medium
	1 cup mashed bananas	3 medium
	2 cups pitted cherries	4 cups unpitted
	2 1/2 cups shredded coconut	8 ounces
	4 cups cranberries	1 pound
	1 cup pitted dates	1 8-ounce package
	1 cup candied fruit	1 8-ounce package
	3 to 4 tablespoons lemon juice plus 1 tablespoon grated lemon rind	1 lemon
	1/3 cup orange juice plus 2 teaspoons grated orange rind	1 orange
	4 cups sliced peaches	8 medium
	2 cups pitted prunes	1 12-ounce package
	3 cups raisins	1 15-ounce package

	When the recipe calls for	Use
Meats	4 cups chopped cooked chicken 3 cups chopped cooked meat 2 cups cooked ground meat	1 5-pound chicken 1 pound, cooked 1 pound, cooked
Nuts	1 cup chopped nuts	4 ounces shelled 1 pound unshelled
Vegetables	2 cups cooked green beans 2½ cups lima beans or red beans 4 cups shredded cabbage 1 cup grated carrot 8 ounces fresh mushrooms 1 cup chopped onion 4 cups sliced or chopped potatoes 2 cups canned tomatoes	½ pound fresh or 1 16-ounce can 1 cup dried, cooked 1 pound 1 large 1 4-ounce can 1 large 4 medium 1 16-ounce can

Measurement Equivalents

1 tablespoon = 3 teaspoons
2 tablespoons = 1 ounce
4 tablespoons = ¼ cup
5⅓ tablespoons = ⅓ cup
8 tablespoons = ½ cup
12 tablespoons = ¾ cup
16 tablespoons = 1 cup
1 cup = 8 ounces or ½ pint
4 cups = 1 quart
4 quarts = 1 gallon

1 6½ to 8-ounce can = 1 cup
1 10½ to 12-ounce can = 1¼ cups
1 14 to 16-ounce can = 1¾ cups
1 16 to 17-ounce can = 2 cups
1 18 to 20-ounce can = 2½ cups
1 29-ounce can = 3½ cups
1 46 to 51-ounce can = 5¾ cups
1 6½ to 7½-pound can or
  Number 10 = 12 to 13 cups

Metric Equivalents

Liquid	Dry
1 teaspoon = 5 milliliters 1 tablespoon = 15 milliliters 1 fluid ounce = 30 milliliters 1 cup = 250 milliliters 1 pint = 500 milliliters	1 quart = 1 liter 1 ounce = 30 grams 1 pound = 450 grams 2.2 pounds = 1 kilogram

NOTE: The metric measures are approximate benchmarks for purposes of home food preparation.

CALORIE CHART

Almonds, shelled, ¼ cup 213
Apples: 1 med 70
    chopped, ½ cup 30
    juice, 1 cup 117
Applesauce, ½ cup: sweetened. 115
    unsweetened 50
Apricots: canned, ½ cup 110
    dried, 10 halves 100
    fresh, 3 55
    nectar, 1 cup 140
Asparagus: canned, ½ cup 18
    fresh, 6 spears 19
Avocado, 1 med 265
Bacon, crisp-cooked, 2 slices ... 90
Banana, 1 med 100
Beans, ½ cup: baked 160
    dried 350
    green 20
    lima 95
    soy 95
Bean sprouts, ½ cup 18
Beef, cooked, 3 oz:
    broiled, sirloin steak 330
    roasted, heel of round 165
    roasted, rib 375
Beer, 12 oz 150
Beets, cooked, ½ cup 40
Biscuit, from mix, 1 90
Bologna, all meat, 3 oz 235
Bread: 1 roll 85
    white, 1 slice 65
    whole wheat, 1 slice 55
Bread crumbs, dry, 1 cup 390
Broccoli, cooked, ½ cup 20
Butter, 1 tbsp 100
Buttermilk, 1 cup 90
Cabbage, ½ cup: cooked 15
    fresh, shredded 10
Cake, 1/12 cake: angel food 140
    devil's food 195
    yellow 200
Candy, 1 oz: caramel 115
    chocolate, sweet 145
    hard candy 110
    marshmallows 90
Cantaloupe, ½ med 60
Carrots: cooked, ½ cup 23
    fresh, 1 med 20
Catsup, 1 tbsp 18

Cauliflower: cooked, ½ cup 13
    fresh, ½ lb 60
Celery, chopped, ½ cup 8
Cereals, ½ cup: bran flakes 53
    cornflakes 50
    oatmeal, cooked 65
Cheese: American, 1 oz 105
    Cheddar, 1 oz 113
    cottage: creamed, ½ cup ... 130
        uncreamed, ½ cup ... 85
    cream, 1 oz 107
    mozzarella, 1 oz 80
    Parmesan, 1 oz 110
    Velveeta, 1 oz 84
Cherries, ½ cup: canned, sour .. 53
    fresh, sweet 40
Chicken, cooked, 4 oz:
    broiled 155
    canned, boned 230
    roasted, dark meat 210
    roasted, light meat 207
Chilies, fresh, 8 oz: green 62
    red 108
Chili powder, 1 tbsp 51
Chocolate, baking, 1 oz 143
Cocoa mix, 1 oz 115
Cocoa, unsweetened, ⅓ cup .. 120
Coconut, shredded, ¼ cup 166
Coffee 0
Corn, ½ cup: cream-style 100
    whole kernel 85
Corn bread, 1x4-in. piece 125
Corn chips, 1 oz 130
Cornmeal, ½ cup 264
Cornstarch, 1 tbsp 29
Crab meat, 3 oz: canned 85
    fresh 80
Crackers: graham, 1 square 28
    Ritz, 1 17
    saltine, 1 square 13
Cracker crumbs, ½ cup 281
Cranberries: fresh, ½ lb 100
    juice, cocktail, 1 cup 163
    sauce, ½ cup 190
Cream, 1 tbsp: half and half 20
    heavy 55
    light 30
Creamer, nondairy, 1 tsp 10
Cucumber, 1 med 30

Potatoes, sweet:
baked, 1 med 155
candied, 1 med 295
canned, 1/2 cup 110
Prunes: dried, cooked, 1/2 cup .. 137
fresh, 1 lg 19
juice, 1 cup 197
Puddings, instant, prepared,
1/2 cup:
banana 175
butterscotch 175
chocolate 200
lemon 180
Puddings, pie fillings, prepared,
1/2 cup:
banana 165
butterscotch 190
chocolate 190
lemon 125
Pumpkin, canned, 1/2 cup 38
Raisins, 1/2 cup 231
Rice, cooked, 1/2 cup:
brown 100
minute 105
white 90
Salad dressings, 1 tbsp:
bleu cheese 75
French 70
Italian 83
mayonnaise 100
mayonnaise-type 65
Russian 75
Thousand Island 80
Salami, cooked, 2 oz 180
Salmon, 4 oz: canned 180
steak 220
Sardines, canned, 3 oz 75
Sauces, 1 tbsp: barbecue 17
hot pepper 3
soy 9
tartar 74
white, med 215
Worcestershire 15
Sauerkraut, 1/2 cup 21
Sausage, cooked, 2 oz 260
Sherbet, 1/2 cup 130
Shrimp: canned, 4 oz 130
cooked, 3 oz 50
Soft drinks, 1 cup 100
Soup, condensed, 1 can:
chicken with rice 116
cream of celery 215

cream of chicken 235
cream of mushroom 331
tomato 220
vegetable-beef 198
Sour cream, 1/2 cup 240
Spaghetti, cooked, 1/2 cup 80
Spinach: cooked, 1/2 cup 20
fresh, 1/2 lb 60
Squash: summer, 1/2 cup 15
winter, 1/2 cup 65
Strawberries, fresh, 1/2 cup 23
Sugar: brown, 1/2 cup 410
confectioners', 1/2 cup 240
granulated, 1/2 cup 385
1 tbsp. 48
Syrups, 1 tbsp: chocolate 50
corn 58
maple 50
Taco shell, 1 shell 50
Tomatoes: canned, 1/2 cup 25
fresh, 1 med 40
juice, 1 cup 45
paste, 6-oz 150
sauce, 8-oz 34
Toppings, 1 tbsp: caramel 70
chocolate fudge 65
Cool Whip 14
Dream Whip 8
strawberry 60
Tortilla, corn, 1 65
Tuna, canned, 4 oz:
in oil 230
in water 144
Turkey, roasted, 4 oz:
dark meat 230
light meat 200
Veal, cooked, 3 oz:
broiled, cutlet 185
roasted 230
Vegetable juice cocktail, 1 cup .. 43
Vinegar, 1 tbsp 2
Waffles, 1 130
Walnuts, chopped, 1/2 cup 410
Water chestnuts, 1/2 cup 25
Watermelon, fresh, 1/2 cup 26
Wheat germ, 1 tbsp 29
Yeast: cake, 1 oz 24
dry, 1 oz 80
Yogurt, 1 cup: plain 153
plain, skim milk 123
plain whole milk 139
with fruit 260

VEGETABLE CALORIE CHART

Artichoke:
  1 lg 88
  hearts, frozen, 3½ oz 26
Asparagus, 1 cup 35
Beans:
  green, fresh, 1 cup 35
  kidney, dried, 1 cup 635
  limas, dried, 1 cup 656
  navy, dried, 1 cup 697
  soy, dried, ½ cup 95
  wax, fresh, 1 cup 30
Beets, 1 cup 58
Broccoli, 2 lg stalks 145
Brussels sprouts, 1 cup 55
Cabbage:
  green, 1 cup 36
  red, 1 cup 28
Carrots:
  raw, 1 whole 30
  cooked, 1 cup 50
Cauliflower:
  fresh, cooked, 1 cup 30
  raw, chopped, 1 cup 31
Celery, 1 lg stalk 7
Chard, 1 lb 113
Chestnuts, 1 cup 310
Collards, fresh, cooked, 1 cup .. 65
Corn:
  cream-style, ½ cup 100
  fresh, 1 ear 70
  whole kernel, ½ cup 85
Cucumber, 1 lg 45
Dandelion greens, fresh, 1 lb .. 204
Eggplant, boiled, 1 cup 38
Endive:
  Belgian, 1 head 8
  curly, 1 cup 10
Kale, fresh, cooked, 1 cup 45
Kohlrabi, fresh, 1 cup 41
Lentils, dried, 1 cup 646
Lettuce:
  Bibb, 1 cup 8
  iceberg, 1 cup 7
  romaine, 1 cup 10
Mushrooms:
  canned, 1 cup 40
  fresh, 1 lb 125

Mustard greens:
  cooked, 1 cup 30
  fresh, 1 lb 141
Okra, fresh, 1 cup 36
Onions, fresh, 1 cup 65
Parsley, fresh, 1 cup 26
Parsnips, cooked, 1 cup 82
Peas:
  black-eyed, fresh, 1 cup 184
  green, fresh, 1 cup 122
Peppers:
  hot chili, ½ cup 18
  green bell, 1 med 14
  red bell, 1 med 19
Potatoes, sweet:
  baked, 1 med 155
  candied, 1 med 295
  canned, ½ cup 110
Potatoes, white:
  baked, 1 sm 93
  boiled, 1 sm 70
  French-fried, 10 pieces 175
  hashed brown, ½ cup 177
  mashed, ½ cup 90
  scalloped, ½ cup 120
Pumpkin, canned, 1 cup 81
Radishes, 10 whole 14
Rutabagas, fresh, 1 cup 87
Spinach:
  cooked, 1 cup 40
  fresh, 1 cup 15
Sprouts:
  alfalfa, 1 cup 10
  Mung bean, fresh, 1 cup 37
Squash:
  summer, fresh, 1 cup 25
  winter, mashed, 1 cup 129
Tomatoes:
  canned, 1 cup 50
  green, fresh, 1 lb 99
  ripe, fresh, 1 lb 88
Turnip Greens:
  fresh, cooked, 1 cup 30
Turnips, fresh, 1 cup 39
Watercress, 1 bunch 20
Water chestnuts, canned, 1 cup .. 70
Zucchini, fresh, 1 cup 22

BREAD BAKING GUIDE

The pleasure of baking homemade bread is matched only by eating it, except when something goes wrong. Most problems can be determined and easily avoided the next time.

Problem...	Cause...
Bread or biscuits are dry	Too much flour; too slow baking; over-handling
Bread has too open texture or uneven texture	Too much liquid; over-handling in kneading
Strong yeast smell from baked bread	Too much yeast; over-rising
Tiny white spots on crust	Too rapid rising; dough not covered properly while rising
Crust has bad color	Too much flour used in shaping
Small flat loaves	Old yeast; not enough rising or rising much too long; oven temperature too hot
Heavy compact texture	Too much flour worked into bread when kneading; insufficient rising time; oven temperature too hot
Coarse texture	Too little kneading
Crumbly texture	Too much flour; undermixing; oven temperature too cool
Yeasty sour flavor	Too little yeast; rising time too long
Fallen center	Rising time too long
Irregular shape	Poor technique in shaping
Surface browns too quickly	Oven temperature too hot
Bread rises too long during baking and is porous in center and upper portion of loaf	Oven temperature too cool

BAKING EQUIVALENTS

	When the recipe calls for	Use
Baking	½ cup butter 2 cups butter 4 cups all-purpose flour 2½ to 5 cups sifted cake flour 1 square chocolate 1 cup semisweet chocolate chips 4 cups marshmallows 2¼ cups packed brown sugar 4 cups confectioners' sugar 2 cups granulated sugar	4 ounces 1 pound 1 pound 1 pound 1 ounce 6 ounces 1 pound 1 pound 1 pound 1 pound
Cereal—Bread	1 cup fine dry bread crumbs 1 cup soft bread crumbs 1 cup small bread crumbs 1 cup fine cracker crumbs 1 cup fine graham cracker crumbs 1 cup vanilla wafer crumbs 1 cup crushed cornflakes 4 cups cooked macaroni 3½ cups cooked rice	4 to 5 slices 2 slices 2 slices 28 saltines 15 crackers 22 wafers 3 cups uncrushed 8 ounces uncooked 1 cup uncooked
Dairy	1 cup shredded cheese 1 cup cottage cheese 1 cup sour cream 1 cup whipped cream ⅔ cup evaporated milk 1⅔ cups evaporated milk	4 ounces 8 ounces 8 ounces ½ cup heavy cream 1 small can 1 13-ounce can

Fruit	4 cups sliced or chopped apples
	1 cup mashed bananas
	2 cups pitted cherries
	2½ cups shredded coconut
	4 cups cranberries
	1 cup pitted dates
	1 cup candied fruit
	3 to 4 tablespoons lemon juice plus
	   1 tablespoon grated lemon rind
	⅓ cup orange juice plus 2 teaspoons
	   grated orange rind
	4 cups sliced peaches
	2 cups pitted prunes
	3 cups raisins
		4 medium
		3 medium
		4 cups unpitted
		8 ounces
		1 pound
		1 8-ounce package
		1 8-ounce package
		1 lemon
		
		1 orange
		
		8 medium
		1 12-ounce package
		1 15-ounce package

INDEX

THIS COOKBOOK IS A PERFECT GIFT FOR HOLIDAYS, WEDDINGS, ANNIVERSARIES AND BIRTHDAYS.

★ ★

You may order as many of our cookbooks as you wish for the price of $10.00 each plus $2.00 postage and handling per book ordered. Mail to:

Telephone Pioneers of America
Alexander Graham Bell Chapter #15
930 H Street N.W., 9th Floor
Washington, D.C. 20001

Save postage and handling by picking up your books at the Chapter Pioneer office or from our Council Pioneer stores.

★ ★

Number of books ordered: _____

Amount enclosed: _____

Please make checks payable to:
Telephone Pioneers of America

Please Print:

Name: _____

Street Address: _____

City, State, Zip: _____

Daytime Phone Number: _____
(in case we have questions)